DEATH BY A THOUSAND CUTS

Jakki Clarke

© 2017 **Authored By** Jakki Clarke
All rights reserved.

ISBN: 1544918798
ISBN 13: 9781544918792
Library of Congress Control Number: 2017904847
CreateSpace Independent Publishing Platform
North Charleston, South Carolina

This is a work of fiction. References to real people and locations are used fictitiously. All other names, characters, and places, and all dialogue and events, are the product of the author's imagination, and any similarity to real people or events is purely coincidental.

*For Michael,
for everything.
Thank you for being you.
xoxoxo
jlc*

"You can fool some of the people all of the time,
and all of the people some of time,
but you can't fool all of the people all of the time."
-- Abraham Lincoln

PROLOGUE

The bevels of Waterford crystal shimmied in a fleeting rainbow as the tumblers of $500 scotch clinked in a toast of good cheer.

They nodded then sipped; no words were needed.

Or wanted.

Though they were the sole inhabitants of the men's grille of the 19th hole that afternoon, they knew better than to let their guard down there, because, well, they never let their guard down – ever – and for good reason.

"I'm fucking impressed, Bruni. Fuck. Ing. Impressed."

Dino was proud of himself too, but he wasn't glowing like a teenage girl with two dates to the prom or anything. He was simply satisfied. And simply glad Sault was on the same page.

For once, accolades were not on his agenda.

"So he's all squared away? This little shit up at the state capital?" Sault asked, swirling his drink.

Then things changed. Not between the two men, but among Mother Nature.

The sky reversed the fortune for the others swinging away on the course and detonated from placid to panicked in an instant.

Lightning blazed, thunder growled, and "O's" popped the lips of the wait staff.

The bartender and his maids scrambled for the onslaught of harried members seeking shelter...then, presumably cocktails.

Bruni and Sault stiffened their spines, knowing they were on borrowed time to conclude their conversation without prying ears.

The rain started. At first it was like soft grapes pelting the glass but less than a minute later it morphed into plums, drowning out the flat screens adorning the walls: the Golf Channel commentators, and Fox News talking heads; even the CNN ones who almost always barked the loudest.

"Listen Sterling. Not only is he 'squared away' but he'd basically suck a dick or shit his pants on command."

Sterling roared with pleasure, downing the remainder of his drink.

Bruni admired his good man's response, as well as his own reflection in the mirrored shelves behind the bar.

He drained his own half-grand glass and grinned: "We're alllll good..."

1

The Mayor was having a bad day.
Not yet even seven in the morning and already a nasty cobra of a migraine was winding its way up the column of his neck, creeping in tendrils before leisurely coiling against his temples, contented, like a belly-full housecat lazing in a slash of sunshine spilling across a hardwood floor.

The 36-point headline screamed before him:

CAMDEN, NJ: MOST DANGEROUS CITY IN NATION

And for the thousandth time that day he cursed the media and their penchant for witch-hunts. The way they meddled, nosy little fucks. He tore off a piece of his English muffin, long-gone cold -- the butter congealed in all the crevices -- and chewed without tasting.

It wasn't the first time his city had been branded but that was of little consequence when he thought of all the future articles on the horizon and the future headaches that would arrive along with them.

The scrutiny over his governing, his supporters, his life...

He cradled his head, imagining with a painful wince the next banners he could expect:

WHERE ARE OUR TAX $$ GOING?

...The outcry over money he'd spent...

...The patronage jobs he'd doled out like Halloween candy...

TROUBLED CAMDEN = OVERFUNDED CAMDEN

...The low standardized test scores that didn't even come close to reflecting the influx of state aid pouring into the city's school system with Olympic speed...

STATE TO JASPER: WE WANT ANSWERS

...The money over the years that had not-so-mysteriously made its way from his campaign war chest to the Zion Baptist CME on Bledsoe Boulevard and into the preacher's pockets, the one who never failed to implore his flock to do the will of the good Lord above and vote once again for Mayor Jarvis Jasper, hallelujah.

The investigation that would surely be launched into his campaign finance records. No stone would go unturned...

A meaty hand rubbed over his shiny baldhead and down his face, feeling the bristle of two days without shaving: two days worth of worry, knowing the only thing the media liked better than championing an under-dog was taking down a *top* dog. A rattling in his bones told him the sharks were circling. They smelled blood in the water and, to his acute dismay, it was his.

Still, he read on. The rankings of the country's "Most Dangerous Cities" were based upon reports made to the FBI, evaluating the crime rate within six main categories: Murder, rape, robbery, aggravated assault, burglary, and auto theft, comparing 350 cities with populations of 75,000 or more. For three of the past five years now his had been number one and was considered more dangerous than Detroit, than DC, L.A., Atlanta, Memphis, St. Louis -- and a whole host of others -- by those who make a living compiling such lists.

"Three hundred and fifty cities," he muttered, both believing and not. "And we're the *worst*. The poorest. The most goddamn dangerous in the whole goddamn country." His voice was plagued with defeat. "In the United States of America!" The pounding of his fist against the table sent his blood surging, then retreating just as fast, leaving him dizzy with fatigue.

His city was even worse than Philadelphia, which was just a seven-minute ferry ride across the river and roughly fifteen times the size.

"God help me," he said, kneading his temples, feeling the film of perspiration all over, the glut of desperation throughout. The Mayor was a well-known fixture at Zion Baptist -- its parking lot playing host to his gleaming Lincoln every Sunday morning, front row, third space to the right of the preacher's himself -- but as he pressed his weary face into his open palms he wished he were a holier man: one that knew both how to pray and how to have his prayers answered.

Jarvis Jasper was the black mayor of a city made up mostly of blacks -- very poor blacks -- ones whose paltry incomes were typically patched together by minimum wage, government checks, hopeful bus trips to Atlantic City, and a smattering of ill-advised ventures, many on the wrong side of the law.

But that hadn't always been the case.

Camden had once been an economic boon, a place where companies set up headquarters and jobs were plentiful; where good people raised good families and neighbors looked out for one another the way neighbors are supposed to. In its heyday it'd been a destination-of-sorts even, a place where Park Avenue New Yorkers packed up their fancy hatboxes and matching luggage and rode trains to visit.

For decades the riverside city was rife with manufacturing companies, too: a secondary hub for businesses spilling over from Philly to a port that soon became home to one of the most prolific shipbuilding yards during the Second World War. It became such a desirable enclave that soon wealthy folk began to build huge, ornate homes along the banks of the Delaware -- one such home the Mayor owned, was now sitting in -- and for ages Camden was known as a city with much of the grandeur and excitement of Philadelphia, but without the burden of great size or slum.

True, it had never been Camelot, but few places could claim so. Camden had simply been a productive sliver of Americana, home to hard work and the solid values that come along with it.

But then things changed.

It didn't happen all it once, but it did happen: As more highways were built, more suburbs sprang forth and city living became a thing to endure rather than enjoy. People moved away and too many companies followed suit, shutting their doors and taking the jobs with them. The fallout was quick and dramatic: unemployment shot moonward and urban decay nestled in, bringing with it a rippling feeling of unease and a certain kind of nervousness that made even the Mom-and-Pop stores put "FOR SALE" signs in their windows and turn their backs on a community they had once loved, leaving Camden frantic in its fight to keep its head above water.

In the sixties and seventies drugs and civil unrest did their thing and made life worse, but they did that everywhere so it didn't feel like such an imposition. That was, until the eighties came along -- bringing crack-cocaine and ruthless, almost undreamed-of street violence along with it. Gang warfare took the city out by the knees with tsunami-sized muscle and, ever since, the pitiable City of Camden was a place drowned altogether.

And entirely the Mayor's problem.

His eyes swept around the splendor of the dining room and a heavy sigh escaped, one that came from a place further than just his mouth, a place where disappointment and despair were known to dwell. Now his was one of only a handful of homes left of the dozens of great beauties that had once stood regally along the water, gracing the riverbanks like elegant ladies-in-waiting. A few had been home to various businesses at one time or another -- a bank, a law firm, an insurance agency -- but they never lasted long, and the structures were left to follow all the other one-time success stories that had plunged into disrepair after their owners moved in the spirit of "white flight", as the sociologists had so deftly termed it.

Some were still standing but that was almost a worse shame: constant reminders of a fall from grace...like a row of pregnant girls in pretty prom dresses. Dishonored, wounded soldiers still upright whose vast lawns had once hosted stately outings of croquet and tea were now nothing more than barren, soiled shelters for destitute squatters, whores, and junkies: Human vermin who thought nothing of tearing down pieces of antique board and beam to fuel the fires they lighted recklessly in the once-gilded foyers to keep the winter at bay. They took shits in porcelain claw-footed bathtubs; fought and bled on opulent marble. They destroyed emblems of history in less time than it took to take a drag from their smokes, had anonymous sex and shot-up and made their way closer to hell in places once home to the dignified, their withered faces and spirits so far gone and menacing they succeeded in scaring away all but the rats.

Jarvis Jasper had grown up in Camden and unlike most folks who found some measure of success in the world outside; he'd decided to return. College degree or no, he was adamant that he would not turn his back on his community, and his Momma wept with pride the day he arrived, cap and gown still creased from the box it came in.

But Jarvis had felt sick. He'd come home to find a reprehensible husk of a society: unspeakable horrors, and the promise of more lurking in every shadow. Running the streets had always had its risks, but now it was almost a suicide mission. And the old neighborhood? Now just a perilous pile of bricks. Not to mention Bruni Park, one of the brightest spots of his youth, where he'd spent who-knew-how-many times at bat -- dreaming of knocking it over the fence, of Jackie Robinson and making the Big Leagues -- was now nothing more than an unapologetic open-air drug market. And what of his friends? The ones still around, not locked up or six feet under? That legion of poor kids he'd played ball with had grown into an army of angry men who sold drugs to poor kids playing ball.

Camden had become a place where decent people were few and far between. A place that made him desperate to recant his offer and turn tail without second thought, handkerchief-wringin', pride-weepin' Momma or no.

Whether it was guilt or bravery, he didn't know but, in the end, Jarvis didn't turn his back. It wasn't easy, but he manned up. Kept his word. Stayed. And after a few years in a law firm spent basically as a do-boy, he made public his personal mission to return the city to the Camden of his youth. A place to be proud of...Or, at the very least, not to be feared.

The previous mayor had just been sent to prison on a litany of well-earned corruption and conspiracy charges, and nobody else seemed to want the job, so a young and naive Jarvis threw his hat into the ring and promised change. That seemed to satisfy the thin trickle of voters –- so drained and disheartened and deadened to the bad the world had to offer -- and it was what got him elected for the first time twenty-six years ago, the event bringing Momma to tears again.

But things had changed since then, so many things. The man who'd once returned fresh-faced with diploma in-hand to a city he didn't recognize, now didn't recognize the man himself. He'd become jaded by the politics of politics, had grown so tired of his self-serving colleagues on City Council, the tiresome way they tirelessly fought, the laborious process of gathering consensus, the principle of serving the people long gone to the wayside, unnoticed, like highway grass uncut.

What was worse was that he'd grown both ashamed by his people and resentful of them. Not to mention the countless hours he spent toiling to try; to help; to do *anything* whatsoever to improve their lives without a single word of thanks. Before long Jarvis began to understand why cops went on the take; propping up their trifling incomes with easy hush money from dealers and thieves who needed a friend on the goody-good side of the law. He "got it" now: why they couldn't find enough half-decent teachers willing to risk their lives on a daily basis to try and teach kids who didn't care much, dealing with parents who didn't care at all.

Not only that, but Jarvis now appreciated why people stayed away; good, happy suburban folk with apple-cheeked babies and Honest-Abe-ethics who couldn't be baited by the latest and greatest government-funded publicity lures. Not the amphitheater. Not the aquarium. Not the cheap "commuter-friendly" ferry-rides to Philly. Not the lower sales tax. They didn't want to come to this godforsaken city for any reason whatsoever...even in broad daylight...and Jarvis couldn't blame them. Hell, *he* had a hard time resisting the urge to park his Lincoln at the bus depot on Hermann Ave., jump a one-way Greyhound to anywhere else, without a second thought to the folks left behind. From roach-infested Main Street to the rat-infested Banks. All the shootings. The homeless whores. The smut houses. The filthy hunger-pleading masses. Even if suburbanites were compassionate of the plight, sheer revulsion kept them away.

And, he thought as he rubbed his face, *Lord knew* these *headlines weren't gonna help nothin'.*

Jasper looked down at the newsprint in front of him and felt every last spark of energy and any remaining thread of hope bleed from his body and fall away, sinking through something absolute, like a diamond ring slipping through the slates of a dirty sewer grate, never to be retrieved.

Masses of clouds and shadows passed by until, after a time, he raised his fatigued head and turned to the row of tall windows (replete with original wavy glass painstakingly restored), past the veranda and the mosaic of varied-colored potted roses his lovely Henrietta tended to like newborns -- to where his lewd city spilled below and beyond...

He blanched at the thought of those vile reporters and all the nasty insinuations they'd make, the stories they'd concoct. *Goddamn snoops'll have my ass outta office and onto the street before*

Christmas... What gave them the right to tell him how to do his job? As if they had any idea what it took to manage a civilian combat zone? *Fuckin' reporters don't have a clue,* he seethed. *Sit in their fucking ivory tower and criticize while we're the ones in the trenches, just tryna survive.*

"Bullshit!" he spat, gathering up an armful of newspapers and releasing them at once, immediately sorry he'd disrupted them. "This ain't China," he said, smoothing them out in a distracted way, thinking of the police and teachers. "They don't got to be here. They volunteerin'." He looked back toward the pages and pages splayed across the long, glossy table and pieces of articles jumped and blazed before his worn, bloodshot, tear-poked eyes:

> *According to US Census reports, 53% of Camden residents are below the poverty line...*
>
> *Out of 25,000 households, 69% have a female as head of the household with no biological adult male present...*
>
> *Per capita income: $9,056...*

He thought of his own income then: The fifty-six thousand he got every year for a job that was technically supposed to be part-time but, in reality, was anything but.

From the outside the Jaspers appeared to be Camden's closest thing to royalty: A pair of shiny Lincolns. A refurbished home on The Banks. A boy in college, studying hard and working to secure loans to go to law school, maybe even follow in his old Pop's footsteps and run for Mayor one day. Maybe even Congress...

But the Mayor knew the truth.

He and Henrietta paid their taxes on time but that was where the good news ended. The bank was threatening foreclosure and Jarvis had the certified letters to prove it, locked tight in a drawer in his office at City Hall, far away from his wife's line of sight. He had a fat state-funded pension of course, but if he'd been smart he would have double-dipped like everyone else. Triple-dipped even.

He also knew he was too old to think of another career, and too tired to even try. He was able to give Henrietta some of the finer things simply by way of his position, but he knew the bulk of people had pathetically short memories and couldn't be counted on for very many things -- returning favors in particular -- especially if he were ever to be voted out. Momma always said: "When you're up, your friends know you. When you're down, you know your friends." Losing his job meant losing clout, losing "friends", thus losing favors to cash in on, and all those "extras" for Henrietta...

And then where would they be? The foreclosure threats would still be there and all of a sudden that fifty-six grand might not seem so shabby.

With a face marred far too deep for a man his age, Jarvis looked back out the window, trying to claw through his memory for any possible escape hatch, some "out" he'd overlooked -- anything at all -- a sliver of oar for the drowning man.

But there was nothing.

In the kitchen Poppy the maid was burning bacon, just the way he liked it. But the idea of eating was suddenly ridiculous. Waves of revulsion overcame him as if dispelled by the river itself, washing over him, threatening to pull him beneath the briny tide.

But then he thought of the Senator, and the Senator's offer.

Jarvis consulted his gold watch -- the one he'd gotten from the County for twenty-five years of service; the same one he'd once worn with satisfaction, with pride even, but was now just a watch -- and picked up the phone.

For just a moment he paused.

Just one.

Before dialing.

The receiver was like an Olympic baton in his hand; once it was passed on the Senator's plan would be off and running and out of Jarvis' control for good. As he stared at it, cognizant of what he was about to do, how it would make a free man a slave, he almost hung up, almost thought twice.

9

But then his mind flashed. The envelopes. All those envelopes –– both the ones hidden down at City Hall and the tower of the ones Henrietta *knew* about –– all those envelopes holding unpaid bills stacked on the dining room table amid the heaps of damning newsprint. He drew the stack toward him, began fingering their corners until their stiff, pointed angles were rounded and the pile seemed less daunting, more attainable.

But they weren't, and he knew that. They never were.

He pictured Henrietta's face if he were ever to come clean: to divulge the true, sad state of their finances. The sag of disappointment in her shoulders, the flare of anger like jet engines as she watched her beloved home taken away; the tamale ire replacing the soft, almost musical Georgian lilt in her voice; the absence of respect in her usually kind caramel eyes. She would scream and cry, bang her fists on his chest and fall to her knees. The news would stagger her, would wound beyond redemption. Jarvis shuddered despite the balmy morning.

Thinking of all the secrets he'd kept, he almost heaved as he felt a well of regret rise up, a mound of hideous bile in his throat skulking forth, threatening escape. His lips parted but nothing but a heavy moan broke forth, scattering the envelopes like dandelion seeds across the dark wood of the room.

He stared at them dully; a catatonic of his own creation.

His bride of thirty years was a good Christian woman, but Jarvis knew she'd swear like a sailor and curse the day she met him. Tell his sorry-ass what she *really* thought of him. Go home to her Momma down south; leave Jersey for good. Maybe go so far as to try to turn their boy against him...

The dark thoughts retreated somewhat as his gaze made its way back to the phone, once just an innocuous household necessity, no different than a teapot; now his only way out.

When Senator Dino Bruni first approached him, the Mayor had thought that the man had finally gone and lost his ever-loving mind and told him so.

But what choice did he have now?

He choked down the doubt that pricked at him like fire ants and began to dial.

There just weren't any two ways about it. Something needed to be done.

⁂

Later that night he found himself peering through plumes of cigar smoke to see the man smiling across the table -- the Senator himself – pleased as punch by the idea of Jarvis finally succumbing to a direction that better suited his plans. "You're doing the right thing," Dino Bruni said, revealing two rows of glossy whites that the Mayor imagined must've cost a pretty penny. "Really. You are."

Jarvis doubted it but took the man's hand anyway; let him shake it with gusto.

"This is a good move," Bruni said, eyes never wavering, but all Jarvis could focus on that picture book smile -- those flawless teeth -- and how most things that looked too good to be true usually were. "You're being smart. You know that, right? You're doing the right thing."

Listless, Jarvis nodded, but he knew he wasn't doing the right thing; he was doing the *only* thing. Just the sight of the Scottolino brothers leaning against either side of the doorjamb told him so; the hulking masses watching him through hooded eyes, all-but blocking the only route of escape. The mafia wasn't nearly as strong as it had been –- everyone knew that -–- but Jarvis was no dummy. They could still break legs and lives and make you disappear deep within the Pine Barrens or the cement column of a bridge somewhere if they so desired, and by the look on the Scottolino brothers' faces, they wanted *him* to know it, too.

The rest of the meeting was a blur. Jarvis sat by while the Senator and that pushy engineer made plans that were not entirely over his head, but none that he totally understood either and, just after midnight, after another round of vigorous handshakes, he was still surprised to find himself there. How he'd barely even shifted in his seat -- "kid-leather" Bruni had told him, chest puffed, bragging as usual. *Might as well be an electric chair,* was all Jarvis had thought.

It wasn't until they all stood to leave that reality dawned and Jarvis knew this was actually happening to him. Numb, he felt almost feeble as Bruni and Sterling Sault -- that nasty blue-blooded engineer -- guided him gingerly through the bowels of Bruni's campaign headquarters, taking him by the elbow as though he were an infirm in their charge. Later that would haunt him: the way they'd treated him; how they hadn't even attempted to hide their dominance over him the way they'd once tried; it was now a given.

Once outside, Jarvis had stared like a vegetable: Bruni and Sterling Sault all hearty back-slaps and shark-tooth smiles as they stood on the stoop, the Scottolino brothers hovering behind, casting inhumanly large shadows like some fucked-up version of Mt. Rushmore. He'd had to force his eyes away from them and to Bruni when the Senator asked: "Now you're sure you won't join us for a scotch, Jarvis? My good man Sterling here has brought a bottle of thirty year old Glen Fiddich, haven't you?"

The engineer smiled wide –- a little too wide for Jarvis' taste. "I certainly have. This day now marks quite a different future –- for all of us –- and I certainly plan to mark it in the manner in which it deserves."

"Now *this* is a man to do business with," the Senator said with a genial chuckle -- luminous smile flashing -- clasping the engineer's hand as the pair laughed. "He's one of us."

As Jarvis watched he felt more akin to the lampposts, to the trees, to the goddamn alley dumpsters –- to *anything* -- than either of them.

After he declined he'd gone home to the old mansion on The Banks to find that Poppy the maid had left dinner wrapped in foil before heading to bed, but the notion of anything but tea was impossible to digest. He'd sat on the veranda, the roses surrounding him like twisted hands ready to grab, and looked at his filthy city sloping around him until the sky began to match the cold Earl Grey trembling in his hands.

A chorus of police sirens screamed through the early hours and jerked him conscious. His hands shook as he closed and locked the French doors behind him. He was almost frightened by himself; *What time was it? How long had he been out here? What was happening to him?*

"How'd your meeting go?" A sleepy Henrietta wanted to know when he crept into bed.

Her words startled him, piercing his loneliness; he hadn't realized he'd woken her, and his reaction was knee-jerk: "Oh fine, sugar," he said before thinking. "Nothin' to worry about. Go on now, get yo' sleep, Henny. I'll see you in the mornin' now baby."

She seemed satisfied by this and leaned over to plant a clumsy, sleep-riddled kiss on his cheek before telling him she loved him.

Moments later he heard the familiar sound of her gentle breathing. He watched her chest rise and fall, smelling the jasmine from the lotion she always rubbed on just after her bath, and the Mayor had never felt more alone.

He would have years to think about that moment, to wonder how it might've all turned out if only he'd turned on the lamp and repeated to his dear bride the words of the Senator, to see the look on her face and to feel her soft, strong hand in his as she told him he'd be crazy if he let Dino Bruni into their lives like that.

Again and again he'd turn the scene over in his mind like an oyster with a pearl, knowing that one single moment was when he'd stabbed a hole straight through the fortress of their marriage –- a great well from which so many more lies would spring forth.

He'd have more days than he'd ever care to count to regret letting her roll to her side and drift off, not knowing of the evil he'd just plunged them into, leaving him awake for hours, his back flat against the headboard -- growing tighter than a bow -- with the sick knowledge he'd just made a deal with the devil.

What finally eased his burden of guilt enough to allow for sleep to take over were the words of Momma, arriving in some sort of subconscious wake/dream. His eye lids fluttered to close, a nervous butterfly landing, as her voice echoed against the tunnels of his sleep-swaddled mind: "The devil you know, Jarvis baby, is 'whole 'lot better than the devil you don't."

2

Five Years Later
Friday, August 29th
10:33am

"Will the defendant please rise?" A smattering of muffled coughs and the rustling of sweltering and anxious people squished too tightly in their seats echoed against the otherwise reverent oak of the archaic courtroom. The heat of the day bore through the wavy glass windows sending the already tense room beyond the bearable.

Late as usual, Ben Campbell slid through the double doors and returned the glare of the sergeant-at-arms with an apologetic smile. A flop of brown curls still wet from the shower fell into his eyes as he eased along the back wall to the only available space, holding his breath against the assault of too many summer bodies too close together, and craned his neck to see.

The defendant, Iggy, the oldest of the Bruni brothers, showed the packed room his back; his lanky frame defeated by an off-the-rack suit with shoulder pads so conspicuous they only succeeded in drowning his birdlike torso further into the polyester.

The room had surpassed capacity and even though Ben knew his boss would be up front with the rest of the family, he had a hard time spotting him. He shouldn't be nervous; it wasn't as though the

Senator wouldn't be there. Of course he would. But Ben needed more than to just see him; he needed to see how he reacted when he heard the verdict.

For months he'd tried not to have any expectations, but it'd been difficult. Everyone knew that dumbass Iggy was guilty as hell. Senator Dino Bruni's reaction today would set the tone for the rest of the campaign, and thus Ben's every waking minute for the next three months. Though, on the whole, Bruni was closer to untouchable than any candidate Ben had ever worked for, it was never wise to make assumptions. Campaign politics were much like the Wild West; there was a large degree of lawlessness, and just about anything could happen. If they returned a guilty verdict, he'd just carry on as though he'd expected it all along, keeping a finger on the pulse of their polling and courting reporters as best he could in an effort to ensure favorable headlines. And, as far as the voting public went, he'd simply employ the best spin his imagination could conjure to keep them on their side and in their pocket. *We'll be okay,* he kept telling himself. *We'll be just fine.*

He'd barely blinked when a stroke of luck materialized: a rather large woman bent forward, affording him a fleeting glimpse of the Bruni clan in the front row -- the Senator included, his perfect silver mane unmistakable. He looked poised but earnest and Ben felt himself relax a bit.

Just six months earlier he'd sat across from the Senator watching him peruse his resume as if seeing it for the first time, when they both knew the truth. Hundreds of candidates had applied, but Ben was first choice. And why shouldn't he be? His years on the Hill and campaign trails of various candidates across the country had earned him top billing as a campaign manager to be reckoned with. And when the Senator asked why he should hire him, Ben didn't hesitate: "Because I'm the best there is."

Bruni had been both amused and curious. "And why's that?"

"Because I hate to lose and I'll do anything to win."

He was hired on the spot, but Bruni still had questions for him, and as he walked him to the door he didn't hesitate to ask.

"So why leave DC? After building up such a reputation?"

"Personal reasons," Ben simply said. "My father just died and my mom needs my help. She's raising my niece." He was careful to leave out the part of his drug addict sister, though he shouldn't have been; Bruni's henchmen had already compiled a file on him *this thick*, detailing every possible thing about his life they could find. But Ben had been none the wiser.

"Loyalty. I like that." Was all the Senator had said, and watching him now stand by his idiot brother as he dragged their family name through the mud, Ben knew his boss had meant it.

Practically every day since that interview they'd practiced for this moment, and Ben had fine-tuned the talking points so many times he could recite at will every possible permutation of every question a reporter might ask.

But that didn't stop his heart from racing. He had, after all, hung his future on this campaign, on Dino Bruni getting re-elected to represent the good folks of the fifth Legislative District of New Jersey. So many people were counting on him, and he was feeling pressure not unlike a slow, pitiless strangulation.

Hating to feel so nervous, he checked his watch, focused on the judge, swallowed hard, and said a prayer, hoping that if God was not merciful, then at least He might have a benevolent sense of irony.

Cracking his knuckles Senator Bruni was as solemn as an undertaker as he watched his brother standing alongside the trio of lawyers the Senator himself had hired, smoothing their silk ties against their chests and bracing for the verdict.

The Scottolino brothers had recommended them and Dino had been hard-pressed to come up with anyone else who had been found on the wrong side of the law as many times as they had. If anyone ever needed good criminal defending, it was them. "These guys do not fuck around," Val Scottolino had insisted. "If there's a loophole to be found, rest assured they'll hang the prosecution from it."

Still, the Senator had a bad feeling.

He didn't dare tear his eyes from the judge, a patrician Ben Franklin-type who wore a permanent scowl as if he were assigned the perpetual task of asking the world: "What *is* that smell?". Judge Abraham Henry had seen and heard it all by now and couldn't be bothered to muster much more than hostile indifference toward those unlucky enough to turn up on his docket. Bruni glowered at the man in the robe –- at the jowly face lined with red fissures well earned from booze and age -- still bitter that the old bastard couldn't be bought.

Bruni noticed the pads of his fingers turning white as he pressed them against the knuckles of his clasped hands and immediately released them with something close to disgust. Anxiety had no place in this situation. Angst was for the weak. Earlier, his campaign manager Ben had tried to tell him to relax, that either way, good or bad, the jury had already come to a decision and there was nothing anyone could do about it. This morning, in the solace of his breakfast nook, this had made sense. Comforted him, even. But now it seemed naïve, a fool's condolence, and it taunted him. Cagey, he thought of reaching out for his wife's hand, but then of course thought better of it, pulling back. The ruby of his pinky ring glinted in a column of morning light, and he glanced at the line of tall arched windows laboring to keep the August heat from intruding. The building was a historical landmark and regarded as a rare jewel amid his rather defective district. How many times had he posed in front of this very building? Smiling and shaking hands...

But nothing from memory lane could calm him now. The Senator didn't like to sweat and cursed the judge for taking his sweet time. The lack of air-conditioning and blasted trail of moisture making its way down his spine led him to recall he'd never spent much time in here during summer. He was thankful there were no cameras; The Judge had seen to that at first blush of the media circus. But who knew when he might find himself here again? He made a note to have Ben look into drafting some requests for some upgrades. Perhaps this would be another feather in his cap. The school was one thing -- shiny new, state-of-the-art; his baby from Day One. But why not take on a historical renovation, as well? Depending on its date of origination, he might even be able to secure some federal funds for it...

"Madame forewoman!" The Judge demanded, and the small Hispanic woman jumped a little in her pumps, the sound reverberating, snapping the Senator to attention like a cadet. "Has the jury reached a verdict?"

She regained herself. "We have, your honor."

"Kindly hand the forms to my bailiff."

The Senator muttered a silent prayer as the nondescript woman began to read.

"The people of state of New Jersey, plaintiff, versus Ignazio Lucio Bruni, defendant, case number 165805, the jury in the above and titled cause finds the defendant guilty of automobile theft trafficking in violation of penal code section..."

The Senator's head dropped. Gasps and murmurs ricocheted.

"On count two, conspiracy in the second degree, how do you find the defendant?"

"Guilty, your honor."

"On count three, receiving stolen property..."

"On count four..."

Dino's head began to spin, the courtroom dissolving into a macabre kaleidoscope swirling before his dazed eyes, his world slapped askew, knocked off its axis, weakening his knees, and just when he thought he might be losing his mind entirely he heard:

"Bail *denied*."

And he was shoved back to reality, the whole thing over almost as soon as it began, and just as he was wrapping his mind around the shock of it all, of bail being denied, he was pulled to his feet and thrust into a hot sea of bodies hugging him, offering teary-eyed condolences. An old pro, he switched into default-mode, smiling –– not too wide, not too stagy -- but appropriately, as though at a funeral –– both accepting and deflecting sympathy in his subtle, artful way.

"...We'll be praying for you, Senator. You and yours..."

"...Not for nothin', Dino, but they got the wrong guy..."

Just when he thought the heat of the day might roast him whole he noticed the crowd had thinned to a trickle. When the last cheek had been kissed and hand shook, the relieved Senator glanced back toward the defendant's table and felt a bad jolt when he realized he'd never even seen his brother led away to the world of the caged. Never said goodbye. Iggy may have been the world's biggest moron and a disgrace to the Bruni family name, but he was still blood. Dino felt a pang as he stared at the empty table and reached to the row of chairs in front of him to steady himself. His composure had vanished and the thought of going before the cameras and answering to reporters suddenly made him ill at ease. For the first time in his twenty-plus years of public service, he considered ducking out through a back door and avoiding the press corps altogether.

Dino looked back toward the table. Only faint watermarks left behind by the pitcher of ice water and glasses were evidence that the entire thing had ever taken place at all.

In a blaze of anger he thought of the lawyers then, in their Ferragamo shoes and Prada suits, smoothing those somber-colored ties against their chests with false gravity as if they actually cared about Iggy. *As if they actually gave one stinking shit.* His uneasiness dissipated and fury lurched into its place. *Five hundred and fifty dollars an hour. Five hundred and...Fucking Scottolino brothers...Two-bit hacks...*

Suddenly a supernova of rage lit up the room like an electric blue fork of lightning in a docile sky, as unsettling as it was unexpected, as he bellowed: "Five hundred and fifty dollars an hour times two years. Two fucking years. And for what? For *WHAT*?"

But he knew what. And the empty walls of the courtroom seemed to know it, too, as they absorbed and muted his rant. Footsteps moved swiftly behind him and he felt a hand on his shoulder. "It's okay, Dino," he heard Ben say. "It's okay."

But it wasn't until he heard the snap of the plastic cap of a hair-spray canister being unhinged (and the hiss of CFC's that followed) and saw his wife showering her platinum hair in a fine mist that he blinked back to the moment and any semblance of sentimentality evaporated. For whatever reason, the sight of the spray catching the light from the windows and making a fleeting rainbow slapped the old Dino back to life like a bull kicked in the balls, and re-lit that Sicilian fire the wise knew to avoid.

"You ready?" Ben asked.

Bruni's nod was curt before striding past him. "You sure?" Ben called after him, but it was more a formality than anything and they both knew it. He was more than ready to face that infestation of gutless predators crawling about outside, microphones in hand, salivating over the verdict. Of putting them in their place. He could hardly wait to take them on.

"Dino, wait!" Micki Bruni demanded as she smoothed her satin skirt against her tan thighs and worked the Barbie-pink nugget of gum among her molars. He ignored her as usual, igniting a droning: "Diiino!" and the old walls of the courtroom seemed to recoil against her nasal-laden *faux-celebrity-Housewives* whine.

The dread was gone and the bravado was back. *What had he been thinking? He wasn't worried.* He almost laughed. *The thought was preposterous. All this heat was making him soft.* Turning tail and being a coward was not in his nature –– *was not, and never had been* in the Bruni blood -- and, he wasn't about to break tradition. For no more than a moment he paused before the set of double doors and straightened himself. Then he was out the door, striding down the glossy hallway in a victor's gait, ignoring the stares of the curious peeking out from doorways and over frosted government partition glass.

By the time he reached the hall's end Dino Bruni all but kicked open the heavy wooden doors to face the cache of reporters and camera flashes waiting for him on the courthouse steps, panting and pacing in the five-alarm heat like hungry swine, ready to feast on what remained of his political career.

3

Friday
12:04pm

A delicate, baby-pink-painted fingernail clicked "refresh" as Sydney Langston hoped for an update on the Bruni trial. She could go down the hall to watch on one of the many flat screens in the viewing room, but she had no interest in seeing the inside of a courtroom -- ever again, if possible –- even on TV. They gave her creeps beyond belief, and for good reason, so she remained at her desk.

Though technically she was a reporter, she was hardly in pursuit of a Pulitzer Prize. And this "newsroom" she sat in, if you could call it that, was void of any buzz of frenzied activity or breaking bulletins. In fact, with its piped-in easy listening and innocuous Office Depot trimmings, it might have been confused with a dentist's waiting room.

Sydney worked at *The Jerzine*, a lifestyle magazine that occasionally featured a scandalous socialite piece –- the one or two a year that cropped up in the mostly idle Delaware Valley -- but, for the most part, focused on new BYOB's and boutiques blooming in the 'burbs of Philadelphia, the best lawyers in the region, the best doctors; photos from each month's yield of fundraisers and galas, discreet personal ads tucked in the back from locals looking for love and apparently lacking internet access.

That's not to say it wasn't successful, or coveted; it was both, and Sydney was one of the most popular features writers, known for her optimism and unique choice of subject matter, her articles generating the highest volume of fan mail with devotees to her monthly column praising her with sentiments like:

"In a time full of so much crime and misery, Sydney Langston is a welcome escape…"

And, a personal favorite:

"Sydney Langston reminds us of the kind of people we want to be, the kind of world we want to live in…"

Her dogged focus on the positive wasn't by accident or design; if you'd had her past, you'd naturally gravitate toward the upbeat, as well. She'd seen enough of the other side to last a lifetime, thanks.

So today's interest in the Bruni trial had nothing to do with her job and everything to do with friendship. Though he didn't show it much, she knew Ben Campbell well enough to know that this trial had been grating on his mind, and though personally she thought it to be silly -— *of course Bruni would get re-elected, everyone knew that* -- she was a worrier by nature, and Ben holding the special place in her heart as he did, was always near the top of the list.

The trial also served as the perfect distraction from her present woes: the current article she was working on. Sir Thomas More Tech, the region's first charter school, had opened its doors six years ago, welcoming its first class of Camden's best and brightest teens. A state-of-the-art mecca for the learning -- one that would put most private schools to shame -- the project had garnered enormous amounts of attention, and was hailed both regionally and nationally for various reasons: its use of green materials, its commitment to a well-versed curriculum, but most of all for its founders for not abandoning a place like Camden, for not abandoning its kids.

Along with Mayor Jarvis Jasper, Senator Bruni had led the charge in developing what *The New York Times* had dubbed "an urban utopia", and her idea to do a "where are they now" piece on that first class of students, the ones who were now a year beyond graduation, should have been a cakewalk: a tapestry of uplifting stories of success, how brilliant minds emerged from such squalor, propped up by the faith these powerful men had in them. But, as she was finding out, this story was anything but easy. Or uplifting for that matter.

Sighing, her gaze snagged the cluster of framed photos alongside her desk. First and foremost of she and Ben in graduation gowns, laughing as they clutched their diplomas and flung their caps into the air, Piedmont High the lackluster backdrop. The next was faded; them on their ten-speeds, their spindly adolescent legs poking alongside the spokes like fawns first learning to walk, big smiles clad in bulky, shiny braces. Sydney felt herself warm at the image, though she'd seen it countless times before. The Campbell's had been like a second family to her; Ben, a brother. And if there was anyone who'd needed a stable family, it was she.

Her eyes travelled to the next frame, of her grandmother, Nana Jean, the one who'd moved to Jersey from Texas all those years ago, as soon as she'd heard the news about Sydney's parents, and taken her in, a child she'd barely known. She was costumed in a red cowgirl outfit, complete with tassels, bolo tie, and jaunty red alligator boots, blue eyes sparkling as she mugged for the camera, on the way out the door to one of her country line dancing parties. Nana Jean may have been a senior citizen but she had more energy and spunk than a lot of people Sydney's own age. Her smile grew soft at the image, and she made a mental note to swing by Nana's on her way home.

And though she'd seen this one as many times as the others, the next photo made her start, freezing the smile onto her lips and sucking away some of the happiness, replacing it with a melancholy that made her wonder for the thousandth time why she didn't just take the damn thing home, shove it in a drawer somewhere -- do *something* with it, for goodness sake -- other than let it claw at her heart, just like it was doing now. Cody Briggs. Her --- what? Ex-fiancé? Almost husband? --- In flip flops and faded cargo's, on the back of someone's yacht holding up a beautiful blue marlin and smiling, it seemed, just at her. He was in Arizona now, possibly forever, at the Cardinals training camp, issuing occasional emails, but mostly respecting her wishes not to contact her.

"Holy smokes, Langston! You're still here?!" a deep voice boomed, and Sydney jumped at the intrusion, yanking her hand away from the photo as if bitten by it.

"Gosh, Roger! You scared me!" she laughed.

Roger O'Dell may have been her boss, but they were just as much friends as anything. Tall and broad shouldered, he had the appearance of a giant teddy bear, and a personality to match.

"Sorry, Syd, I'm just surprised to see you, is all. It's –- what?" he said, consulting his watch in a stagy way. "After twelve on a Friday in August? Labor Day weekend? I'd say you're taking this project a little *too* seriously," he chuckled.

She laughed too, but then it snagged in her throat: a hook tethering a harmony. "I guess I just lost track of time, is all. What's your excuse?"

The smile faded but didn't fall away altogether; Roger O'Dell was the smiling kind. "No reason to go home."

"Oh I'm sorry. Things with Ellie? Are they...?"

"Over," he sighed. "Movers come tomorrow."

Sydney's heart ached for him, for the death of his marriage. Breaking up with Cody had been hard enough for her and they'd only been together for three years. She couldn't imagine ending things after thirty, especially the way Ellie O'Dell had chosen to do it: by complete sneak attack, with a brand new boyfriend in tow.

"How are you holding up?"

"Oh I'll be alright. What else can I do? Just keep on, keeping on, I guess." He sighed. "But enough about me. Back to you. Why aren't you headed to the beach or a barbeque or anywhere else but here?"

"I was waiting for an update on the Bruni trial, but actually this assignment is..." she didn't know how to proceed, the words dying in her mouth, and simply waved a hand at the pile of papers strewn before her. She looked up at him, tucking a wayward strand of her flaxen hair behind her ear. "I just don't know how to make heads or tails of it, if you want to know the truth."

Roger O'Dell cleared his throat, his brow cinching together as he grew solemn. "Listen Syd," he began, his voice sinking, drawing her towards him. "I didn't want to say anything because you...you seemed so...I don't know...*into it*. Which is great," he said, holding his palms up toward her, not wanting to offend. "Don't get me wrong. I'm just as liberal as the next editor. But this project you've taken on...well, I've just had my reservations about it, you know?"

She felt a mixture of mild curiosity and annoyance, the latter surprising her, and her face screwed into an expression she hoped conveyed the former. Her tone was slow, but firm: "No. I *don't* know."

He chose his words carefully, gently. "It's just that, well, we're talking about Camden here, Syd. Not exactly paradise, as we all know. You're always dead set on finding the pot of gold at the end...And I just -- well, we *all* just feel that you're going to be disappointed, is all."

Sydney settled back into her chair and fixed her arms across her chest, her eyebrows arched.

A deep flush crept up his neck. "Syd, you know I'm in your corner no matter what. You're the best features writer on the team, and you've never let me down. *Ever*," he added as he noticed that one of the most laid back and kindest women he'd ever had the pleasure of working with -- or knowing, for that matter -- was currently shooting him daggers. "Listen, I know your heart is in the right place, it always is. But I just feel like this time you've got it set on a fairytale ending, and that's probably not in the cards. That's all."

She went to reply but then his cell rang. He checked the number and frowned. "Sorry, Syd. I gotta take this. Divorce lawyer. God help me."

As he made his way down the hall, she felt a little guilty. She knew she shouldn't be so defensive. And why was she feeling defensive anyway? Resting her elbows on her desk, she pressed the heels of her hands against her closed eyes and took a series of deep breaths, hoping to channel some of the clarity and positive energy her yoga instructor was always going on about.

Maybe it was because there was a kernel of truth in what he was saying. She already *was* disappointed, or maybe not disappointed exactly but something -- dismayed? -- At her progress with the article thus far. *The Jerzine* gave her free reign when it came to choosing assignments, although the brass always went through the formality of "approving" it before she got started. Remembering the way Roger and the others had exchanged uneasy looks before giving her the go-ahead, the way they had looked at her with something like sympathy now made sense.

She hadn't imagined it'd be difficult; in fact (she'd admit a little sheepishly) it seemed the absolute *perfect* project to work on during the lazy dog days of August. Especially with everything she'd been through with Cody lately, she imagined it to be exactly the kind of pick-me-up feel-good story that'd brighten her spirits, not to mention the timing was just right, coinciding with the arrival of the new school year. But, for reasons she couldn't put her finger on, much less understand, things weren't working out at all like she'd planned. And failure wasn't something Sydney was used to.

For one, she was having a hard time tracking down a lot of the kids. So many phone numbers had been disconnected and emails unanswered and letters returned to sender that she was beginning to question the reliability of the school's administrative staff she'd considered saintly just weeks ago, the same ones who'd told her if there was anything, *anything at all* she needed, just ask.

Then again, this was Camden, where she imagined necessities such as phones and electricity blinking off and on with a tiresome irregularity.

Then there were also the few she *had* found, had already talked to. True, only a handful so far, but she'd noticed something odd in the way the few of them had interacted with her. What it was she couldn't say, but it was beginning to irk something inside of her.

Take Cyrus and Cedric Ashe, for instance. Twin brothers, standout turn-your-head-then-shake-it-in-disbelief star running backs that'd had college football recruiters watching them with visions of National Championships glinting in their eyes ever since sophomore year. Eager scouts from University of Miami, Florida State, Texas, Alabama — you name it -- breathless as they watched the pair dodge mountainous blockers, defying gravity as they danced and dove past defensive lines so deftly you had a hard time accepting the fact that they were still just kids and not vets of the Pro Bowl, now simply an interchangeable duo sharing janitorial shifts at *So What Johnny's*, the local rib and BBQ joint, nowhere near a co-ed dorm or quad, ivy-laden halls, let alone the NFL.

And it wasn't just what they did for a living, or even how their futures had failed to materialize so spectacularly that troubled Sydney. It was the odd way they had regarded her and her most basic questions, as if tricked by even the most rudimentary forms of interactions, incapable of anything more than perfunctory communication.

"We don't play ball no more," Cedric had told her plainly, his voice as sharp as moss, eyes gray and dead, while his brother kept his head down and mopped, his back bowed like an old man's. No sooner had the interview concluded than Sydney locked herself in her car, unnerved beyond comprehension, her hands shaking like maracas as she tried to place the key in the ignition and failed.

Of course explanations could be given; justifications so obvious it both pained her to acknowledge them, and also pleased her — signaling in the latter that all hope was not lost. First, she'd never heard the boys speak prior. Who knew? They could've been *even less* forthcoming and contemplative four years ago and had made great strides since. Or, they might not have ever been, and thus explained the retreat of any offers for scholarships. For all she knew, they could've had the opportunity to create their own version of the SATs and *still* failed, too dumb to remember the answers to their very own questions. There were also a myriad of permutations on their personal situations — a child on the way (commonplace for teens in

Camden), career-ending injuries (although she thought her research would've revealed such news by now), a sick mother at home that prevented them from leaving town...After all, her own best friend had just jumped ship on a moonward career on Capitol Hill to return to Jersey and help his newly widowed mother take care of his niece. Speaking of which...

She pressed the refresh button again. Ben had been in her corner for longer and throughout more than anyone she'd ever known, save for Nana Jean. But even then. Nana Jean, godsend that she was, had been estranged from Sydney's mom and knew nothing of her murder until a good eighteen months later, and by then Sydney had endured who knew how many foster homes and family court rulings. Meanwhile, Ben had been there all along; everything from Syd's partner-in-crime, alibi, big-brother bodyguard, confessional priest and yes, even stern parent at times (a laughable idea, no matter what she had done, given all his exploits) as well as everything in-between. If it hadn't been for Ben and the rest of the Campbell family there's no telling where she might've ended up, how many governmental cracks she would've slipped through, how many bureaucratic blunders she would've been wounded by...and God-knows how many hands would've had the opportunity to touch her again, to taint her, sapping any last scrap of virtue from her.

If it hadn't been for the Campbell's she had no doubt she'd be a statistic by now, of one sort or another. And like so many of the kids from Camden, she would have been yet another child enslaved by the failures of the adults entrusted with her care.

And for a time she forgot about the Ashe brothers and the high-tech school, her boss' wavering faith in her current project and Iggy Bruni's trial, and instead remembered how she could have easily been another Camden story –- a tragedy so heartbreaking in its familiarity that most were never even moved to tears.

4

Friday
2:11pm

Leaving today of all days was not ideal but the Senator had given Ben his blessing so many times the burden of guilt was all but erased. He'd even hugged him, called him "son", and wished him the best of luck.

"I can handle these schmucks," Bruni had said with a dismissive wave toward the stack of messages from reporters.

But by sheer force of habit and a blue collar work ethic rooted deep within his DNA, Ben had made a pact with himself that he *would* do work while in Boston, which is why he was now in Bruni campaign headquarters, piling aside various documents to take along: the weekly gang report issued by the Camden PD and gathered it; the Attorney General's most recent report on the state of prisons. Ben had already read both, but needed to create talking points for the Senator. As soon as the furor over the verdict died down they'd be right back at his throat wanting to know why crime was on the rise. But Ben would take it, whatever they threw at him; anything was better than having his candidate be associated with a now-convicted criminal, a blood relative no less.

As usual, the ringing phones were relentless. Up front there were two receptionists at any given time, as well as a gaggle of volunteers, mostly made up of devoted party-faithful blue hairs and a smattering of fresh-faced high school kids earning credits. Ben felt sorry for them, thinking of the barrage of calls they'd be buried under until the bloodthirsty press found its next victim. But he felt worse for himself, knowing the lion's share of the calls were for him.

The intercom buzzed and the voice of his assistant Millie came through: "Ben, there's a Herb Heim on the line for you."

"Reporter?"

"No, but this is probably the tenth time he's called in the past couple days. The twentieth this week, easy."

Ben paused in his frenzy, brow wrinkled. The name did sound familiar, now that she mentioned it. He looked to his list of "return calls to make" -- the bane of his existence most days -- and saw the guy's name and number appeared a dozen times, at least. But that was where the recognition ended.

"Take a message, please."

"Right-o."

"And Millie?"

"Yes?"

"Have you seen the latest poll?" Muttering to himself: "It was right here yesterday..."

"Probably on the Senator's desk. He was looking over it this morning."

Of course he was, Ben thought. *Probably trying to soak up all the good news possible before the verdict.* They'd anticipated a bit of a drop in numbers in the event of a guilty verdict, but it was still early. Labor Day was Monday. Voters were still in summer-mode; kids coming home from camp, families at the Jersey shore, the boardwalks packed with people more interested in bumper cars and hot dogs than guilty verdicts and headlines. There might be a delay in backlash but they still had plenty of time to bounce back for Election Day. He was sure of it.

Checking his watch, he jogged down the short hallway of the 100-year Colonial-turned-campaign-headquarters, the old floorboards creaking beneath the threadbare Oriental runner, and darted into Bruni's office. The grandfather clock in the corner stood in judgment, a solemn reminder that his flight was set to leave in just over an hour. Thinking of the eternal line at airport security, he groaned as he pawed the Senator's desk in search of the binder.

Sweat trickled down his back as the clock ticked along in even measure until Millie came through the intercom again. "Just a sec," he called before spotting the binder: relief washing over him like a summer storm on a muggy day as he scooped it up, not noticing the additional documents from Dino's desk stuck to its plastic bottom: the email printouts marked CONFIDENTIAL not meant for Ben's eyes, or anyone else's for that matter.

Trotting from the office with an armful of it all he called, "I'm coming!"

The traffic was light as Ben careened down Admiral Wilson Boulevard, the wind whipping through his Jeep, the music shaking from his speakers, the sun warm on his skin, and he had to smile. In just a few short hours he'd be in Boston, and he'd have a fiancée. It was a notion that was both terrifying and thrilling.

His decision to propose to Kat had come rather suddenly, surprising even him. She had been dropping hints about as subtle as those cartoon pianos plummeting to sidewalks for who knew how long, but he had just never felt the same urgency. Or any, really. The thing was, she was completely out of his league. But for a long time he still hadn't been sure he wanted her. After all, Kat was never someone he'd normally date.

DC was a tough town to make friends in, particularly friends you could trust. Digger Vance had been one of Ben's few and one night after more than their fair share of pints of Guinness at some smoky bar, Kat had come up and hugged Digger, an old friend from her interning days, before turning to Ben and offering up one of her smiles, the kind that told the world she was unaccustomed to hearing the word "no".

"I'm Katherine Van Horn," she'd said, her giant blue eyes dancing with a mixture of chardonnay and something like mischief. "But you can call me Kat."

At the time, Ben was well on his way to being drunk and not thinking of her in any terms other than what she might look like naked back in his apartment just a few blocks away, getting familiar with his sheets from Target, her blond hair loose and splayed across his pillow, those low-slung jeans in a tangle on the floor, discarded in a haze of lust.

Truth was, he never thought of *any* girl much beyond that, because he'd only ever thought he'd end up with Sydney. Through all the years they'd been best friends, he'd never had any doubt. None. They'd make the perfect couple -- everyone said so -- but then she'd met Cody Briggs and suddenly everything changed...

For a while he'd just stood idly by, waiting for it to fizzle out like all the rest, but by the time they got engaged it finally became clear that she was gone for good. And he'd done what any self-respecting brokenhearted man would do: he went out and got good and stinking drunk.

He was drunk the night he'd met Kat, too, just two months later. The three had chatted a bit -- Kat laughing at all his jokes, using any excuse to touch his arm, and then she was gone, leaving him and Digger to continue their drinking.

At some point Digger got into a dart match and Ben got into a flirting match with a perky brunette barely of drinking age who said "like" so many times that he'd balled up and tossed her number before he'd even rounded the block on the way back to his apartment, alone.

And he'd never given any of it a second thought until the next day when Digger forwarded an email:

Hey Digger,
    So good to see you! Hope all is well in research land. Quick question for you – is your friend from last night single? If so, please give him my number. He's a cutie.
XO
Kat

On the phone milliseconds later, Digger had been indignant: "Kat Van Horn and *you*, Campbell? She's practically New England royalty for fuck's sake. They're like the Kennedy's, Campbell. The *Kennedy's*. And she wants *you???*"

Ben had laughed and told him to go to hell and called her anyway, but even back then he'd never thought things would move much beyond casual. He didn't want them to, anyway. Sydney was still taking up most of the real estate in his heart and mind, and he figured probably always would.

But somehow that was exactly what happened. Before he knew it, they had keys to each other's apartments and Saturday night sleepovers extended deep into the workweek. And at some point it occurred to Ben that he was totally and completely content; happy, even.

But.

There's always a 'but', isn't there? He thought bitterly. She'd grown wistful watching her friends getting engaged and married –- a string of giddy toy soldiers falling in line, covered in tulle -- both the ones back home and from DC, and the pressure was on. He'd be in Illinois or Vermont or New Mexico or some other far-flung place working on the campaign-of-the-week, in some godforsaken motel room, cradling the phone between his ear and shoulder, trying to forget about his relentless eighteen-hour day. Flipping through the muted channels, landing on a football game, he'd ease back against the nest of pillows he'd built, grateful for a familiar voice. Then, after the first few minutes or so of listening to her bitch, happy to ignore her.

"But Ben," she'd say, her voice growing dangerously close to a whine. "You just don't understand. I'm not getting any younger. *You're* not getting any younger..."

Here we fuckin' go, he'd say to himself with a swig of his old friend Jack Daniels.

"...I'm *way* prettier than her. Why is *she* getting married first? I just don't get it... "

Touchdown. End zone strut. Swig. Field goal.

"...And we could settle down in Chevy Chase..."

Cell rumbling next to him, ignored.

"...Or, wherever, you know..."

Knock at the door. Room service. Greasy cheeseburger. Salty French fries. Sweet ketchup. A healthy dose of JD washing it all down.

"...And she has like, *zero* taste. I can't even *imagine* the god awful dress *she'll* show up in..."

Half time. Cheerleaders. Swig. Long legs. Long hair. Short skirts. Boner.

As Kat would natter on, he'd try to picture her: Prim blond bob, matronly suit skirts grazing her knees as she pumped through the halls of DC's most prestigious buildings with the tenacity of a rabid mutt -- a girl he never would have asked out in a million years if he'd met her there, on the job, watching her bust balls for a living.

But then there was the other side of her, the one in a pale yellow sundress, bare feet tucked under her as she read on the Parisien balcony of her apartment, face void of makeup and exquisite in its simplicity. Eyes closed he would see her so clearly he could almost smell her: Aristocratic nose, high cheek bones, rosebud lips moving silently along with a biography of FDR, or James Carville, or whatever dull piece of partisan literature that was her passion of the moment. He would see her in his mind and a serene, almost nostalgic smile would ease onto his face; a dopey grin he would've been embarrassed by if he hadn't been alone. *Aw Kat,* he'd muse, eyes still on the cheerleaders, imagining a sudden knock at the motel room door and Kat standing there in nothing but a raincoat and a dirty agenda for the night...

"...Knowing *her*, the rehearsal dinner'll be at the shittiest country club this side of the Mississippi, no doubt..."

Goodbye boner. Swig.

Pass rush. Flag. A pair of drunk chicks caught by the lustful cameraman, big boobs bouncing in time with Guns-n-Roses. Swig. *Welcome to the Jungle* and welcome back, Mr. Boner.

"...And I love you, Ben. I really do..."

Fumble. Swig. Recover.

"...Are you even *listening* to me?"

Swig. Cigarette. Touchdown.

And the thing was, Ben hadn't been opposed to getting married at all. Just not to her. Kat was beautiful, no doubt, but she was also whiny, difficult, and often caught hanging on the every word of her father, whom Bend tell had higher hopes for his daughter than the likes of some blue-collar kid from Jersey. And more than anything Ben was deeply embarrassed by that: by the idea of his life sounding like the lyrics of a Springsteen song.

But this summer all that had changed. Sometime around Memorial Day they'd arrived at a mutual decision to "take a break" and Ben had been fine with it at first. He'd just gotten the job with Bruni a few months earlier, after all, and was happy to focus just on that for a while. Well, that and helping his Mom and Zoey. The first few Kat-free weeks had been relaxing, even, and in some vague sense he figured this break would eventually evolve into a break-*up*, but he had neither the inclination to initiate it, nor break her heart.

But, though they were apart, they still talked. And that's when he learned about Tad Ernst.

His blood surged at just the thought, his hands all-but strangling the steering wheel of the Jeep, his lighthearted gaiety obliterated by a roundhouse to the gut, a reminder of the boarding school scumbag who'd moved in on his girl, who'd mistaken him for some chump who'd just roll over and let them sail off into the sunset together. *What kind of fucking name was* Tad *anyway?* Ben answered his own question: *It was the kind of name that almost demanded a punch in the face.* Ben had never met him, but almost didn't have to. He knew the type. Polo shirt with the collar flipped up, Nantucket red pants, boarding school breeding, cleft chin and witty banter. The exact opposite of himself. And Kat was cozying up with this dipshit, this guy who probably took her on picnics and played golf at The Club with the Old Man. In the worst moments he thought of her in her yellow sun dress, and then easing out if it, Tad getting ready to know Kat -- *his* Kat -- on a primal level...

It was enough to make Ben crazy.

Though he'd never admit it, he supposed that was what had prompted this hasty proposal. The idea of letting her go, of letting someone else 'win', was too much for him. Losing just wasn't an option in Ben Campbell's world.

It wasn't romantic, but he wasn't exactly a romantic guy. He'd invested two years with her –- most of it good. Well, about half of it –- and he wasn't about to let some Brooks Brothers douchebag sweep in and take off with his girl. Because she *was* his. Even though she often mentioned Tad, every call would end with a teary goodbye, her telling him how much she loved him and lamenting at his choice to move back to Jersey.

"But I had to, Kat. My mom needs me. Zoey needs me."

From four states away he'd feel her resentment, a blistering silence followed by an exasperated huff as if she just *couldn't believe* what an idiot he was. "But it's a state senate race, for Christ's sake, Ben. I've never *heard* of someone making such a colossal career fuck-up in my entire life. You were on the fast track on The Hill. You were a rising star. You were..."

He hated that, how she talked about his career. Yes, politics was something she'd grown up with -– or more precisely *in* –- and her family had more connections than US Air. But he was still a man, and it was still *his* career, and he'd be damned if he'd allow someone to second-guess his decisions. Or worse: have the *audacity* to judge them. His jaw would tighten then. "I know what I'm doing, Kat," he'd say, and mean it.

But now, looking in the rearview of his mind, dredging up all the past with her, he wondered if he really knew what he was doing *now*. After all, Sydney and Cody were no longer together...

But then: *Tad.* Just the thought of him...And yes, damn right he knew what he was doing. He was going to put a ring on *his girl's* finger, the twenty thousand dollar one all but burning a hole in his pocket. His adrenaline was coursing now, and he cranked the music, letting the speakers thunder, AC/DC ruling the day.

No sooner had he sped through EZ-Pass than he noticed the red and blue lights flashing in his rearview mirror. "Oh great," he moaned as he eased to the side of the base of the Ben Franklin Bridge. Peering in the rearview mirror he saw the City of Camden leaking away from its sides like toxic waste and thoughts of Kat were replaced by ones of Bruni.

Of all the things he could say –- *I'm late for my flight, I'm on my way to propose to my girlfriend* –- he said the one thing he *knew* with 100-percent certainty that would get him out of a ticket. The cop approached and he turned down the radio, leaning an elbow on the open window. "Good afternoon, officer. I work for Senator Dino Bruni."

Thirty seconds later and a friendly wave goodbye, Ben was back on his way to Philadelphia International, and Boston was just a few hours away.

2:44pm

The Senator's office was a torrent of strewn papers and upended files, scattered piles of documents and wadded up newsprint. It looked trashed beyond repair. Dino Bruni sat on the floor, his tie yanked askew, his normally coiffed hair mussed and jagged at points from his endless tugging on it. He knew *exactly* where he'd left the printouts of Heim's emails. Exactly. And now they were gone. And if anyone ever saw those...Just the thought of such a thing made his insides churn ghastly with nausea...

No, he wouldn't go there. He couldn't...

His cell disturbed the quiet of his defeat, and he recognized the number at once. "Wrigley!" he spat. "Where THE FUCK have you been? I've called you fifty fucking times and you --"

"Easy, Dino-baby. I'm here now. What's the problem?"

"Don't call me that."

"You need something, or what?"

Bo Wrigley had the upper hand and they both knew it.

The Senator attempted to compose himself. "Yeah, I need something," he said, the frustration and fatigue in his voice betraying him. He hated being in this position, desperate. "I need you on the next flight to Boston."

"A tail?"

"Yeah."

"Stats?"

"I'll get all the vitals over to you in a minute."

"Description?"

"I'll send a photo, too," Bruni assured him, then muttered: "I think he's got one on his desk of him and his girl..."

"His desk? You have access?"

"Yeah. He works for me."

"Name?"

"Ben Campbell."

"So what's the deal?"

"It seems some important shit made it into the wrong hands, and I need it back, or I need it destroyed. Whatever's easiest."

"And if this important shit can't be separated from this wrong pair of hands?"

"You know the drill," Bruni's eyes flashed: "Destroy his ass, too."

4

Friday
6:17pm

The New Jersey Department of Environmental Protection was housed in a section of the Statehouse built sometime during the Johnson Administration and scarcely touched since.

Surrounded by the fuzzy gray walls of his cube, Herb Heim stared at his computer monitor without seeing. It was well past quitting time, but he was in no hurry. Most state employees left at five o'clock sharp, but Herb had always been a workhorse. Not that he was really working much at the moment –- or would ever again, for that matter. His reason for lingering? A list that he needed to accomplish without the prying eyes of people with a penchant for gossip and too much time on their hands. And, on a picturesque Friday afternoon in August like this one, the Statehouse was about as busy as a church on Super Bowl Sunday.

Ever since the parade of his co-workers had filed out over an hour ago, Herb had been sitting in his worn tweed roller chair, staring at his computer monitor and plotting. His entire life he'd never been relevant, never had any sort of power. Now he had so much of it he tottered between exhilarating intoxication and utter terror. But the latter feeling had begun to dwindle in recent weeks, so much so that he barely felt it anymore, it only twitching against his mind every so often, like a lazy bee eying an abandoned glass of cola. He'd swat at it and it'd retreat, only to come back again a while later, suddenly remembering it was still thirsty.

No, these days he felt like the superhero version of Clark Kent. Gone were the days of taking orders; now he gave them. In fact just a few hours ago he'd sent a very specific list of them to some of the people who had kept him under their thumbs for all these years, and from his work email address no less, imagining them soiling their drawers when they noticed *that* little detail. Especially Bruni. And especially that asshole Sterling Sault.

A small but satisfied smile wormed its way across his lips.

These thoughts brought with them a new gush of bravado and in that moment Herb plucked the phone from its cradle and began to dial the number he now knew by heart. Though he'd made this call at least two dozen times this week –- twenty six, actually, at last count –- and four times today alone -- he still felt the clamminess of his palm against the plastic, his throat growing dry from nerves and a lifelong cloak of debilitating shyness he'd never been able to shed. He moved to push back the black frames of his glasses -– the kind Buddy Holly wore, that he himself had worn since he was a kid –- but they slid right back down, and it was then he realized it wasn't just his hands that were sweating; his entire body was covered in a tangible film of dread. *Old habits die hard,* he mused, and dialed anyway.

"Bruni Headquarters," an efficient voice barked on the other end of the line, and Herb straightened. It was the same voice he'd heard many times over the past week, the one who was undoubtedly getting pissed at his tenacity.

He squared his shoulders and puffed himself up; hoping it would rush of confidence to his voice, knowing it probably wouldn't. "Ben Campbell, please. It's Herb Heim again."

A maddened sigh. "Mr. Heim? Ben has left town for the weekend on a personal matter. May I ask what this is in regards to?"

"Have you...has he been getting my messages?"

Her tone was clipped, almost military in its efficiency: a quality he'd normally appreciate if it weren't currently inhibiting him from getting his way. "He has, sir," she replied, indignant that someone might doubt her competence.

"Then I..."

"Mr. Heim? We'd probably get a lot more accomplished here if you just told me what this is in regards to. I'm Ben's assistant and he is adamant he does not know you. I can assure you that he would be much more likely to return your call if you'd just..."

Herb was almost offended by her brusqueness, but he was sure he was being a nuisance, and it was something new for him. His whole life he'd made it his mission to be nothing more than wallpaper; the human form of beige. Someone people forgot was in the room; a thing people only noticed after the fact.

But those days were over. Without another word he replaced the phone back in its cradle, ending the call, her words flapping in the air like forgotten laundry on a line.

He felt himself smiling. Hanging up on someone -- being so incredibly rude -- felt almost perverse. He smiled at this grandiose departure from "beige". It was so unlike him and he was loving every minute of it.

A rare surge of bravery came then, and he pushed his chair away from his desk, his sweaty hands only slipping a little against the aged Formica. He stood for a moment in his cube, the same one he'd had for nearly a decade, stretching his back, surprised to hear it crack. The janitors had already made a cursory sweep through his department and thus many of the lights had already been turned off, leaving only the main corridors illuminated with a kind of gray glow: a combination of the same sullen shade of the walls, the cubes, and the carpet so powerful it could permeate and tarnish even the most brilliant Tahitian sunset...

It was funny to him how he'd never even noticed before. Employed by the Department for twenty years -- his first job out of college was to be his last -- and he'd never even noticed the hideous gray, the suffocating blandness, the utter oppressiveness of the place.

But, if he were being honest, he had never been very observant in general, and surely not in the past few years. Ever since Bruni and Sault had first propositioned him he'd spent his life stranded in some sort of forest that he hadn't been able to find his way out of, a frame of life that had sucked the ability to sleep from him, that hollowed his cheeks and blackened his eyes to the point where people were constantly asking him if he felt OK...

And he hadn't, not at all. It didn't help that he'd spent most of his waking hours away from work drunk; or, while at work, hung over. Which was odd, too, because all his life he had never been a drinker. That was not to say he hadn't ever drank; he had of course, every single time a social obligation cropped up, in fact. It was the only thing that made him feel less like himself and more like the sort of person someone might want to talk to. But that was social lubricant, plain and simple. A crutch to help him hobble through whatever horrid display of phony camaraderie Marcie had signed them up for, her knee bobbing on the inevitable drive toward it, hoping like hell, he could tell, he wouldn't embarrass her *again*.

"Can you at least *try*?" she'd ask him, as if imploring a twelve year old not to wet the bed. "I *need* you to try. I really do."

But what did she know about need? About *true* need? Even he himself hadn't understood it entirely until someone had needed him. He had been thirty-five years old when, for the first time in his life someone had needed him -- needed him bad -- and he'd risen to the occasion. Not that he'd had a choice in the matter. But still. They'd chosen him. Powerful men had. Bruni, Sault. They could've picked anyone, but they'd picked him.

And then, about a year ago, it dawned on him *why* they'd chosen him. He and Marcie had been at the Heeper's Christmas party, an annual event Herb loathed in a way that was almost depraved. After enduring hours of inane banter he'd begun looking for her, hoping to leave, cradling his hot toddy as he threaded through the crowd, imagining her ire if he spilled on that absurd sweater she'd forced him to wear, the green and red one with those ludicrous googly-eyed reindeers kissing on the front. God, he'd felt like a dope in that thing. But she'd insisted, rolling her eyes and saying, "Jiminy crickets Herb, it's *festive*. You just don't know how to have a fun is all." And because he was sure she was right -- he *didn't* know how to have fun, never had -- he didn't question her judgment, nor substitute his own, and wore the stupid thing on faith alone, only to suffer through an uncommonly ruthless ribbing from every man in the house for the duration of the evening, most of which came from Del Heeper himself, having obviously missed Etiquette 101 on how-to-be-a-gracious host. Beer had nearly shot through his nostrils when he'd opened the door and seen the Heims on his stoop, Marcie's chipmunk grin poised above a homemade fruitcake and Herb in that ridiculous sweater. "Honey, honey, get over here," Del had nearly choked. "You have *got* to see this." And Marcie, traitor that she was, offered nothing more than a near imperceptible shrug of her shoulders at Herb by way of apology before laughing gaily at every last one of Del's humiliating, emasculating jokes.

But that wasn't the worst of it, not by a long shot. No, the worst came later, when he was looking -- no, *searching* by this point -- unable to find Marcie in the pressing crowd of drunken neighbors, thunderclap laughter exploding around him, sure every peal of it was directed at him, the social lubricant working on all cylinders but still unable to quiet the horrid discomfort he hadn't felt in his bones since adolescence. His anger flared with every step he took along the corridors of the Heeper's tacky split-level, anger at Marcie for dragging him to things like this only to ditch him for more exciting companionship as soon as they crossed the threshold.

With each new step it became clearer that the anger and alcohol was making his gait unsteady, and he found himself using the walls for support. He'd been ready to give up, thinking she must've gotten sick or something and been unable to find him as well, and took off, hoping he'd figure it out eventually and follow. His anger was replaced by sympathy then, at the thought of a pale, nauseated Marcie darting for home, having to miss one of her favorite parties.

But then he'd heard the laughter. Soft at first, almost like chimes from a distant porch. But wait...it was Marcie's laughter, he was sure of it, and whether it was the booze or the way the Holidays always brought on nostalgia, he felt himself smile –- soft and serene –- and rested his head against the wall, eyes closed, as if listening to a Master tickle the ivories, thinking of her head resting on his shoulder as they danced to "Smoke Gets in Your Eyes" on their first date, almost eighteen years earlier. *Oh Marcie,* he had thought. *My sweet, sweet Marcie.*

Her giggling was suddenly eclipsed then and he was jolted from his wake/dream with such abruptness it was almost cruel. It was the sound of Del Heeper -- the vocal equivalent of a bull in a china shop -- and at once Herb was alert, any uncertainty dissipating *like that,* as he followed the sounds of their muffled laughter and whispers volleying back and forth from down the hall. He paused in a shadow and saw the door to the bedroom was open just a crack, the bedroom where earlier Del had added their coats to the heap already on the bed. Herb's heart was a piston, steam blasting from its valves as he moved closer, pushing his Buddy Holly's back, needing to see...

And there it was: Del Heeper's fat ass pinning his wife to the wall, kissing her neck, his tongue darting like a revolting piece of liver against her white skin, moving down to her bare breasts, milky pale, Marcie groaning as if she'd never known anything so sweet, the Christmas lights strewn to the gutters outside twinkling through the drawn country curtains illuminating the cozy pair like some sort of illicit Amsterdam red light district attraction smack dab in the middle of yawn-central suburbia...a cliché in motion –- a horrific, ridiculous, fucking *pathetic* cliché in motion –- literally –- that might have made him laugh out loud if it hadn't been right in front of him and so utterly incomprehensible...Watching, Herb tried to bat at the cobwebs of booze and disbelief, trying to discern what was real and what was not...and then he saw Del was getting aggressive now, yanking at her pants, at his zipper, hungry to get the show on the road, and he knew it was real. *He fucking knew.* And though he should have been enraged, afraid -- so many things -- he simply moved closer, a drunken Jane Goodall moth mistaking a forest fire for a flame, and unable to tear away...

Herb's praise for the performance was a repetitious chorus of: "Uh, yeah, uh, fuck yeah" that was so boring and typical it nearly had the ability to re-trance Herb but not now. Not anymore. He was 100% back-in-business, drunk or no, the shock was shed, and his eyes were glued to her -- to Marcie, his bride, the fucking mother of his children, for Chrissakes, the one who --

"Ohhh Del, wait, hey..."

Marcie was resisting a bit, but not nearly as much as a husband would've liked. Not at all. In fact, her opposition -- if there was any -- was woefully overpowered by her moaning like a whore in heat, and Herb had felt himself falling away, back into the husk of nothingness that had sheathed him his whole, pathetic life...

That incident launched him into a depression almost subterranean it was so deep. The way he wasn't even man enough to fight for his own wife. The way his wife didn't seem to want to be fought for. Not by him, anyway. Not anymore. He just hadn't been able to climb out from under the memory of how he'd just walked away, letting them have at it, slipping out the sliding glass doors off the rumpus room and wandering through their neighborhood until the snow turned to rain and that ridiculous sweater of his was soaked all the way though.

Later, in bed, it was worse. She'd wanted to make love, that much was clear -- nudging her way closer in the dark, clumsy in her pawing, remnant yarns of cheap chardonnay tickling his neck as she whispered her quasi-naughty requests -- the same ones he'd heard a million times before -- and at first he'd resisted, still a-shiver from rain and the memory of another man dry-humping her, Marcie, his *wife* for fuck's sake -- against the wood-paneled wall, Brenda Lee crooning in the background as he'd stood silent, impotent.

Beige.

But not just any man, either. Not just any dry-humper. It was that super-sized douchebag Del Heeper tugging at his zipper as he thrusted his fat khakied-ass toward Marcie, toward *his* Marcie, that shit-stained dirtball that borrowed everything not nailed down, only to return it broken or never at all, pushing Marcie's panties down, neither considering nor caring that Herb could walk in at any moment, always daring Herb to defy him, his arrogance an affront at every turn, and suddenly Herb had risen to the occasion, the booze egging him on to give her the banging of her life, cheering him on to make her forget every dick she'd ever known but his and then he was on her, fucking her like he meant it, imagining each thrust was a pummel into Del's fat, red face, her squeals of surprise and delight barely registering as he moved faster and harder, adding Bruni and Sault into the mix, smashing their faces into hard, unforgiving concrete with every push, drilling them into submission, sweat coursing down his back, winning this fight, showing the world a thing or two, *Take that Bruni you fuck, you fucking...fuck!* And then, before he knew it there were those fuck-face Scottolino Brothers and he was ready to show *them* who was boss, too, and somewhere in his mind he heard Marcie shrieking she was almost there when suddenly and without warning his rage was uprooted and tossed aside in favor of fear...true fear...as the image of the Scottolino Brothers now dancing before him made him shrivel on impact, his manhood vanishing in an instant (both figuratively and literally) and he felt Marcie deflate beneath him, knowing it was over before he did, pushing him off and letting the knowledge settle over him as she muttered, "Whisky dick," to an invisible spectator, pulling the coverlet over her shoulders as she turned her back against him as he still tried to catch his breath.

And then he heard: "It figures." And knew his demotion back to beige was complete.

And that's when he realized: they'd chosen him because he was beige. Just like Del Heeper hadn't been worried he'd walk in, Bruni and Sault had seen him for what he was and knew they could have their way with him, just like Del had with his wife. It was a thought so depressing his entire world had morphed to black and white. To eating, sleeping and shitting. And drinking. Lots and lots of drinking.

But then he'd come up with a plan, and suddenly life had turned Technicolor. Somewhere around February he'd come up with it -- a brilliant plan, if he did say so himself, albeit a bit on the macabre side. But that was what he liked about it. It was as if he'd spent his whole life being of complete and utter unimportance, plodding along in a monotone as lackluster as the very walls themselves, only to end it all in the most spectacular display of drama nobody could have possibly seen coming. And with this plan, the forest fell away. The color came back to his cheeks, his eyes rose from the pits, and he began to make lists, create strategies, and follow through with them, just like now...

As he navigated the corridors of the Statehouse he ran through his checklist: The documents were organized and sealed away in the cavernous maze of safety deposit boxes in the bowels of his bank, Garden State Trust. The note had been written, the ammo bought. The emails had been sent to all concerned parties...

He had to chuckle at that last one: *concerned parties.* Oh they'll be concerned all right. Just thinking of the looks on their faces as they read the email he'd sent was enough to make him laugh out loud. It surprised him, the volume of himself, usually so quiet, and he recoiled at the sound when he noticed a State Trooper standing guard by the Governor's office giving him the kind of look only men of great authority seemed capable of. A look that caressed the gleaming piece in its holster and said: "Come on, punk. Just give me one good reason not to use this thing." Herb offered a quick, congenial nod and ducked his head, hoping his Statehouse ID card was visible from where it was clipped to his belt loop.

Now around the corner and in the clear, he felt a nugget of pride come into flower within his chest. They had chosen him because he was weak. Because they knew they could scare him into submission, into doing anything they wanted. And they had. They had been right on both counts. But now here he was, slipping by some of the most well-trained law enforcement in the whole state –- unnoticed, unassuming –- and in less than a week he'd be one of the most notorious men known to man. He imagined the ruined careers of the Mayor, the Senator, and the engineer, all because of him. His only regret would be not seeing the fallout himself. It was likely to make Hiroshima look like a pool party. Jarvis, Bruni, Sault. Those hideous thugs the Scottolino brothers, who seemed to live to make him shit his pants in fear. The thing that assuaged him was that he –- little Herbie Heim, peon, piss-ant, nobody Heimy-boy –- would be the one dropping the bomb.

Thinking of the Trooper he smiled then, imagining yards and yards of yellow police tape surrounding his tidy Colonial, the neighbors with their mouths agape as the white-sheeted gurneys rolled past, all the Heim's, dead at last. The evidence he'd squirreled away in the safe deposit boxes, the cache of weapons they'd find. The bodies.

Allllllll...the bodies. He'd never thought Trudy Heeper was much of a looker, but there was no doubt he had it in for that dickhead Del. He'd tie that fat bastard up, fuck his wife right in front of him, singing "Jingle Bells" the whole damn time...

And Herb Heim began to laugh.

Imagining the almost inhuman amount of carnage he was about to invoke, he laughed until tears streamed down his cheeks, fogging up those Buddy Holly's.

5

Saturday
9:49 am

As Sydney drove she was thinking: the thing about poverty and most bad things in general is that the line is fine between "I'm sorry it's you" and "I'm glad it's not me".

She followed the curve of the exit ramp and slowed her Cabriolet to a stop sign, standing like a beacon, red and alarmed, almost as if to say: *You sure you want to do this? Think hard now. It's not too late to turn back, you know.*

The City of Camden was crawling all around her: broken buildings in various stages of decay, a thick mantle of trash coating the cracked, uneven sidewalks, the gutters, the sewer drains; rot squeezing itself into every available inch of split cement and mortar, seeming to both seep through and sprout forth from the earth.

In an anonymous apartment somewhere a radio whined to life and salsa music broke the yolk of the morning, mixing together with honking horns and the shrieks of hungry babies and hungrier junk yard dogs catapulting against the brick walls, pinballing through the of Section-8 housing; neighbors shouting for them to shut the fuck up, all of 'em.

Although she wasn't a hard-hitting reporter hoping to expose the scandal of the century, that didn't mean she hadn't won accolades.

She had, numerous times. Various plaques and framed commendations covered the walls of her office, a patchwork quilt of rectangles and squares of pine, cherry, walnut, all of which she'd publicly accepted with the same graciousness that, predictably, only resulted in the masses loving her more, truly thankful for the opportunity to do –- and succeed at -- something she loved, that she believed made a difference –- a profoundly *positive* difference –- to the people and the world around her.

But in private, there was one that she cherished most, which was perhaps why this story about the school meant so much to her. In many ways she felt invested in the school, but it wasn't just that, it was something more *primitive*, if she had to give it a name; a Momma Bear-like quality that made her want to protect it, see it flourish.

When Dino Bruni and Jarvis Jasper had set out to build an innovative, state-of-the-art high school in the heart of the state's eyesore and cash drain, the City of Camden, it seemed wildly ambitious at best, foolhardy at worst. It was to have all the same trimmings as the schools of the wealthier districts, the theory behind it being that the playing field would now be leveled, so to speak, and the disadvantaged and disinterested kids of Camden might have a renewed magnetism to education. But before long, the liberals caught wind of it and loved it, naturally, and soon psychologists and pundits from Newark to Cape May sang its praises, about what the boost in morale could mean in terms of drop-outs and teen pregnancy. And just as naturally, the fiscal conservatives cited study after study as if it were Scripture, pointing to the lack of any semblance of correlation between increased spending and standardized test scores, let alone teen pregnancy rates. But the latter petered out quickly –- they always did when it came to Camden, always worried their opposition to funding it's projects would be perceived as something as radioactive as racism -- And before everyone knew it, the land on the Banks was cleared away and Senator Bruni's school was off and running.

Things progressed swimmingly for a while, with legendary engineering powerhouse Sault & Sault taking the lead on the project, beating out nearly a hundred other bids. Elected officials from the Mayor on up to the Governor spoke with pride at the number of out-of-state firms that had expressed interest -– that's how exciting their plans for this new school were, they assured the public –- and Sydney had copies of never-ending newsprint to prove it. Moreover, Sterling Sault, President of the firm, had even managed a way to get promise of funding from the federal government in exchange for his pledge to use "green" materials whenever the opportunity presented itself.

Most surprising, however -- and the thing Sydney loved most about the entire enterprise –- was how the City –- nay, *community* of Camden –- emerged, as if awoken from a horrid dream. Bake sales and car washes began cropping up where teachers and students and even a smattering of parents stood alongside one another on Camden streets on Saturdays, hoping to raise money for new band uniforms, new football equipment –- intent on showing all the naysayers that they weren't just looking for a handout, that they were willing to roll up their sleeves and pitch in. That this new school meant something to them. It was a bright spot in the otherwise bleak terrain of their existence. It was something they could be proud of, that they'd take care of. It was hope. (As Pollyanna as Sydney could be even she didn't believe that the citizens of Camden consciously believed this or, more accurately, could even articulate it -– so she did it for them.) And that was one of the things that was driving her crazy about her article. It had held so much promise for her at first, and now was just a jumble of dead ends, inconsistencies she hadn't anticipated and, just, well...plain confusion.

Not unlike the story of the school itself. For all its positivity, there was still controversy. Like the hiring of the Scottolino Brothers to take the lead on the construction, for instance. Their criminal pasts and penchant for playing fast and loose with state and local building regulations was certainly no secret, and though Sydney guessed much of it to be myth and something more apt to take place in fertile imaginations or an episode of *The Sopranos* than real life, the Scottolino Family was widely rumored to be one of the last bastions of the mafia in New Jersey; a thing all but dead in this day and age, at least as far as the Italians went. True, many of the brothers and uncles and cousins had been charged with a litany of crimes over the years, but Sydney was a firm believer in giving the benefit of the doubt; and besides, most of them had never been convicted. Not of anything serious, anyway.

The appointment of the Scottolinos seemed like a terrible decision; one so bad it might kill the entire project before it was barely born. But to everyone's surprise -- the Governor, the press, Sydney, perhaps even the Scottolino's themselves -- the people of Camden rallied around them, going so far as to pack Greyhounds to *picket* in front of the Statehouse for weeks on end, chanting and demanding for them to get the job. Why? Because in the end, they were hometown boys, Camden-born-and-bred, and that meant something to those people; something golden. The people who'd ever had a sliver of opportunity, real or imagined, beyond the City's limits, usually took off and never looked back. Left that cesspool and didn't even have to hope for greener pastures, *knowing* they'd find them, knowing any*where* was better than the filth and destitution and complete absence of anything worth remembering they were leaving behind. Camdenites had seen it so many times they didn't even pretend to count anymore...and so, when one of their own found success and stayed (or at least returned), it was respected like few other things. And, despite all their faults, the Scottolino's stepped up to the plate, bringing in enough legitimate subcontractors to assuage the opposition.

But even the Scottolino's weren't the biggest controversy. No, the biggest controversy was the *name*. What to name this urban fantasy of a school, this beacon of optimism that had grown to near-mythic proportions before even the first shovel had broken ground? The location and demographics meant all the usual suspects were suggested: Martin Luther King Jr., Nelson Mandela, Booker T. Washington, John F. Kennedy, Bobby Kennedy, Stokely Carmichael, Malcolm X. Trouble was, all those names and every other one with a similar connotation were already in use in Camden, whether at another school, a library, or park. Given that this all occurred prior to Barack Obama, Bill Clinton was the only person to be considered the "first black president", and his name was tossed into the ring, along with Jackie Robinson, Michael Jordan, and even, to the disgust of many, Al Sharpton.

Then there was the Senator, of course. His appetite for leaving a legacy was a well-known quirk about the man, and Sydney had little doubt as to just how hard he had fought in the trenches to get his name on that school, despite the well-practiced air of humility he donned whenever a reporter inquired.

The press detailed the back-and-forth name-game as if it was Wimbledon, and countless op-eds were issued highlighting the brilliance of some over others. There were detractors, of course, grumbling to one another over morning coffee at local diners, along the sidelines of suburban Saturday morning soccer games and over power lunches in Center City Philadelphia, muttering at the absurdity of the debate as the stalemate dragged on month after month, catching regional then national attention, even going to far as to prompt publication of a *Wall Street Journal* op-ed titled "What's in a Name?", its author emerging as pied piper of all of the thousands of people perplexed over why there was such an intense debate in the first place, let alone one halting construction and costing the taxpayers untold amounts of money.

But Sydney was not one of those people. She understood the point of the discussion, the reason why it was so important. To the people of Camden, this was more than a school; this was a chance for the kids the world had forgotten about to break out, to prove themselves as worthy, as equal, as good enough. This project would offer the opportunity for the chance to compete, maybe even get a leg up -- or at least allow them to *catch* up: so much more than they'd ever had before.

And that's what she had been thinking about at two o'clock in the morning back in 2004; sleep evading her as though she were a clingy ex-lover. *The WSJ* article had just come out and something about it wouldn't stop nagging at her until she'd finally thrown the covers off in frustration and padded to the kitchen, brewing herself a pot of Tim Horton's and settling down at the antique architect's drafting table where she spent most of her time working: the one smack dab in the place where a dining table should have been, refusing to budge until she came up with a solution, at least one that would satisfy her personally. It turned out she hadn't needed the whole pot of dark roast after all; a resolution came almost at once and, giddy with delight, she'd found the most difficult part of the night to be waiting for daylight, when she could call her best friend Ben in DC without him going postal, when she could sail through the front doors of *The Jerzine* and see the excitement alight on Roger's face, the happy thrill she'd feel from her colleagues, many of whom who'd been just as invested in the hope of finding a solution as she.

In hindsight it was sort of silly it was so downright simple, and she was reluctant to take credit for it. The overwhelming reaction she'd received was so fervent it was a little embarrassing, as though she'd cured a world epidemic. But, regardless of her feelings, her idea to hold a contest for the children of Camden to name their own school had elicited a stunning tsunami of praise and accolades –- both locally and nationally -– that she'd soon found herself weary from fielding phone calls -- from reporters, from far-flung friends, from prestigious national publications eager for her freelance work. She'd even been on *Good Morning America,* Nana Jean's favorite because of Diane Sawyer, whom she'd dubbed with a reverence not often seen in a woman like Nana Jean: "the last true American lady". As *The Jerzine* and Sydney Langston became sudden (if fleeting in the endless loop of 24-hour global news) household names and circulation of the magazine sky-rocketed, Sydney found herself ducking away from the glare of spotlight, a garish thing for a behind-the-curtain girl like herself. And then came the day of the press conference -- three long, exciting and jittery months after the contest was first announced -- when thousands had gathered in Bruni Park, right by the river, waiting beneath a cornflower sky with bated breath to hear whom the panel of judges had chosen as winner from the list of finalists, any one of which she thought would have been a spectacular choice. Mayor Jasper had given her a key to the City, held out his meaty hands that all but drowned hers as he'd handed it over. Even now she could see it: a sparkling spangle of something in his russet eyes that had spoken to her of dignity. Hot on the extravagant words of the Mayor fresh from the podium, feeling unable to measure up to all the superlatives he'd laid upon her, it had taken all that she had and a good stretch more to give her acceptance speech.

But then something happened. Looking at the crowd that day, hearing her name chanted by a thousand children or more, she'd forgotten to be nervous, had somehow shed her terror at being the center of attention, and tears had flowed freely down her cheeks, her entire being never feeling so...*full,* and then it came over her: the exhilaration of the occasion, the weight of what it -- and the school, and their ability to name it themselves –- really meant to the people of Camden –- a people so often shunned and spit and shit upon they were rarely regarded with any sense of humanity; a tragic lot so resigned to their station on the bottom of the shoe of the social hierarchy that it had simply rocked her to her core to look out over the sea of faces and feel the unadulterated purely *pure* happiness radiating from them.

Of course there was also the admiration and pride from her bosses and Cody and Nana Jean; as well as genuine friends like Ben Campbell who'd driven hours and/or taken trains or planes to see her accept the honor, but it was knowing that she'd made a difference -– truly *knowing* it, rather than just praying and hoping –- in the lives of an oppressed people that had left her weak with gratitude, and she had meant every single word when she'd concluded her heartfelt but brief speech by saying: "From the bottom of my heart, my cup hath runneth over, and I thank you."

Thinking of that day always brought with it a rush of emotion, tinged only at the edges by a touch of sadness at the thought of her mom not being alive to see it. But now, today, baffled by the pathetic lack of progress she was making on her current article about this place she cared so much for, it brought a new sentiment, one she couldn't quite place; an uneasiness she imagined came upon anyone stuck in Purgatory.

Ultimately the school had been named Sir Thomas More Tech, the winner a short but wiry eighth grader named D'Quan Jackson who'd had the biggest, brightest, most beautiful grin she'd ever seen. From the very first moment she'd heard it, she'd loved the name, and when the mild-mannered boy had given his speech, detailing the meaning behind it, she'd marveled at the evenness of his voice as he articulated the notion of an urban utopia, relating the story of the fictional island Sir Thomas More's imagination had created nearly five hundred years earlier.

Her current article was to coincide with the start of the new school year, and was to chronicle the whereabouts -– or, if she were being honest, the great accomplishments and stunning societal feats she hoped members of the first class to have begun at Sir Thomas More Tech and graduate would share. A simple but eloquent "where are they now" piece of the human interest variety –- right up her alley in general, and close to her heart specifically -– but to say she was finding it quite thorny already was a grand understatement.

Sydney's goal for the day was simple: meet with some of the folks from Sir Thomas More Tech who'd actually agreed to an interview (not many), and simply knock on the doors of the addresses she had obtained from the school, hoping for the best. She liked to be methodical, beginning with the A's and was making her way one-by-one through the list. But this was no ordinary project, and she was quickly learning that beggars couldn't be choosers. First on the docket for today was Marion Jefferson, the grandmother who had raised standout student and aspiring actor, Sherrod Jefferson.

Flipping down the visor to keep the sun's glare at bay, she pressed down the street until she came to a red light. Her gaze drifted: Stoops sagging in front of mashed-together row-homes where a dreary rainbow of old, pilled blankets served as curtains across windows –- fractured and spider-webbed, or missing altogether. Faded bloodstains on the concrete. A complete absence of any greenery. Hunched-over junkies weaving their way down the alleys and through weed-laden vacant lots, searching among broken bottles glinting in the sun for loose change, walking past heaps of their sleeping brethren curled in doorways and on church steps like crescent moons, their faces stained by filth and years of straining among the shadows.

Just then a body filled the driver's side window, casting a shadow across the dash and beyond, and Sydney jumped. It was a man knocking frantically, his toothless mouth jawing, waving a rag and bottle of what looked like dingy dishwater.

Against anyone's better judgment, Sydney rolled down the window a crack to try and make out what he was saying. It was a frenetic jumble, but she was able to understand that he wanted to wash her windows: a red-light stint crack heads were famous for, though usually they started washing them before you had a chance to decline, demanding payment for a service you never even asked for in the first place. Recalling that if you said no, or refused to pay, they were known to wipe something across your windshield that even the world's best carwash was unable to remove, she wedged a few bills through the crack of the window into his eager, soiled fingers –- able to smell the putrid stink of him even through those few inches -- and took off the second the light turned, only feeling slightly guilty.

Typically she felt a great deal of compassion toward all the people of Camden, including every last beggar and addict. Truly, she did. But that didn't make them any less unpredictable, any less worrisome. The stories this city emitted were the stuff of urban legends; so scary and ludicrous they couldn't possibly be true, but were. Just last year *The Philadelphia Inquirer* broke a story about how gang lords were enhancing their drug trade fortunes by dabbling in the human body part trade. She'd read with shock and disgust at how black market buyers were willing to pay ridiculous figures for things like kidneys, and the thugs were only too eager to supply them, after harvesting them from the homeless and desperate, who didn't even seem to miss them, until they died of infection not long after receiving their pittance for participation. The city was teeming with stories like this, steeped in various kinds of unspeakable horror that one found hard to believe given that they were taking place in the United States of America. It was enough for her to give up reading the newspaper for good.

As she slowed to the next light she surveyed the surrounding sidewalks chock-full of ticking time bombs, knowing that at any moment, from any angle, she could be under siege. She was already a gigantic slow-moving target simply by virtue of being white and in a decent vehicle. Oftentimes little else was needed by way of provocation. Anything was possible. She knew most of the people of the city were victims of some sort of undeserved circumstance, but they were scary as hell just the same.

Sydney's heart leapt as a horn blasted behind her, jumping her foot from the brake through the green lighted intersection and sending a smattering of loose papers from the front seat onto the floor. Her little compact responded to her gassing the pedal as she groped the mass of papers on the floor, hoping to come across the directions she had printed out. She shouldn't be lost right now; she had been here before, of course, countless times, especially lately. Mainly to see the school, though, which was on The Banks, in a decidedly better part of town. But Camden being the neglected dump that it was, offered no street signs; they'd all either rotted away or been shot clear off in the heat of vengeance or boredom, or stolen in the night in some crack head's misguided attempt to make a profit.

Her cell sprang to life just as she turned onto MLK Boulevard and, for a moment, was drowned by the clatter of garage-like storefronts being peeled back in a jarring chorus of aluminum rattle along with the thin, defeated shouts of shopkeepers shooing away the homeless human shells collected on their doorsteps. She didn't recognize the number, but answered anyway.

"Sydney Langston."

"This, uh, Cindy Lan'ston who writes for the, uh, thing? The uh, magazine?"

Sydney ignored the error: "Yes it is. May I ask who's calling?"

"This is uh, Shanice. Shanice Hopkins. You done called 'bout my son? T-Ray?"

Sydney flipped through a mental Rolodex. "T-Ray?"

The woman sighed, impatient. "Demetrius."

Sydney brightened as she recalled the name. "Oh yes of course. Thank you so much for returning my call, Ms. Hopkins. You have no idea how much I appreciate it."

There was a pause, but Sydney didn't know what to make of it, if anything. "Yeah, well. He gone for a while, but you can still talk to me if you want."

Gone for a while? Probably to jail, Sydney thought with a sigh, but quickly dismissed it. She'd been having such poor luck getting interviews; she'd jump at the chance for any nibble. "That would be wonderful! How does tomorrow sound? Say, one o'clock?"

"Yeah, that's fine," the woman said, an ambivalent air of boredom, defensiveness, and defeat in her tone. "I'm guessin' you got my address since you got my phone number."

"I do, yes, thank you," Sydney said, though she was pretty sure the woman wasn't trying to be all that helpful.

"Fine," the woman said, audibly taking a drag on her cigarette, and before Sydney could thank her again, the line went dead.

The home of Marion Jefferson was an ancient narrow tenement tucked between dozens just like it. Though it was old, it was not among the projects of Camden, and was shipshape as far as cleanliness, orderliness and, well, *everything* went, and Sydney scolded herself for forgetting that there were lots of good, hardworking people of Camden. You just didn't usually hear about them.

A sturdy, matronly woman in her sixties, Marion sat on a sofa (which she called a chesterfield) across from Sydney (whom she referred to as a journalist) in the tidy living room (which she called a parlor). The bright day pirouetted through delicate lace curtains, illuminating the paintings of a black Jesus engaging in the Stations of the Cross, shining against their gilded, chipped frames, and highlighting the arrow-straight vacuum lines in the faded peach carpet.

She had a tight helmet of dyed gray hair that looked slightly purple in the light, a Sunday church dress and a simple gold cross glinting between the lapels of the Peter Pan collar. Her square-toed pumps were old, likely from the days of Eisenhower, but they shone like oil slicks just the same. Her face was smooth, belying her age, but there was something about it -- in her eyes, maybe -- that radiated the glow of the wise, making Sydney respect her instantly.

"I so enjoy your columns, Miss Langston," Marion said with the warm yet restrained smile of a woman who has seen much of the appalling the world has to offer, but has too much dignity to give it credence. "You're doing the Lord's work, you know."

Sydney blushed at the compliment, and thanked her sincerely.

There was a parcel of silence then between them, peppered by the din of the street outside.

"You're here about Sherrod," she said, but it was not a question for Sydney; it was a statement.

Sydney began to shuffle through some papers, though she wasn't sure why. Perhaps it was because she had found Sherrod Jefferson to be one of the most disturbing cases to come through Sir Thomas More Tech, even worse that Cyrus and Cedric Ashe, which was saying something. Straight-A student, aspiring actor, member of the school's Drama Guild, Youth Ministry, Color Guard...

Now his only membership was to the Olde Gate Cemetery on Quindlin and Ross.

Marion Jefferson straightened her spine as if to steel herself while Sydney went through the usual questions -- all benign and nothing more than confirmation of her research -- before Marion interrupted.

"Miss Langston. While I appreciate your journalistic thoroughness and integrity, it'd probably do us both more good if I just told you the story. Get the big pink elephant out of the room, as they say?"

Sydney felt relief. "That would be fine," she smiled warmly. "Thank you."

"Well," she began, gathering up her small stature in an effort to draw the strength she anticipated she'd need to get through the whole sordid tale. "My daughter, Sherrod's mother, was a beauty. Everyone said so, from the day she was born. I could barely make a trip to the market without a half a dozen women stopping me, peeking into her pram and showering her with compliments. Do you have children, Miss Langston?"

"No, I'm not --," she went to continue but stopped herself, and blushed as she said: "No."

"Well," Marion said quietly, her smile maternal, as her eyes swung heavenward. "He has a plan for each of us."

Sydney swallowed hard and nodded, trying desperately not to think of her own mother. Of Cody. Of their marriage that almost-was.

"Leonetta was named after her father who died in a work-related accident at The Port when she was just two. Of course I thought mine was the most beautiful baby in the world, like all mothers do," she chuckled, "But it was still so nice to come home and tell Leon about how the ladies at church would dote on her..."

"Oh, I'm so sorry to hear about your husband."

"It was many moons ago. But I thank you, dear." Ever the gracious hostess, Marion stood then: "Would you like some tea?"

"That would be lovely."

Sydney followed her into the tidy kitchen as she continued. "Leonetta was blessed with beauty, but she was a handful from Day One. She had a neediness about her -- an *insatiableness* -- that far surpassed any other child I've come across, before or since. She was like a bottomless pit. Nothing was enough for her: no amount of attention, praise -- you name it. It was as if she needed constant approval from the whole world, even from the people no one should pay no mind.

And you've never heard such a temper tantrum! Leonetta had lungs like cannons. The whole street would come running; fearing the worst, and there'd be little Leonetta crying over the most trivial thing. It got so folks stopped liking her as much. Stopped being enchanted by her good looks. And I couldn't say I could blame them. She just took so much from everyone and gave so little. There was simply no pleasing her.

And forget about any type of criticism, no matter how well meaning. Goodness, you couldn't even give the child a compliment without her looking for some ulterior motive. Today they'd likely call it low self-esteem or some such but back then all I knew was that she was just exhausting. Utterly, entirely exhausting." Marion exhaled then and Sydney felt the weight of it. "This void she had, this...black hole... It did get filled. Eventually. She was about twelve or thirteen, I'd say, when she first discovered men, and the change was almost palpable. It was like a light went on within her. But it was the wrong kind of light, you see. It served no purpose but to illuminate the neediness within her. The desperation. And any kind of man worth something saw it and stayed away, leaving wide berth for the predators to come forth. And prey they did." For the first time in the interview Marion's eyes dipped away, disgraced, and the whistle of the teapot relieved them both.

They took their cups and saucers back into the parlor, steam winding around them in delicate tendrils, the pair of them settling back into their perspective seats among the well-aged furniture and the cozy camaraderie that had grown between them.

"My beautiful daughter became a junkie who sunk to new and more depraved depths with every passing day. Try as I might to raise her right, she fell into the Devil's grip; a hard enough thing for any mother to bear witness, but even more so because of her tender age. Running the streets, lying, stealing." Her eyes narrowed, as she began almost spitting her words, disgusted by them. "Getting caught doing the nasty with every two-dollar nigga who looked at her twice..."

The words hung in the air as Marion collected herself.

"I knew it didn't bode well, that it was only a matter of time, and sure enough she came home pregnant," she shook her head with regret. "I never found out who is father was, probably because Leonetta didn't have a damn clue herself. We didn't bother with the formality of the courts because she was happy to get rid of Sherrod, and I was happy to have him." A smile came then, with remembering. "Sherrod was such a joy. *Such* a joy. Nothing like his mother whatsoever. From the first day he arrived, he never gave me a moment's worry. He loved school and loved his family. All his cousins. His aunts. He loved to read, loved to write. Oh he won spelling bee after spelling bee. All the teachers loved him. The preachers, too. He loved church as much as I did. We were two peas in a pod," she said, her eyes glinting with tears — though whether they were sad or happy ones, Sydney couldn't say.

"He always had a flair for the dramatic, was always making people laugh with his antics. He played Joseph in the Christmas pageant — beat out all the older kids every year. And that show draws a huge crowd. Huge. But you think he was scared? The boy never got stage fright a day in his life. It was like he was born to be there, center stage in front of all those people. He just loved it. When he was eleven I was able to find a scholarship for him to a drama camp in the Poconos. I hated to part with him all summer long, but I knew it was the best for him. To get out of Camden, and get around other kids who had a future. And oh how he loved it. Four straight summers I sent him, and he was like belle of the ball there. I'd go up at the end of the summer — all the parents would — to see the final performance. Afterward, they would come up to congratulate me. Tell me how talented he was, that he was going places. The boy was a born ham," she chuckled fondly. But then a shadow came over her face. "It was about this same time I realized what Sherrod was."

A veil of quiet fell over the room, and Sydney shifted in her seat, uncomfortable but knowing she had to hear what Marion needed to say as much as Marion needed to say it.

"I'm sure your research has revealed that Sherrod was a homosexual?"

Sydney cleared her throat. "Well yes. It has. Did that have any effect on him as far as his schooling?"

"Well. The gangs never wanted him because of it, so that was one less worry. But every school has its share of bullies and, like any other child who's different, Sherrod suffered from time to time... but it was nothing he couldn't handle. That sense of humor of his melted even his enemies. And by the time he was accepted into Sir Thomas More, it was a moot point. Let's just say that he had more friends than not."

"That's great," Sydney said, meaning it, as she scribbled in her notes but when she looked it up and saw the look in the old woman's eyes, she felt foolish. The eyes said: *What difference does it make now?* And Sydney supposed she was right.

But it *did* matter. At least to her. She decided she needed to shift the tone of the conversation –- the last thing she wanted was for this woman to suffer anymore than she already had, especially at the hands of Sydney. That was most certainly *not* her objective, no matter how badly she wanted the story.

"I saw that he petitioned for the Band and Color Guard to go to Washington, DC. That must have made you proud."

Marion beamed. "Oh it did. And to play for the first African-American President, to boot." She motioned to one of the many photos hung in even rows against the rose-patterned wallpaper: Sherrod was positively sunny standing there in his uniform –- big toothy grin, chiseled chin tilted with pride. You could almost feel his delight through the glass. "Yes. That was a blessed day, indeed."

"He was a handsome boy. Definitely had those movie star looks."

"Oh and didn't he?" Marion said, glowing. "That was one good thing his mother gave him. Probably the only thing."

A silence passed between them before Sydney asked whether Sherrod ever saw his mother.

Rolling her eyes Marion released a scornful snort then, and Sydney cringed: it was a gesture beneath a woman of Marion's worth, but she did not judge.

"Leonetta cared about nothing. Not me, not her child. She was a drunk and a whore and unless you were giving her what she was after, she had no use for you."

Sydney nodded, and deftly moved to change the topic. "Mrs. Jefferson, did Sherrod have a job?"

"Not during the school year. His extracurricular activities took up too much of his time. On any given afternoon you could find him out on that football field, practicing. Sometimes with other members of the Color Guard, but many times alone. I used to kid him that he was like the mailman; neither rain nor sleet nor snow could keep him from practicing." She chuckled, but it had a hollow ring to it. "I had such high hopes for him."

Sydney let the silence settle between them before she ventured her next question, the one that had to be asked. "So what happened?"

Marion Jefferson had expected the question of course, but she drew in a quick breath anyway -- the blow of it still sharp against the rawness of the ache.

"At the time I thought it just happened so fast, that it had to be drugs. Nobody turns from day to night like that unless it's drugs. But, looking back, I've come to realize that there were signs over time. It was more gradual than I'd initially thought. Hindsight's twenty-twenty, I guess." She said this last part with great effort, an admission of defeat, and Sydney had to will herself not to go over and embrace the woman.

Her voice was gentle. "Could you be more specific? Maybe give me an example?"

"Well the winter play, for one. He was having trouble remembering his lines. At first I just thought maybe the pressure was getting to him. Graduation, his future. Waiting to get accepted to seminary school. Even the prom was a quandary; it wasn't like he could bring his boyfriend. Even a progressive school like Sir Thomas More has its limitations. And then the spring musical came and he didn't get a lead. In fact, he was reduced to playing a bit extra part, something he hadn't had to do *ever*. Something was wrong. I just assumed, once again, that it was preoccupation. Oh how I wish I'd seen it then, that is was so much more than that. I would have taken him to a neurologist. I have good insurance, you know, working for the State. It wouldn't have been a hardship. But I just didn't see it for what it was."

A bolt of surprise struck Sydney, making her lean forward with concern. "So you think something was going on in his brain? Like a tumor?"

"Well the autopsy has since ruled out a tumor, but I think it would have been a starting point at least. To get to the root of what was making him act so crazy. A place from which I could move forward, go to specialists. Experts. That sort of thing. Instead I thought the worst of him." She shook her head dully; regret emanating from her like toxic gas. Her voice, once strong and sure, was a mere thread of itself: "He was forgetting things, mixing things up. Small things at first, but they got bigger, more important, and it was just so strange. He was like a zombie. I constantly felt uneasy. Mother's intuition was speaking to me, but I ignored it. And, I suppose, my experience with Leonetta clouded my better judgment, and so when he began to behave so unlike himself, I just assumed he was lying. I thought of all that I'd been through with his mother and just assumed history was repeating itself, and I did all of this without even giving him the benefit of the doubt."

An embroidered handkerchief dabbed at her eyes and nose, her face now crumpled in upon itself, compounded by sorrow and looking much older than when Sydney had first arrived. It was heart-wrenching to listen to, and Sydney yearned for it to stop. But she knew she needed to hear this.

"Then money turned up missing. And by the time his final report card came and he'd gotten 3 D's and an F, I'd just about had it. To top it off I found a letter from the Seminary School, stuffed between his mattress and box spring, telling him he'd been denied admission. It had to be drinkin' or druggin', and I was furious. How could he *do* such a stupid thing? He'd seen what had happened to his Momma, what had happened to this whole city," she said, sweeping her arms around. "How could he fall prey?! Oh I was beside myself. Then, one Sunday, Reverend pulled me aside. He said a member of the congregation, a policeman, had seen Sherrod wandering along by himself, talking to nobody, late one night. They wanted to charge him with prostituting and the officer said Sherrod seemed surprised. But Miss Langston, you know as well as I do that nobody in their right mind goes out for a stroll in these parts. They're either looking for trouble, or they've already found it. Ultimately they let him go. They simply didn't have the proof.

He had lost weight and had a vacant look in his eye for more than a month, he was a regular ghoul. But this was what confirmed it for me. Reverend Morehouse and I go way back. He knew Sherrod was the light of my life and would have rather eaten tacks than told me something bad about my baby. I asked if it was drugs, and the Reverend said he thought so, so I felt I had no choice but to practice tough love. I kicked him out the next day.

He denied it, but they all do, don't they? How was I supposed to know? He begged me to get him help, said he didn't know what was wrong with him but it wasn't drugs. I spent every waking moment on my knees, asking for strength. I never once thought to ask for..." she trailed off.

"Mrs. Jefferson, if this is too painful..."

Marion held up a hand, and pressed her eyes closed. "It's okay. This is a story that needs to be told." Her exhale was deep. "I wouldn't talk to him, refused his calls, let him wail against my front door, pounding, begging. I told myself 'he just needs to hit bottom, then the Lord will save him'." She snorted again then, and the hint of bitter sarcasm in her tone left Sydney ill at ease. "When they found his body, I was at church. He'd jumped off the bridge the night before. His body surfaced sometime during the sermon."

Sydney drew her breath. She knew what was coming next but felt powerless to stop it.

"My Sherrod, my baby, God rest his soul, had been telling the truth all along. Toxicology reports came back and he was clean as a whistle. I even paid for a hair analysis, the kind the FBI uses, and it showed he'd never touched a drug in his entire life. I'd thrown him out, turned my back against him. My own flesh and blood. Denied him. And here he'd been telling the truth the entire time. He was sick, I know he was. He was sick, that was all, my baby was sick and I was supposed to take care of him, and I didn't. Oh that just about did me in. Every day, it's still a battle within myself. A war."

Sydney got up and sat next to the woman, whose quiet sobs were reverberating so deeply in Sydney's heart she imagined she'd always hear them. She covered the older woman's hands with her own, and said, "Marion, you have to forgive yourself. You did the only thing that you...you did what you thought was right..." Sydney fumbled for the right words, hoping that she'd be able to give this woman some semblance of peace. She looked to the floors, the walls of photos, everywhere, groping for something to say.

But when her eyes swung back around and landed on Marion's, she knew there was nothing that could comfort this woman.

"Forgive myself?" Marion asked, the falsetto in her voice glass-breaking and incredulous. "Forgive myself? Could *you*?"

6

Saturday
10:19 am

Poppy the maid wasn't really a maid; at least, not in the traditional sense. Sure she cooked and cleaned and did all the laundry, polished the silver and made the beds, scrubbed the toilets, and...

But she did it for free. Had she known the correct term, she would have called it "indentured servitude", but her education barely eclipsed the sixth grade of rural Georgia's finest one-room school house, and so her fate was sealed. The thing that bothered her most wasn't the hard work, or even the absence of a paycheck. It was that her own sister was responsible for the whole thing.

Yes, she'd gone and gambled away a king's ransom, but it had been Henrietta's demand that Poppy attend Zion Baptist CME in the first place. But if Poppy'd had her way she would've never stepped foot inside; that oily preacher was slicker than Satan himself.

"We have a *name* to protect, you hear me? A *name*." Henrietta had explained in her haughty way, as if taking the time to elucidate things to Poppy was a chore that exhausted her. "My husband's the Mayor, and if you want to live here in *our city*, your black ass better be front and center in that church each week."

Poppy never would have become destitute if it weren't for that church. If it weren't for that church she would've never known about twice-weekly bingo, and if it weren't for that church she never would've taken all those congregation-sponsored bus trips to Atlantic City. She would've never maxed out thirteen credit cards and been forced to become a virtual slave to her own sister if it hadn't been for that damn church.

She'd gone out of obligation, plain and simple, though who knew why when it seemed pretty clear that neither her sister nor the Mayor wanted to be there either. No matter what the season, there was always something better to do on Sunday. In the fall and winter, Jarvis wanted nothing to do with anything besides football and politics. And in spring and summer, all Henrietta cared about was her garden. For the longest time Poppy had just assumed they went because they wanted to show off their Cadillacs and clout; but then, after a time, she'd heard them from behind their bedroom door, fussing to get into their dress clothes, and she knew there was more to the story. (How she'd seethe when she heard them bitching when things were too tight. "Damn that Poppy! She done shrunk my drawers again. Don't she know how to do nothin' right?" and "That crazy bitch's tryna put me in an early grave with all that damn fried okra she be feedin' us". As if she had any control over the menu or food shopping; Henrietta's lists were precise and uncompromising. She'd probably get a whipping if she deviated, as if it were 1810 and not 2010.) She'd hear one of them bellyache about not wanting to go and, inevitably, the other would gently coax, saying, "You know what Dino said," or "Dino'll be on our ass if we don't" and she'd wonder *Who cared what that smarmy-ass Senator wanted anyhow? He ain't even Baptist.*

Only to her closest friend LaShay Dupree would Poppy whisper the "name" her sister had been trying so desperately to protect: Uncle Tom. Then they'd laugh the way girlfriends do, until their considerable bosoms shook and Poppy had to use the corner of her apron to wipe at her eyes.

Her employers were always nasty to her, but today was extraordinary. All morning the Mayor had been pacing the house like a cat on a hot tin roof and when she'd suggested he was going to run a groove in the floor with all that back and forth she'd actually flinched, thinking he might slap her.

And all for what? *For the Senator's dumbass brother getting locked up?* The Mayor didn't even like him; she'd heard him say so a thousand times. *What do he care?*

But he did care. He was nervous and jumpy, as if he expected the cops to come bust down *his* door, too. Poppy could hardly take it anymore, all the tension in the house. It was so bad she almost wished her sister were home to explain, or at least create some sort of buffer. But Henrietta was off with her garden club. Camden of course didn't have such things, being the urban landfill that it was, so Henrietta was off in the suburbs, pretending to fit in, and likely wouldn't be home until suppertime. Poppy was on her own, and if she wanted to escape the suffocation of the Mayor's dark mood, she could only rely on herself.

"Mistah Mayor?" she ventured from the doorway of the living room, peeking her way around of the jamb in the event he launched something at her as punishment for the interruption. Lord knew it wouldn't be the first time. She stole a glance and saw he was still in his bedclothes, splayed out on the couch like a manatee, a scruffy beard at least two days old, staring vacantly at the television.

Her nervous eyes glanced over to it: It was turned off.

"You okay?" she asked, but one look at him and anyone could tell he wasn't. There was a huge mess of papers on the coffee table that he'd been pawing through all morning that she didn't dare touch, remembering that he'd even turned down a piece of apple crisp she'd made just that morning -- something he never did, no matter how sick he was -- and knew things must be real bad.

Damn! Was all she could think as she looked at him, the way his shoulders sagged like a discarded puppet's, shapeless and without life behind them. *He depressed as hell.*

With those heavy velvet drapes pulled closed so tight, the room was like a tomb, though it was a bright and sunny and perfect-day August just beyond them. Poppy moved slowly amid the creepy scene, afraid of what may happen next, because when she looked at him, she felt a cool chill of anxiety weaving through her neck hairs like some kind of snake charmed, giving her the shudders despite the heat of the day. "Mistah Mayor?"

He didn't seem to hear her.

"I'm goin' off to the store now. There anything you need?" She lingered a minute, awaiting an answer, and when none came, she scuttled out of the house before he could change his mind.

There was something strange and awful brewing, and Poppy wanted no parts of it.

"Thought she'd never leave," Jarvis grumbled as he tossed and turned against the cool velvet of the couch. "Damn fool's always underfoot."

Having his sister-in-law move in was not a choice he'd make again. Her housekeeping skills were not nearly good enough to surpass the sheer revulsion he felt whenever he looked at her. How she and his lovely Henrietta had come from the same woman was beyond him. That fat-ass Poppy was enough to make a man impotent.

"Who she think she foolin', sneakin' off like that? Tryna slip away undetected?" he mumbled to the empty room. "That overgrown rhinoceros could play offensive line for the Philadelphia Eagles."

But Poppy was not the problem, at least not today. Oh how he wished it were that simple.

No, Jarvis was defeated. Crushed. And as he lay there, he watched as the walls moved in, inch-by-inch, slow and steady and determined to destroy him once and for all, and he didn't even have the strength to look away. He was pathetic, and he knew it, and his ability to extract himself from it all was nil.

And he knew this, as well.

The latest report from the Attorney General lay in a heap on the coffee table before him: a two hundred and twelve page brief detailing the escalating mayhem in the Camden County Jail, his prison, where the gang activity was reaching a fever pitch, and the Task Force was demanding answers. From him. He gave it one last mournful look before closing his eyes and turning over, drawing his knees closer to his massive belly, burrowing his withered face in the nook of the brittle velvet.

The prison's most recent problem was cell phones. Friends, family, and fellow gangsters on the outside were finding newer, sneakier and more daring ways every day to get pre-paid phones into the hands of prisoners, allowing them to conduct business as usual from the inside, without threat of detection. Lately, the report said, these friends on the outside had taken to standing on the roofs of their Section 8 housing and launching –- literally *launching* from various formations of homemade cannons-of-sorts -- the phones through the air and over the fences into the yard where prisoners were supposed to be getting their daily exercise, and they were nailing their targets with alarming accuracy. Guards risked being shanked if they intervened, though most were being paid on the down low to look the other way anyway, and so the thugs got their phones quite easily. The phones were considered throwaways; none could be traced, and thus were the favored mode of communication for the Bloods, Crips, Mexican Mafia, you name it. Thanks to these devices all of the inmates were able to call the shots on the streets without ever leaving their cellblocks. Hits were ordered, retaliations planned, and the drug trade was flourishing as if all those gangbangers were simply on a Carnival cruise rather than doing hard time.

And, according to the AG and the Task Force, nobody seemed able to stop them. Jarvis remembered an exchange just last week when the Warden had told Jarvis with tears in his eyes that he felt like the little Dutch boy. "No sooner do we plug up one method of the drug trade, the murder trade, the human horror trade, than those wily little shits find another way." Jarvis had watched him, dumbfounded, as the round little man paced his office, fidgeting and forlorn and lost, looking like someone on a ledge high above a metropolis contemplating a swan dive.

Despite the alarming turn of events, or perhaps in spite of them, Jarvis couldn't help but wonder what kind of innovations and advances in society these convicts would've been able to make if they had simply used their ingenuity for good rather than anything and everything else.

But that was on the backburner. What was of most pressing concern at the moment was Iggy Bruni and his conviction. There had always been a chance -- fifty percent, really, when you thought about it -- that he might get locked up, but nobody had anticipated he would be denied bail. That meant a year or more awaiting sentencing. A year or more behind bars in the County lock-up, the same place phones were being launched into the hands of bloodthirsty gangbangers at this very moment. Men without souls, lost long ago to the streets, who sliced necks first and asked questions later. A year was plenty of time to get scared -- (hell! A day was!) -- To get your ass beat, get angry, get raped, get so ungodly uncomfortable in your own skin that you just might be willing to cut a deal, even if it meant sharing secrets. Nasty secrets. The kinds of secrets men kill to keep. Even if it meant feeding your own brother to the wolves. Even if he was a senator...

And Jarvis was no fool. He knew what that meant: if Iggy sold Dino out to the Prosecutor and his team of pythons, everyone ever connected to him would go down, too. Jarvis included.

Originally he'd lain down on the sofa to take a nap, but that was out of the question. There was just no way, with all these visions of Iggy dancing through his head. Of all of their conversations he'd been privy to over the years. Jarvis could kick his own ass for not being more discreet, for not thinking that maybe one day it'd come back to haunt him.

The Mayor rolled over, back and forth like an injured animal, clutching himself, sick to his stomach, thinking of the emails from

Heim, thinking of Iggy calling the Prosecutor and singing like a bird. Thinking of Henrietta and his Momma and all the people he'd let down. Who'd soon know what kind of man he *really* was if any of the past five years came to light. And then where would he be? Right alongside the likes of these creeps with their cell phones, plotting murder and rape and deals with the devil...and the Mayor would no longer be the Mayor, would no longer have any power. He'd just be regular old Jarvis Jasper, identified by an inmate number. He would be unable to stop a thing. Unable to protect even himself.

A long, low wail filled the room, reaching every crevice and cranny the old house had to offer. It was the cry of a wounded soul, and it took several startled moments before he realized that it was coming from him.

Alarmed, he shot upright. No, there was no way he could sleep. Not now. He needed to talk to Bruni, and it couldn't wait.

Though the City of Camden was worlds away from rural Georgia, Poppy had adjusted quite well. It had taken some time, of course, but after getting over the initial shock of all of the filth and crime, she'd made a nice little life for herself here, with good friends like LaShay Dupree and Mr. Wu who ran the grocery. She'd carved a niche for herself, and despite her wretched employers, it wasn't a place she altogether disliked, even if she didn't always understand it.

He looked up as soon as the bell on the door jingled, alert as prey behind six-inch-thick bulletproof glass.

"Afternoon, Mr. Wu," Poppy called as she scooped a red plastic basket into the crook of her hammy arm.

His face relaxed. "Miss Poppy, we have fresh peaches in the back."

She smiled at this, loving his thoughtfulness. She didn't really need much of anything, but she had the money her sister had left her this morning and figured she might as well use it. At least it got her out of the house for the afternoon. Just thinking of Jarvis laying there like a beached mammal, whimpering like he had been all morning long, was enough to give her nightmares, and as she navigated through the small bodega, picking up something here and there, she persuaded her thoughts to move elsewhere. But then she spotted the Mallomars, the Mayor's favorite, and her mind was right back where she didn't want it: picturing him in his dingy Jockeys, wallowing on the couch, popping migraine medicine like jelly beans, wailing in his sleep; all those inhuman noises. She shuddered at the memory of it. As she grabbed two boxes, a wistful thought came: *Maybe this'll help calm his fat ass down.* She meant to move on but then stopped, turned on her heel and went back for a third, just in case.

The fresh fruits and vegetables section of Mr. Wu's store was limited to a sorry-looking heap of collard greens and the half dozen peaches he always ordered especially for her. She loved this reminder of home, and loved him for providing it. She couldn't blame him for not having more; most folks in these parts ate fast food or no food, depending on whether or not they'd spent their monthly check yet.

She paid at the counter and chatted for a minute before waving goodbye and making her way down the block. The day was hot but, being a southerner, she was used to it; plus there was a nice breeze coming off of the river, and so Poppy decided to take the long way home.

The beauty of the day drew people to their stoops, to lean out open kitchen windows, bringing with them laughter and conversation and children shrieking in the streets, splashing in the water from the fire hydrants they'd hijacked. Poppy stopped to chat and was filled in on some local gossip: who was locked up and who was set to come home, who was messin' with who these days, who's pregnant, who's the daddy, who's causing trouble. There was always an earful of delicious news, and today was no different. But what most people wanted to talk about was the Senator's brother, whom they claimed was yet another victim of police corruption and authoritarian brutality in general.

"Must be a set-up."

"The Bruni family is good people."

"Ain't that just like The Man to try'n take down the good folks of Camden."

All this talk about Bruni made Poppy think of the Mayor then, of him flopped on the couch like some drunken cow, and then of the Mallomars -- the salve that might save the day, that she couldn't afford to have go melting in her bags -- and so she quickly said her goodbyes and made her way back toward the direction of the river.

During the day, with the junkies asleep, she could almost picture what the homes along The Banks might've looked like before they became crack dens. She wondered how it all happened, how something once so pretty became something so vile. Who'd let it get that way, and why. This was the type of thing that baffled her: New Jersey was the richest state in the entire country –- she'd heard it enough times to know it was true –- and yet here was Camden, just five miles away from a plethora of prestigious towns and darling hamlets, of country clubs and private schools. And there, just across the river was the birthplace of the entire country, letting a piece of itself fall down and die in such a spectacular way. Watching it wilt away like a once healthy rose now dying from neglect –- or no, something worse. Like watching an innocent man get kicked and beat for a crime he didn't commit. *Philadelphia oughtta be ashamed of itself,* Poppy thought, imagining what they'd think if they could see it now –- Jefferson, Adams, Franklin, the whole lot of them. How disgusted they'd be. How angry with their modern day countrymen. How sad that everyone seemed resigned to the situation.

They didn't have problems like that back home in Georgia, at least none that she ever saw. Towns were either poor or rich, but they didn't settle side by side one another, displaying the inequity as brazen as a face slap, as though it was nothing to be ashamed of.

She thought of her sister then, and what she must've seen that first day when she stepped away from the bus from Georgia and onto the depot on Herman Avenue, what she must have thought. Poppy imagined Henrietta questioning her sanity at first, wondering what she'd gotten herself into by following some college boy back to his hometown –- a *Yankee* hometown at that –- having only the best intentions, a heart full of young-girl hope, and arriving on Camden's doorstep. *She must've stepped off that bus feelin' like she stepped in a pile a' dog shit,* Poppy mused, her thoughts pierced by blasts of gangsta rap shrieking from the glossy Range Rovers and BMWs of the drug dealers speeding by, leaving thuds of bass in their wake.

She had been gone for nearly two hours before the notion to worry niggled its way into her mind. Checking her Timex she realized with sudden dread that Henrietta would be home soon, and she'd expect dinner to be well underway. Nervous now, she decided to cut through the abandoned lot by the bridge to make up for some lost time, and just as she negotiated her way through the hole in the chain-linked fence, the sight before her made her stop dead.

There, beneath the base of the big bridge that led into Philadelphia were two cars. One she didn't recognize, but there was no doubt as to whom the big shiny Cadillac belonged to. She could hear her heart beating in her ears as she slid down to avoid notice, watching the Mayor and that slimy-ass Senator talk, desperate not to be spotted, hungry as hell to hear their words.

"...Jarvis, you're being ridiculous..."

Poppy marveled at the way Bruni was speaking to her boss; it was the same way Jarvis talked to her. *This gonna be good,* she thought with a wry smile as she hunkered down amid the tall weeds and broken glass to get a better view.

"But what about the election?"

"Jesus Christ, Jasper, I'm not going to tell you again. Just shut up about the election. *I'm going to win.* Nobody gives a shit that Iggy's in jail. You think they care? I own this fucking city."

"But what if you don't win? Someone'll start snoopin', then we'll all be..."

"But nothing!" the Senator bellowed, and though she may have only wished it, Poppy was almost sure she saw the Mayor flinch. *Damn, I wish LaShay was here with me to see this!* She was nearly giddy when she thought about telling her best friend about this scene, imagining the way she'd re-enact it, and how LaShay would throw her head back and laugh.

Jarvis grew quiet then. Solemn. His head bowed like a schoolboy admonished to a corner. "And what about your brother?"

Bruni's face contorted into a snarl: "What about him?"

It was hard to stay focused with the roar of cars passing across the bridge overhead making the steel grates rumble, but Poppy inched forward, doing her best not to rustle too much, wincing as the serrated weeds sliced into her ashy heels and calves.

"Man, you saw the AG's report! That prison might as well be Hades. Ain't nobody sane lastin' down there more than five damn minutes."

"And?" The Senator rocked back on his heels, the sun glinting from the buffed black leather, making Poppy squint. Mosquitoes feasted on her flesh but dared not slap at them as she shifted her considerable weight from foot to foot, trying to forget about the rats that loved these parts, the way they weren't afraid of nothing.

Like a riverboat paddle wheel her mind turned over and over again one thing and one thing only: *What on God's green Earth were they talking about...?* It was as though she needed subtitles to follow this conversation. *Might as well be in Greek.*

Jarvis was scared, she could tell, but he was animated, too. Frantic. "What I'm sayin' is that's a long ass time to be waitin' on sentencing. Your brother might go on an' have a change of mind is all I'm sayin'. That jail ain't fit for nobody. You know as well as I do that it ain't nothin' like what he's used to. He probably never even thought it'd be as bad as it is. It's bound to be so bad that he might get the idea to start talkin' to somebody. Start lookin' for ways to get out a whole lot earlier. Start telling folks in the Prosecutor's office —"

"Enough!" Bruni roared, the veins in his neck purple and thick even from where Poppy sat hunched. "You don't know a goddamn thing about my brother, Jasper, and for you to be so bold as to insinuate he's some kind of rat is enough to make me shut *your* fat ass up for good."

Damn! He mad as hell! She thought, excited to tell LaShay, wondering if *she'd* be able to figure out what any of it meant.

But what she heard next made her shudder; it sounded nothing at all like the man she knew, whose booming voice carried from basement to beam in that old house on The Banks, demanding to know where his socks were, and where she'd moved his eyeglasses to, and *who the hell ate the last damn piece of cobbler?*

"But what about Heim?" the Mayor asked in a high-pitched whine; a child's anguished cry. "You read his email! From his work address, no less! We're gonna be –-"

"Forget about him. I'll take care of him. Enough of this shit, Jasper. I've had it!"

Feeling her girth begin to wobble upon itself she reached out a hand to steady herself, but fell forward anyway, the weeds and rocks and who knew what else biting into her knees like millions of grains of uncooked rice. But the pain was secondary to the eavesdropping.

"But your –-"

"I said *enough*, Jasper, and if you don't stop asking so many stupid fucking questions I'm going to hurt you in a way that you'll feel for your whole fucking life," Bruni hissed, and Poppy felt it ripple throughout, fear rising within her like a roller coaster, leaving her throat prickly and dry: the man meant what he said, and only a fool would doubt it.

7

Saturday
4:59pm

The mellow melodies of Jimmy Buffett sailed among the jolly din of the revilers savoring the last of summer as Herb Heim wove his way through the crowd.

The block party existed each year within a time warp; the same music, same food. The same goofy middle-aged men hiding their beer bellies behind Hawaiian shirts, trying in vain to remember what it means to be cool. Only thing you could really count on to change among the Grassy Glen sub-division was the kids, and the thought of this almost made him tear up. An urgent need to find his girls came over him then, and he cupped a hand along his eyebrows to search.

He found Olivia almost at once; girls her age were more prone to lounging about and talking with their friends than anything. Her braces glinted in the sun and as she laughed he watched the smooth curve of her throat, the shudder of her budding chest, and wanted to sear it into his mind, the way she looked when she was happy, because she hardly ever looked that way at home anymore. "She's just going through a stage, Herb," Marcie had told him. Then, to his annoyance she'd added: "She's growing up, you know."

You know. As if he was so stupid he'd somehow missed the almost cartoonish angst over Olivia's pining for the elusive Connor

Romaine that had overtaken the entire Heim household for nearly four months. The endless tears over his lack of returned affection set to an unbearable soundtrack of sad, whiny music that haunted their house for a whole semester. Her agony over waiting for her boobs to arrive; the tampons, the cramps; the constant texting and subsequent bills that made Herb's eyes bulge; the 'mean girls' whom she alternately loved and hated, depending on the day. The lemming-like devotion to ludicrous icons created by the culture of consumerism. As if he was so obtuse that...

Oh who cared anymore? He thought as he watched her on the grass. He felt his heart leap as he caught a few snippets of conversation carried by the wind, of Olivia chattering about their trip as she showed them mobile uploads taken on her cell.

He felt his chest puff. He was proud of himself for thinking of Paris. It'd come to him one day while he was nestled away in his gray cubicle, staring blankly at the computer screen, his eyes burning from twelve hours worth of peering at it, his brilliant plan still in its early stages. *I'll take them to Paris,* he'd thought suddenly, and everything was jarred back into focus. Marcie had always wanted to go, but once the girls had arrived, they'd never found the time. (Or the money, as Marcie so often liked to remind him.) And just a few months back –- when she was still in the throes of puppy love with the infamous Connor Romaine, Olivia had squealed: "Paris is the most romantic city in the world!" Ever since he'd announced it, only the promise of going had made her happier at home than he'd seen since grammar school, at least at any notion that included him.

Lucy, of course, being Lucy, was happy to go anywhere. Though, when it came to travelling, Herb knew she would've rather spent two weeks at space camp, or hiking, or on a ranch in Montana learning to fly fish. But in true Lucy-fashion she'd gone along gamely. Herb had known she would, of course he had, and had made it a point to take care of her big dream, too. "And when we get home, Luce, you can get a puppy. You can even pick him out and name him yourself!" He'd nearly toppled at the sheer force of her hug, and the way her eyes shined when she finally let go had made his heart ache. She was still young enough to not realize that she should be embarrassed by him, and he supposed that's why he loved her best.

In February he'd broken the news: If the girls had good report cards, they'd be going in August. Olivia and Marcie were like two best friends the way they giggled about it, poring over *Lonely Planet* guidebooks and looking up stuff on line, shrieking over the high-end boutiques, the cafes, the celebrities they might see.

"Money's no object," he'd said casually, vaguely sure Marcie was too excited to remember to ride him about every penny. "Got a big raise." The lies came easily now; after so many, they slid right out and never even made him blink anymore.

He finally made his way to the keg. These suburban attempts at camaraderie never failed to remind him of college or, if he were being honest, stories he'd heard from guys in his college classes. Though he'd watched and marveled and envied the co-eds and Greeks and arty liberals as they threw caution to the wind, he'd never been brave enough to attempt to ingratiate himself into the social scene. Nobody in his section had ever much ventured beyond a school-sanctioned mixer or two, and he was no different. Somewhere along the line, however, good old osmosis must've taken hold, because at some point he'd learned that a shy man's wisest first move was always toward the liquor.

As he poured himself another -- His what? Fourth? Fifth? -- He spotted Lucy rounding the bases in the Miller's front lawn, her lanky limbs moving easily with speed. Where she'd gotten the athleticism gene from was anyone's guess. Must have been buried somewhere on Marcie's side, because there wasn't anything remotely sporty about the Heim clan.

She's so beautiful, he thought as if seeing her for the first time. *I'm going to miss her the most...*

"Heimy-boy!" A raucous voice bellowed along with a staggering clap on his back, and Herb cringed. Del Heeper. "Was wonderin' where you were!" Herb stiffened at the lie, but tried to remain natural just the same.

"Hey there, Del," he said in what he hoped to be a jovial tone.

"How was your trip to the Land of the Frogs?" Del asked, but before Herb could answer, he launched into his own long-winded diatribe. "I gotta tell ya, I didn't think you had it in you. You must've really been in the dog house to agree to that trip!" His laugh was as hearty as it was insufferable. "Although I'm sure you fit in just fine with all those faggot Frenchmen, eh Heimy-boy?!" Del threw his head back and guffawed, all three hundred pounds of him a-jiggle, showcasing the remnants of the potluck buffet in his teeth, elbowing Herb, as if they were friends. "Aw shit," he said, wiping his eyes. "So Herbie my man. What's new at the Statehouse? Still full of crooks and lackeys?"

Herb had the intense desire to stab him repeatedly. "Business as usual," he said through gritted teeth, his blood pressure rising.

"I'm just joking, Heimy-boy! No offense, no offense. You're not a lackey."

Herb was offended more by the lie than the put-down. Del grabbed for one of Herb's arms, spilling his freshly poured beer down the front of his shirt, the one Marcie had warned him not to muss. *Why do you have to be such a slob?* She'd surely groan, unadulterated disgust lacing her voice, leaving no doubt as to just how much he annoyed her.

"Yep, just as I thought!" Del boomed. "You're gettin' guns there, Heimy-boy!" Herb fucking hated that nickname, and Del knew it. "Yo Jerry!" He called across the street to the row of fathers sitting in their lawn chairs in the shade of Mrs. Abella's ancient Maple. "Old Heimy-boy's finally got some biceps! All that pencil-pushing's finally paying off!"

The laughter came in a sharp burst, like an air horn. Herb felt his face grow scarlet when he noticed some of the women had heard and were laughing too. Then he watched Marcie turn her back on the entire scene, her face red, marred by contempt.

"Anyhoo," Del resumed casually, as if he hadn't just humiliated him in front of the entire neighborhood, glugging like a glutton on his beer stein. *A regular silo cup was no good for Del Heeper,* Herb thought nastily. *Nooo, he needed to get as much alcohol into his gigantic fat ass as possible.* This made him smile a little.

"--I just don't know how you do it, is all I'm saying. Your pensions are robbing us taxpayers blind, you know."

Herb worked to keep the anger from his voice. He'd been bullied by brainless assholes like Del Heeper his whole life, and now that there was an end in sight, it was as though he'd suddenly found his backbone. "I work in the Department of Environmental Protection, Del. Not the Division of Pensions and Benefits."

"I know, I know. It's just that all you people kill me." How Herb hated that expression: 'you people'. It was always said in such a vile manner, the speaker practically spitting it.

"Yeah?" Herb asked as he took a sip of his beer, "How's that, Del?"

Del looked at him sharply, his eyes narrowing as he sensed defiance from his prey. But then Herb pushed his glasses back on his nose, and the gesture seemed to remind Del that there was no way Herb Heim would ever venture back talk.

"You know. State workers. You get every freakin' holiday off, only work 9-5, get fat-ass pensions, take the wife and kids to *Paris,* for *Pete's sake,* while the rest of us humps gotta work overtime just to survive anymore in this shithole state. I don't know what kind of numb-nuts keep re-electing these assholes..."

Talk of re-election brought Bruni to the forefront of his mind as pleasantly as a hammer to the thumb. Only after he'd fired off those emails in a fit of bravado had it occurred to him that he'd made a very bad mistake. And if the Scottolino brothers caught wind of it, a fatal one. With a hanky, Herb blotted at his forehead, wondering if it was just him or it was getting hotter? Because suddenly the sun seemed to sear right through him, scarring his bones. *What was I thinking?* He hadn't wanted to carry out his plan until he got Lucy her puppy, until he made good on this one last promise. But she had her heart set on some new type of hybrid: a Labradoodle or some such, and the only local breeder he could find with a litter was unavailable until Tuesday.

That left three days for the Scottolino Brothers to do significant harm to him. Oh God, why hadn't he thought of that? His legs began to play tricks on him: one moment they were steady, the next: jelly. *Oh God.* The Scottolino's were all but a given, but who knew what kind of depraved thugs Jarvis Jasper could round up in Camden, bring up to the Grassy Glen cul-de-sac and turn it into Compton? He'd jumped the gun too soon, and now he was going to pay...

Herb took a long pull from his beer hoping to compose his thoughts; in an instant they'd become overrun and clouded...

But wait. He still had control. He might not make good on his promise to Lucy, but he could carry out his plan tonight and all would be good.

His heart was still a snare drum in his bony chest but he felt a new calmness was easing over him like a salve. He hadn't had a thing to eat yet, and with all of these beers, in the sun this hot...He was just being paranoid. *Yes, that was it.*

But then, in his mind's eye he pictured a long-drawn out torture session led by some punks who'd seen too many *Scarface*-type movies and the dread was back so fast it nearly gave him whiplash. He pictured his girls dying, or worse: surviving with unmentionable wounds and scars so deep and debilitating that their hate for him would last until their graves.

The street became a wicked circus then; everything suddenly too loud, too bright, and the smell of Bob Carroll burning hotdogs on the grill suddenly smelled to him like burning flesh, and he looked heavenward, in prayer, willing this wretched feeling away. But it was useless. Instead the sun struck his eyes hard and he had to bend over, his Buddy Holly's tumbling to the asphalt, and the sounds closing in from all sides were draining him of everything normal and human, making him feel weak with nausea and, as he stumbled away -- returning a day's worth of block party food onto Mary O'Ryan's orange day lilies -- he heard Del Heeper laughing like a wild rhino, calling after him, "Don't worry Heimy-boy! I remember my first beer, too!"

8

Saturday
7:11 pm

The wan slip of sleep cocooning Ben Campbell was first shaken with the grating launch of the loudspeaker whining to life, then shed entirely when the pilot's irritating voice followed, cavalier and bedroom-like, permeating the interior of the fuselage like dime store cologne.

Ben slid out of his dream and heard: "Ladies and gentlemen, it appears as though the City of Brotherly Love isn't nearly as excited to see us as we are to see it." The words came with a velvety *heh-heh* chuckle, as if the pilot were wooing the rows of weary travelers rather than guiding them through the night sky. Annoyed, Ben cringed, eager to find sleep again but acutely aware it was gone for good.

"Looks like we'll be circling for a bit, folks," the pilot warned, and the people released a collective groan. 'Circling around for a bit' at Philly International could mean hours and they all knew it; they'd already been delayed taking off from Boston which, when you added it all up -- including time spent in an endless helix of security checks -- and Ben counted five hours since his last cigarette.

"But don't let the nighttime fool you, folks," said the pilot, with another raspy *heh heh*. "There's still ample opportunity for sightseeing..."

As if we give a shit, Ben mused, peeling his face from the narrow space of plastic next to the window and rubbing where coarse lines had been left along his cheek. He knuckled the sleep from his eye and stretched his wrinkled spine: the city was shrouded in charcoal, pricked by a million small, winking white lights. He thought of all that waited for him below: the voicemails, the emails, the calls to return, the eighty-hour work weeks...

The election.

He turned away.

At once his head began to pound, the last twelve hours assaulting him in a relentless wave, and he found it near impossible to suppress the cringes.

He thought of Old Man Van Horn then: tanned ankles crossed beneath pleated khakis, patrician hands folded over his considerable belly clad in Facconable, the unimpressed smirk evident amid sun-splashed jowls. Day was setting on the eighteenth hole, and though Ben had a twenty-thousand dollar diamond ring in his pocket –– more than he'd ever spent, or could have imagined was possible for him to spend –- he was still fairly certain his worth was negligible, particularly in the eyes of the Old Man. He was going to ask for Kat's hand in marriage, and while Ben felt his heart jackhammering, he assumed a mask of tranquility, as if he did such things every day, as if he felt perfectly at home here at a place where annual dues exceeded most annual salaries.

They had consulted their menus in silence, and only when the waitress arrived did Van Horn finally acknowledge Ben's presence.

"The Kobe beef sliders are excellent," he said, almost in passing, and Ben nodded with vigor -– *perhaps too much vigor,* he thought now, despising the shame of being such a suck-up.

The waitress, a timid wisp of a girl, announced the specials in a voice just a shade above a whisper, and Ben had thought to himself as he glanced around one of America's most exclusive and expensive clubs, *Sweetheart you are in the* wrong *job if you're easily intimidated.*

"Vichyssoise." The Old Man corrected, his tone so curt it yanked Ben from his thoughts.

"Um, pardon me?" she asked, her nervous-rabbit eyes darting.

"You said vicchyssway. It's pronounced vichyssoise."

Her face bloomed red. "Oh, I apologize sir. I'm sorry, I..."

Van Horn waved a hand as if swatting a bug and Ben felt indignity rise within him, entangled with a white-hot anger that took all of his strength to suppress. Maybe that should've been his first clue...

"At the moment our passengers on the right can see where some the greatest athletes of all time hailed from," the pilot announced. "Philly's one of the craziest sports towns ever, and...Well, if their walls could talk," (heh heh) "they'd have quite a few tell-all books up their sleeves..."

Ben was a huge sports fan but he rolled his eyes nonetheless and didn't bother to join the other rubberneckers contorting themselves to basically see nothing more than a couple of roofs.

"Let's just hope they don't make us circle too long. We hear thunderstorms are on the way and, I don't know about you folks, but I'd prefer not to have to return to Boston, lovely as it is this time of year."

As other passengers grumbled, Ben leaned over to retrieve his carry-on from beneath the seat in front of him.

"You from Philly?" came a voice.

Ben looked over to his right: a jolly sort of fat man who seemed affable enough, but Ben was in no mood for making new friends. "Sort of. Jersey," he replied, hoping his terseness would be enough of an indicator that he had no interest in conversation.

The man laughed, oblivious, double chin bouncing. "Jersey, eh? I used to do a route in Jersey. Back in the eighties..."

Ben rolled his eyes. *Oh great. Here we fuckin' go.*

Without prompt the man went on: "...I was with Tastykake for years. Knew every cupcake and crumpet like the back of my hand..."

Ben eyed the man's girth and thought, *No surprise there...*

"...Used to cover all the way to the AC Expressway, if you can believe it..."

Just then Ben noticed a tidy redheaded stewardess primly making her way down the aisle and he leaned across the empty middle seat to flag her down.

"Yes, sir?" she asked in a prudish tone, penciled-on eyebrows arched into improbability.

"Jack Daniels," he said in a rush as he fished into the back pocket of his jeans for his wallet. "Make it a double."

The flight attendant eyed the quartet of empty bottles already amassed on his tray table with scarcely masked disapproval before turning on her heel and disappearing into the galley without another word.

Determined to converse even without participation from anyone else, the fat man continued talking and Ben continued ignoring him as he pawed through his carry-on for his phone. He pulled it out and sat back. It blinked to life and he was avalanched by dread as he read: 143 new messages.

"Fuck me," he grumbled; it had only been two hours since he'd last checked.

Scrolling through, he stopped only at the emails from his assistant Millie, updating him on his messages from the office phones. Most were predictable: reporters, reporters, and more reporters. Their opposition research guy, their media consultant. Every one of them demanding something from him.

His head thumped as he swam through the list until one name leapt forth and snagged his eye: a name that was increasingly becoming more familiar with every batch of new messages over the past few days:

Herb Heim.

"Guy's relentless," Ben muttered as he sat back, exasperated. *Who the hell is this guy and why's he keep fucking calling me?*

"Excuse me, sir."

Ben looked up; the redhead again, her pale face screwed into reprimand: "Sir, you'll need to turn that off," she admonished. "No electronic devices until we land."

Ben grumbled but didn't bother with an argument. He knew the rules, of course; he was just trying to break them. He dropped it into his open carry-on and handed her a twenty in exchange for the tiny bottles in her hand.

"Do you have anything smaller?" she wanted to know, growing more annoyed with him with each passing second.

Feeling's mutual, lady, he thought as he turned to the window, began unscrewing the cap of the first bottle and said: "Just keep the change."

The liquor burned, but Ben welcomed it. He wasn't supposed to be on this flight, after all. He'd just left Philadelphia the day before, intending to stay in Boston for the duration of Labor Day weekend, but Kat apparently had other plans. Like dumping him.

He exhaled and closed his eyes.

Maybe he should have just taken his lumps from the Old Man, taken his medicine when he'd told him: "No, you most certainly do *not* have my blessing."

Chalk it up to his Irish stubborn streak, or perhaps plain old hubris, but Ben Campbell was not about to go out without a fight. He'd continued on with his plans, taking Kat on a horse-and-carriage ride around Boston Common, to be followed by dinner at the swanky Parc 23 in Beacon Hill and then, the proposal.

Of course they hadn't gotten that far; they'd made love in his hotel room and set off for the horse-and-buggy ride, and the sun hadn't even set when Kat turned to him and said, "My father's right, you know."

The smell of manure rising from the cobblestone was mingling with the late summer flowers, and Ben turned to her, his mouth an 'o'. *Had the old man really gone and blown the surprise? Could he really be that evil?*

"W-what?"

Kat sighed then, and a breeze wrapped around them, lifting her blonde bob around the edges, her wide blue eyes twinkling with... what? *Tears?* Ben wondered, almost relieved, thinking there might be hope yet...but then remembered her allergies, and they way they flared year-round.

"You have no job stability, Ben. You bounced around the country from campaign to campaign for how many years? Only making pit stops in DC long enough to do your laundry. But at least on The Hill you were on your way. Now you're back home and I...well, I could never live in Jersey. It's just...not me, you know? And yeah, maybe you've got a good thing going as far as Bruni. I don't know. I mean, the guy can't lose. But it's still. It's...(sigh)...you see where my dad's coming from, don't you? You *must*."

He did not.

"It's *Jersey*, Ben. A state senate race, for God's sake," she said, exasperated. Almost ready to give up.

"Yeah and if I win –- *when* I win -- I'll have my pick of any job, Kat. *Any* job."

"Any job in Jersey." She retorted a little too quickly. Then she saw his face and sighed. "Look, if you win and get a job with the Governor or something, maybe he'll come around. I'll see what I can do, but honestly Ben, it's a big 'if'. For me, too."

And then, all at once, he *did* see where the Old Man was coming from. Although now he saw that Van Horn's train wasn't just a one-man show after all; Kat was on-board, too. He felt his knees weaken with knowing and anger and humiliation, and was grateful to be sitting in the carriage, not sure his body could've sustained the impact on solid ground. *He just wasn't good enough for her.*

But Kat loved him. He knew that much. And as the tears streaked her sun-kissed cheeks she gave him one long, last kiss goodbye and said: "Call me when you win."

And he loved her, too. He did.

Didn't he?

Ding! Ben's head snapped up and he saw the sign illuminated above. *Oh goody. We're no longer allowed to take a piss. We must be on our way to landing.*

He sighed. He'd just endured a brutal trip and was now on his way to return to a brutal life where the next three months would make "brutal" look like baby's breath.

The good news was that nobody expected him back until Sunday morning so, for the first time in a long time, he'd have one day and two nights of solitude, something he wouldn't get again for a while.

143 new messages.

He took another sip of bourbon, not bothering with to mix it with the half-can of Coke from earlier still sitting on his tray, and thought of his messages. He hadn't been able to peruse the entire list but he could guess who'd sent the bulk of them: his old pal Chip Wesley calling from the Governor's mansion wanting to know when he'd be back, did he see the latest poll, and *Why aren't you answering your phone, Campbell? Don't they have cell service in Beantown?* Fundraiser extraordinaire Marlena Torres wanting to report the take from the week's fundraising, did he really need to spend that much on the new ad, and *You'll be back on Sunday night, right Ben?* Their media consultants wanting to know if he'd seen the latest TV ad, heard the opponent's radio spot. Digger Vance from DC: *You getting my fucking emails dude? Why the fuck haven't I heard from you??*

In campaign politics, time was accelerated. Returning messages in a near-instantaneous manner was not only critical but downright expected. He spent his days and nights glued to screens. No sooner than he made a dent in the pile of messages than the gap would be filled. It was a grueling profession in general, magnified tenfold during the three months leading up to Election Day. Labor Day was the official kick-off for campaign season -- just two days away -- and Ben was already exhausted.

He took a long, searing sip and drained the first mini-bottle. From the corner of his eye he noticed the fat man eying him as he opened the second.

143 new messages...

None of these mattered, though. The only communiqué of real importance was from his boss, who penned emails in the same choppy, barked manner in which he spoke. The Senator himself. The last one Ben received before boarding had read: "New Ad = mediocre. I'm paying for what exactly? Step up the game, Campbell. D Day in 61 days. Am I clear?"

D-Day being November 4th, of course, when Ben was expected to get Senator Dino Bruni re-elected to the New Jersey Legislature for his ninth term. And not just win, but by a wide margin, delivering the same embarrassing landslide of votes to ensure this opponent would be obliterated and scared away from politics for good, just as all the others had been.

Ben had beat-out hundreds of applicants for the job of campaign manager, but he was beginning to wonder if he was better off back in DC. When he'd accepted the job in the spring, this campaign had looked like a cakewalk; nothing more than an easy means to an even better end. But the conviction of the Senator's brother had Ben worried. Not a lot, but his confidence was shaken just enough to keep him on his toes.

The good news was, he was home. Who could guess how many nights he'd spent in the pubs of Georgetown, watching the hordes of co-eds walk by -- arms linked and highlighted heads thrown back in laughter as they graced the cobblestone streets, their tight, trendy denim hugging all the right places -- and thinking of Jersey. Though he was thirty now -- and despite having spent the last ten years working tough campaigns and earning a sterling reputation as a top-notch operative -- he'd never been able to shake the fish-out-of-water feeling in DC. It wasn't an easy town for a blue-collar kid to like, and he'd spent most of his time on The Hill feeling as though he was walking around in another man's suit, another man's life.

His return to the Garden State was expedited by the sudden death of his father, of course, but he wasn't trying to be a martyr. When he really thought about it, how much could he have really expected to continue to accomplish on The Hill knowing his mother was back home, needing him?

Despite Kat's reservations, landing a coveted position with a premiere campaign straight-off-the-train had been an accomplishment. What was better was that no one in their right mind would try to take on this particular district and expect to win. The only elections that were ever tough for Dino Bruni were primaries, and he'd sailed through the last one, even though Ben suspected the Governor herself had handpicked the opponent.

The opponent running against him now, one J. Harrison Almond, a political greenhorn, had about as much of a chance as Mickey Mouse of triumphing over Dino Bruni, and Ben might have felt sorry for the poor guy if he didn't find him so profoundly stupid for even trying. Almond was a retired stockbroker nobody had ever heard of, while the name Bruni meant something in Jersey -- especially South Jersey -- and *especially* The City of Camden, where the Bruni family had lived in the same neighborhood since the first Roosevelt was in office.

Ben's plan had been to return home to help Mom, coast Bruni to victory, then have his pick of the litter of cushy Jersey government jobs, guessing he'd likely land in the State House, chief-of-staff or consultant or some other six-figure post, maybe even a lobbyist. Either way, he'd be close enough to help out Mom. Hell, it wasn't like DC was going anywhere. He could always go back. But, for now, he needed to be here. He *had* been bouncing around the country, living out of a suitcase, and getting congressmen and governors elected for so long now it had come to seem normal to not know what time zone he was in. But he'd made a decision: this was his last campaign. Bruni would win, and Ben would sail into the job of his choosing.

People in DC had thought he was nuts for taking the job, but Ben had known what he was doing. Bruni was a powerhouse in a state full of them. He'd get Ben any job he wanted.

And it wasn't just his buddies in DC who'd thought he was crazy, either. Take Chip Wesley: a close friend since Rutgers Poly-Sci 101, now the Governor's right-hand. He'd laughed when Ben had told him, laughed right to his face: "Bruni? You won't last two fucking seconds on that campaign. The guy's a complete narcissist, Campbell. Wants his name on everything. Every bill, every building —-"

Ben had snorted. "And that makes him different from all the rest *how* exactly?"

"Touché. Look, I know you've met your fair share, but this guy is a Grade-A dickhead. You'll hate him, Ben. Trust me."

He took this with a grain of salt, thinking of the Governor's contemptuous relationship with Bruni, doubting Chip would be able to maintain any sense of neutrality on the subject.

"Thanks for the heads up," he'd said, figuring there was no way this guy could be any worse than the other mega-egos he'd successfully herded into office over the years.

But Dino Bruni wasn't nearly the asshole Ben had expected. There were rumors of a hair-trigger temper and a scorched-earth resolve but as far as politicians went, he wasn't half-bad. Maybe a little crazy at times, the way he constantly talked of legacy and loyalty —- obsessing about it, really —- but his little tangents were mild compared to some of the self-important freaks Ben had had the misfortune of dealing with in Washington. Ben had met more prima donnas in DC than at a debutante ball. Assholes he could handle.

And, asshole or no, Ben had suffered through worse. Every campaign brought with it long hours of putting out fires, but at least Dino Bruni was a legend, a legend the public loved; a man who hadn't forgotten his roots, who toiled to bring economic-vitality to long-struggling Camden, and the people there worshipped him for it. When he died, there was no doubt there would be a statue erected in his honor, gleaming from its post along The Banks with the caption eulogizing his public servitude. That's what Dino wanted anyway: immortality; a noble way to carry on the family name.

Legacy.

He'd told Ben so on many, many occasions, and Ben could now understand why: Lord knew his brothers weren't doing much to further the cause.

"So what about you, pal?"

Ben turned away from the window, from the city swirling below. "Hmm?"

It was the fat guy in the aisle seat again, apparently finished with his monologue, and now ready to ask questions. "What line a' work you in?"

"Politics," Ben said curtly, hoping as he always did that he wouldn't regret it, wouldn't get sucked in to some long conversation...or worse: a debate.

"Who for?"

"Dino Bruni."

The man nodded and regarded Ben in a different way all of a sudden.

"You heard of him?"

"Bruni?" the fat man said with a vague smile, as if recalling a fond memory. "*Sure* I know him. Helluva guy, that Bruni. Shame about his brother, though."

No shit, Ben thought. Convicted on all six counts, facing prison *was* a shame, and possibly the one thing that would derail the smoothest-sailing campaign in history. Ben could just about *kill* Iggy Bruni for being such an idiot. Generations had toiled to foster the Bruni name, and Ignacio "Iggy" Bruni might have just pissed it all away.

"Money makes people do crazy things, ya know?" the man mused.

"Yeah," Ben said in a noncommittal way, when really he was trying to contain the rage he felt at the moment; everyone knew about the case against Iggy, and, before he'd been hired, Ben had been relentless in voicing his concerns about how it might impact the campaign. Ever the salesman, the Senator had offered him his best smile and assured him he'd hired the best defense money could buy and there wasn't a chance in hell his brother would get convicted.

"I'd bet my life on it," Bruni had said, his smile ricocheting against the light shed from the Tiffany lamp on his desk, bathing his face in the warm, nostalgic kind of light that made him seem almost fatherly, and Ben grimaced now, thinking of how he'd bought it hook, line and sinker.

And now look at them. Ben could kick his own ass for being so naive. No sooner had he taken the job than Bruni began to backpedal, and now that Ben's worst fears had been confirmed, they'd be spending who-knew how many hours deflecting questions and spinning the story, doing everything in their power to get reporters to forget the trial and instead focus on their platform, their plans to continue redevelopment of The Banks, to bring sorely-needed economic growth to that grotesque cesspool Camden...

"...Comes from good people, though. My grandmother grew up in Camden an' everything I ever heard was how the Bruni family was good people."

Ben smiled, the bourbon kicking in, and said to Tastykake Guy: "Your grandmother is a very wise woman." He tilted his tiny bottle forth in mock toast, neglecting to realize he was drinking alone.

So the story went Giancarlo Bruni, Dino and Iggy's grandfather, had taken all the money he'd saved from working on the docks at The Port of Camden and set up the first funeral parlor in town. At the time the next closest one was eleven miles away and, like so many proud immigrants, he put his name in the biggest letters on the biggest sign he could find, and business boomed for years.

The Senator's father, Alfredo, had taken it over once Giancarlo got too old and sick (and, before long, became a client himself) and made a good business better with one very simple sales strategy, and word spread quickly there was a generous man in the City of Camden who would bury the poor for free. Alfredo's business plan might've been simple, but it was ingenious; the new business he received for his generosity far surpassed the costs for the pine boxes he doled out to the poor, and the name Bruni was solidified at once as a fixture among the people of South Jersey, a name that evoked gallantry and kindness: a community man that cared.

While maintaining their rapidly flourishing business, Alfredo and Marie Bruni bore two sons, Ignazio aka "Iggy" and Alfredo, Jr.(A.J), who would go on to run the family funeral home and die of AIDS, respectively.

Then there was Dino. A short stature had given him a Napoleon complex, and a keen mind had deemed him destined for things greater than stagy condolences and overpriced urns. His mother had been the one to urge him into politics -- *He's got a face that would give JFK a run for his money* -- and so, after a lackluster career working in the family business under brother Iggy's clumsy charge, Dino had taken her advice.

Lucky for Ben, name identification was key to mounting an effective campaign, and creation of a Bruni "brand" had been done by others over the years and eliminated a lot of work on his part.

Well, not too much...because while since the turn of the century, the Bruni name had meant something, Ben wasn't so sure he liked the new meaning.

His face contorted into something like pain as he remembered the morning's headlines.

BRUNI: GUILTY.

But Ben could still breathe easy. Cautiously, but easy. It was still early, and there was a hope that the trial wouldn't follow them all the way through to Election Day. The story would likely grow stale and, with a little luck, they'd go from distancing themselves from it to skating away from the scandal altogether.

As far as he could tell, the people of Camden still loved Dino Bruni, and Camden still comprised the bulk of his district. Of course the Senator didn't live there anymore; and who could blame him? No matter how you were raised -- praising Allah or Buddha or spinning the dreidl or, like Ben, dragged by the collar to Catholic mass every week to spend Sunday morning on your knees hearing about how full of sin and unworthy you were it made you wonder why God had bothered making man in the first place -- the notion of hell is a pretty clear concept. A final destination for the wicked. A dungeon of gloom. A lake of blood and guilt, no different than the Ninth Circle in Dante's *Inferno*...

Or Camden, New Jersey.

Ben sat back, letting the booze introduce itself to his brain and tug the tension from his shoulders. His eyes fluttered to a close and a fast but hollow sleep ensued, and the next thing he knew, the fat man was shaking his shoulder telling him they'd landed.

Grabbing his bag, Ben followed the line of weary travelers streaming from the plane into Philly International. Along the concourse he stopped only to go to the bathroom, clicking his phone on at the urinal, and made his way toward baggage claim.

The 143 new messages had only grown by twenty, most of which came from his assistant Millie.

> WIMBERLY MEYER: DAILY NEWS. 215.555.6875 STILL WAITING FOR COMMENT ON THE VERDICT.
>
> JOHN DAVID MILLER: PHILA. INQUIRER. 215.555.1008 WANTS COMMENTS ON THE VERDICT.

And a dozen more from publications around the tri-state area, all wanting the same thing.

> YOUR MOTHER CALLED. SHE WANTS YOU TO COME FOR DINNER ON SUNDAY.

Ever since spring when he'd packed his Jeep and left his Capitol Hill apartment for the last time, Ben had tried to make it to Sunday Dinner at Mom's, but whenever he had a rough week looming ahead like the one facing him now, he risked hurting her feelings and begged off. He made a note to decline, but then he read on: SHE NEEDS TO TALK TO YOU ABOUT ZOEY. *Uh-oh*, Ben thought, hoping his niece wasn't in trouble again. Lately she'd been running with a bad crowd and it was worrying his Mom to death.

That was another reason he'd come back from DC, to help with Zoey. It went without saying that his sister was useless in that department. He scrolled through to reach his calendar, and flipped to Sunday: Dinner at Mom's, he typed.

He dreaded going, though, if only for the reason that Mom would ask about Kat, and Kat was something he did not want to discuss with anyone right now. He hated himself for getting involved with her in the first place, let alone letting it drag on for two years. Now he was reassessing *everything*. Regret was doing some sort of Mexican Hat Dance on his psyche, having the time of its life while Ben was brought to his knees by self-pity.

His phone bleated, bringing him back to the moment. Boston was behind him and now he was back home, business as usual. There were at least fifty calls that could wait until Monday, and a good chunk he might not return at all. But there was something that bothered him: 17 messages from this habitual caller that seemed to be haunting him. This man –- this stranger -- named Herb Heim.

Ben groped through his memory, trying to recall a time or place where they might've met. Whether it was his fatigue, the bourbon, or both, he was drawing a complete blank. For all he knew it might not have to do with the campaign or politics at all. It could be a guy he played ball with, an old landlord, the cop who'd pulled him over for speeding last month, a frat brother, a kid he'd coached in Little League...

At precisely the same time Ben felt his head begin to thump the emblem of *TGI Friday's* blazed neon and beckoned him in for a touch more booze to quiet the ache. A stitch of relief came at the thought of not having to dodge and compete with a hundred other tired and impatient people trying to fetch their baggage; By the time he'd have drank enough to wash away the head-pound, his bag would be the only one left on the carousel.

He ordered a drink and the bored-stiff bartender seemed almost grateful for something to do.

His attention turned to the Phillies on the TV and he relaxed: the curse had been lifted in 2008 and his boys no longer had to endure the taunts of other cities regarding their sports teams. All he needed now was the Flyers to win the Stanley Cup and he could die a happy man.

Ben fingered the glass growing ever more sweaty by the second, his thoughts drifting from Kat to the Senator and back to the stranger named Heim that apparently had the tenacity of a stalker.

"Need a menu, hon?" the frizzy-haired waitress wanted to know, pausing only for a second on the toes of her high-tops to watch him shake his head 'no'.

After another drink he came to the conclusion that no matter who this guy was, Ben guessed he probably wasn't important. After all, every campaign was known to attract their share of nuts: people who got fixated on one issue and made it their life's crusade to pursue it. Lots of folks with too much time on their hands and not enough friends or interests, who felt it necessary to waste the valuable time of other people by banging on the door of the campaign headquarters with complaints about everything from the price of eggs to the price of healthcare to the pothole on their street. The Senator had an office full of government-paid employees to handle that kind of minutiae; Ben had neither the staff nor the time to care. But their votes were still needed, so the nuts that walked in off the street were kindly shuffled out of the building, and sent on their way with a promise their concerns would be relayed to the Senator.

But the nuts who called or came by never asked for Ben by name -- or any other campaign staffer specifically -- and maybe that was why he was so bothered by this. He was a behind-the-scenes guy who hated dealing with the masses, so aside from maybe reading a quote Ben had made in a newspaper article, how would this guy even know who Ben was? Cranky constituents only wanted to talk to the Senator or to "go on record" about a certain issue and, as difficult as Millie herself could be at times, she was a good assistant and usually did an excellent job of screening his calls, demanding to know how they knew him, what they were calling in reference to, if they had a deadline (for reporters only) and, on a scale of one-to-ten, how necessary was a call back -- and Ben loved her for it. This Heim person would have never been able to get by Millie that many times unless he convinced her it was urgent.

So who was he?

Ben checked his watch: it was after nine now and Millie would be long gone, home with her husband Walt in their bungalow, probably watching this same game. No need to bother her. It could wait. Besides, the area code Millie had recorded indicated Heim was somewhere up in central Jersey. Not a constituent. It's not like they needed his vote or anything.

Ben paid his check and his legs were only a little unsteady as he made his way down the concourse. He thought of the remainder of the night that lay ahead and the following twenty-four hours of freedom, of nobody knowing he was back in town, and he felt a smile eek its way into the corners of his mouth.

A jovial spring found its way into his gait until he reached the baggage claim, now emptied clear of people, travelers from his flight long gone to the parking garage or whisked away by taxis, well on their way into the hazy summer night.

But then he looked at the empty carousel, looked to the sign above (Boston, Flight #3331) and his buzz evaporated with two hard, subsequent jolts of realization: first, that the carousel was bare, its silver glint magnified by the fluorescent lighting overhead. And second, why he was here, back home, at the airport, in the first place (Kat). He looked over his shoulder: he was alone, and a guillotine of dread fell from above.

Of all days they had to go and lose my bag, he thought as he looked around for an airline representative -- a porter -- *someone* who might be able to help. *Of all fuckin' days.*

So much for rest and relaxation until Sunday morning; he'd likely be on the phone all weekend long with useless automatons from Go-Screw-Yourself Airlines.

He noticed a small, glass door and the words etched into it, and dragged himself over. Inside, he filled out the necessary paperwork and was told to return in the morning, they might have it then.

Goddamn airlines, he seethed as he walked outside, lit a cigarette and inhaled like a prisoner recently paroled. The sultry heat of nighttime August meandered around him as he dialed the only person on the planet he wanted to see, the only one who would not want to talk about Kat or the election, the one who would get good and stinking drunk with him tonight.

"Sydney," he said when she answered.

"How's Beantown?"

"Wouldn't know. I'm back. How do you feel about Chinese?"

"Wwhoa, wait a second there, Romeo. Thought you weren't coming back till Sunday...?"

"Change of plans," he said as he exhaled a plume of smoke.

A short, plump lady with a nest of thin red hair made a face and waved her hand dramatically, her distaste centered squarely on Ben and his cigarette.

He turned his back and took another drag.

Sydney chuckled. "Trouble in paradise?"

"Something like that," he muttered. "Listen, I didn't call you so you could bust my balls, I just wanted to see if you wanted to hang out tonight."

"You're assuming I don't have plans."

"I *know* you don't have plans."

"Ouch. Okay. You're on. But how 'bout Mexican?"

Glancing to and fro, hoping for a cab, he passed a man on a bench, decked out in full military fatigues, whistling merrily as if this was his weekend hotspot and immediately stuck his finger in his ear to banish the unsettling tune as he flagged down a taxi. "Mexican works. See you in twenty, Scoop."

As he hopped in the cab Ben didn't bother looking over his shoulder, or else he would have seen the man in the fatigues watching him, smiling and whistling as he dialed the Senator's number.

9

Friday
10:39pm

"So what really happened?" Sydney wanted to know. The enchiladas were long gone and she and Ben were now halfway through a case of Corona, sitting on the roof of her building, feet up, ankles crossed on the milk crates she'd brought up to serve as makeshift ottomans, watching the lights of Philadelphia glittering in the distance. Santana was rocking out on the old radio and the street below was animated with people determined to make the best of their Saturday night.

"C'mon, Syd," Ben replied, tugging on his beer. The night was warm and comfortable and he was grateful to be off the plane, far away from Boston. From Kat. But he still didn't want to talk about it.

"What? I just think an explanation is in order, is all. You were gone for less than a day, Campbell."

Looking at her, he could nearly make out each her features through the navy-colored night; a face he knew almost as well as his own: the long eyelashes casting shadows down her cheekbones, the sprinkling of cinnamon freckles across her nose, the faint scar on her chin from when she fell out of his tree house in the third grade and needed seven stitches.

She re-crossed her endless legs, the ones emerging from a pair of faded and frayed cut-offs -- and he noticed her bare feet, tanned to golden brown, just like the rest of her, her silver toe-ring from Costa Rica glinting in the bath of street light from below...

Then he heard her laugh –- loud and genuine, like she just couldn't help herself. "You're ogling me, you know," she said, a teasing lilt to her voice, the trace of dimple in the left cheek deepening. "You must have beer goggles, Campbell."

He laughed. He was drunk and they both knew it, and it mattered not. He released a wide, toothy grin. "Sorry."

"'Sokay," she said, and he noticed a shy smile appearing, the dimple faint, but still there. "I've always known you had a gutter mind. So where were we?"

"You were about to give me a cigarette," he lied, hoping the shadows cast by the potted Ficus trees circling the perimeter of the rooftop would hide the embarrassment rising red in his cheeks.

"Thought you quit," she said, handing him a pack of Camels.

He took one and leaned over to light it.

"I did," he said as he exhaled.

She did the same and said: "So did I."

"Alright, so where were we? You were grilling me about Boston. About Kat. And I was avoiding you. Like the fuckin' plague, in case you hadn't noticed."

"Ahh," she said with a slight smile, "Now I remember." Then it faded. "I'm not trying to be a pain in the ass, I just –-"

He waved her away. "Don't worry about it, Scoop. You'll get all the juicy details one of these days. Suffice to say, I should've known it was doomed when I first heard her use seasons as verbs."

Sydney choked on her beer as she laughed. "She *what?*"

"You know. Her family *winters* in Palm Beach. They *summer* on the Cape."

She roared. "Good *gawd*, Campbell!!!" Then, after she mopped off most of the spilled beer from her chin: "You sure know how to pick 'em..."

He waved her off. "Yeah, yeah, I know. What can I say?" He drained the rest of his beer and reached for another. Down below a group of couples spilled out on to the sidewalk from the Italian restaurant, laughing and making their way down the block toward the coffeehouse where a jazz band was entertaining the ones lucky enough to have snagged seats at café tables along Center Street.

The town of Piedmont they now surveyed was different than the Piedmont of their youth. They'd grown up on these streets, had ridden their bikes down them more times than they could ever count; but in those days the streets didn't house trendy bistros and jazz bands, boutiques and manicured lawns. Back then, Piedmont was strictly working class, a town rife with firefighters and policemen and their nurse or schoolteacher wives, a place where neighbors cut their own lawns and kids wove red-white-and-blue streamers through their bike spokes for the annual Memorial Day parade downtown.

Then the gentrification happened. Progressive and homosexual couples had been the first to spy the potential: the magnificent (if aging and neglected) Victorians and center-hall Colonials. They moved in and began renovations and, within five years, the town had attracted an array of art galleries, coffee houses, and specialty shops, even a few fine dining spots, and Piedmont was a place reborn. Real estate skyrocketed and when Ben moved back from DC he'd found his hometown had morphed into "the place to live" in South Jersey.

Ben could see his apartment from where he sat: he lived in the building across the street from Sydney's, two doors down. The difference was that she had been smart enough to see the handwriting on the wall and buy before anyone else besides the gays wanted to and now owned her entire building, while Ben just rented an apartment in his.

Just then he thought of the "For Rent" sign that had been in the window and asked: "So you find anyone to rent this rat trap yet?" He was teasing and they both knew it; her building had been restored to such a pristine state that she had to laugh when she looked at him.

"Not yet. I got a guy coming by tomorrow to take a look, but it's been slow."

"Maybe he'll be just your type. Nice and hunky. You can kill two birds."

She swatted him. "Go to hell, Campbell."

He shrank away, pretending to be surprised, feigning innocence. "What? What'd I say?"

"You *know* what. When it comes to my love life—"

"—or lack thereof—"

"—I'll ask if I want your opinion. Got it?" she laughed.

"I got it, I got it, jeez."

She went to say more but just then a stupendous rip of thunder made them jump as it rumbled around them, and a prong of lightning followed suit, illuminating the sky.

"Should we go in?"

But before he could answer, the clouds detonated and a heavy summer rain emptied the sky.

They jumped to their feet, him grabbing the beer and her scooping the boxes of take-out as they hurried toward the fire escape, knocking the hibachi over as they ran. The sky electrified from gunmetal gray to pink with each new debut of lightning, and the thunder seemed to grow louder with each pant of their breath.

"Oh, no!" Syd yelled, and he could barely hear her over the clamor of Mother Nature and her footfalls clanging against the fire escape.

"What?!"

"The radio!"

Ben dashed back up to the roof to grab it, though he didn't know why — it was probably only worth about a five spot on EBay, thing was so old — and caught up with her in time to help boost her back inside the window they'd left open. Pulling the window shut behind them, they stood in her living room, shaking themselves off like dogs after a bath.

He tried to rub the wet from his mass of brown curls and, as he did, caught a glimpse of her faded red tee-shirt, tight against her curves, the rain making it cling, that read: *Mamas Don't Let Your Babies Grow Up to be Cowboys.* "Nana Jean?" he asked, nodding toward it.

"You know it," she grinned. "Gosh, look at you!"

They caught each other's eyes and began to laugh.

"You're a mess," Sydney said as she moved toward the hallway.

She came back with an armful of towels and tossed one; he caught it and got busy wiping his soaked cargo shorts while leaning across the drafting table situated beneath the bay of windows in what was supposed to be the dining room.

"So what's the latest project, Scoop?" he asked, eying the spread of papers across and rubbing a pink towel against the back of his head.

"Actually, it has to do with your boss."

Ben's head shot up. "What about him?" He asked, unable to hide his surprise.

She smirked. "Don't worry, big shot. I won't mess with his re-election."

Ben felt foolish for even thinking it, and even more so for her having known it.

"His school. I'm doing a follow-up on the first class to go through Sir Thomas More. A 'where are they now?' type of piece for the back-to-school issue in October."

"You're planning to interview him, I assume?" he asked as he fended off her pair of Bassett Hounds licking the rainwater from his legs.

"Of course," she said with a sly grin. "Him, the Mayor, the Governor. And you're going to help me do that, aren't you?"

"Of course," he said, matching her grin. "Are you kidding me? We can't buy this kind of publicity. October is perfect, too. Just in time for the election. Remind all the voters of the crown jewel of Dino Bruni's long, illustrious career at the Statehouse."

She snorted. "Oh, like *that's* the reason why I'm doing it. No offense Campbell, but getting party bosses and political parasites re-elected is not my goal."

"Ouch. Jeez, can't you at least take pity on us? I had this election in the bag until that dipshit brother of his decided to go get himself convicted."

She shrugged. "Sorry, but the main focus is on the kids, you know? How this state-of-the-art facility has prepared them for life. Did it make a difference, or would they have been better off at MLK High with all the other Camden kids?"

"Bruni's school cost the state more than three hundred million dollars. It damn well better've helped them," Ben grumbled, eying her pages of notes.

"Yeah, well. We'll see," She said as she stooped down to scratch behind the floppy ears of both Woodward and Bernstein. The hounds conveyed their appreciation with long, generous laps against her bare feet. "But so far it hasn't seemed that way."

"What do you mean?"

She was pensive. "I don't know," she said slowly, with a shake of her head. "There's just something really weird about the whole thing. You'd think these kids would be doing really well, right? They were handpicked, passed all the right tests, and spent four years at one of the most premiere facilities on the East Coast, maybe the whole country...They should be going places –-"

"Now Syd," Ben insisted. "Let's be reasonable. These kids were from Camden, let's not forget. They ain't exactly Harvard material."

"But they should be able to hold down jobs, right? Even you could agree with that. Minimum wage, at least. Who can't handle minimum wage?"

Ben was genuinely surprised. "They can't?"

Her face was the picture of frustration as her glance glided across the desk piled high with books on the history of Camden, her notes, pages of interviews and emails. "Well a few have, but most of them...I don't know. Seems like their lives have gotten worse instead of better."

She sounded defeated, sad, and rather than do what he *really* wanted (which was wrap his arms around her), her gave her a soft punch in the shoulder and softened his voice: "Don't worry about it,

Scoop. They can't *all* be failures. You still have a bunch more to go, right? You'll find your success stories. I promise." He said, wanting it to be true.

She shrugged. "I guess so. But hey -- Enough about work. It's Saturday night, right?" And her toothpaste-ad grin was back as she steered him away from the table.

Ben's smile returned too...that was, until his gaze caught a photo sitting on the shelf above: Sydney and Cody Briggs. Her ex-fiancé. The one she'd caught cheating just three days before their wedding...

"Aw Syd," he said, the lament in his voice sounding whinier than he'd intended, a thin moan amid the raindrops pelting the windows, tiddlywinks against the glass. "Please tell me that's not who I think it is."

One glance and a shadow crossed her face. She turned away. "Leave me alone, Ben, okay?" Her voice had a tired, ragged edge to it. "You've said your piece about, oh, I'd say, a hundred freaking times now. Just leave me alone about it, okay?"

He looked as though he were about to say something then stopped, thought better of it. A few moments passed when the tension swung between them, heavy and awkward, a bundle of emotion neither of them wanted to face.

She sighed. "I'm soaked. I'm going to change."

Ben sighed too. It was a sore subject he shouldn't have touched. He took a slug of beer. He was drunk but he didn't care. He took another as he flopped onto the couch and turned on the TV.

Now in an oversized long-sleeved tee and her old college mesh shorts she went to the kitchen and began rummaging through cupboards. A moment later she appeared, blocking his view of the TV, a bottle of tequila in one hand, two shot glasses in another. She lifted the trio and said: "Truce?"

He grinned -- relieved -- and pressed the mute button. "Truce."

She had swept the great bulk of her wheat-colored waves back into a hasty ponytail and as she cocked her head back to swallow the shot, a strand fell loose and, before he realized he was doing it, Ben's hand reached out to tuck it behind her ear. "You were too good for him," he said, his voice coming out in hoarse, weathered threads as he slowly tucked and re-tucked the stray strands of hair behind her ear. "You know that, don't you, Syd?"

She looked up, eyes wide.

"You were too fucking good for him," he said, his words coming out in more of a slur than he would have liked.

Her honey-brown eyes shone in the glow of the TV. She placed a hand on his chest.

"Ben, I—"

Just then his line of sight caught something on the TV screen behind her and he was jarred in the same way he'd be if he'd come across his own obituary in the newspaper. Totally, thoroughly aghast. He leapt to his feet and moved to see around her to see the screen completely: It was a photograph, one clearly transferred from some sort of government-issued ID; a face of a man he did not know, but he certainly recognized the name beneath it.

"Quick, the remote!!" he demanded and, confused, she fumbled for it. With trembling hands he took it and re-instated the sound and moved towards the television, as if being pulled against his will. A Poltergeist calling just to him...

"...Police sources say evidence indicates this was clearly pre-meditated," the anchorman was saying from behind the news desk, a grim expression fixed to his face.

"Ben, what?" Sydney asked. "What is it?"

"Shh!"

"...We go live now on the scene with reporter Shannon O'Shaughnessy."

"Thanks, Graham. Behind me is the home of Herbert Heim, where he lived with his wife and two daughters until earlier this evening. At approximately nine p.m., several neighbors called 9-1-1 to report hearing gunshots in this otherwise quiet bedroom community. Police arrived on the scene to find what appears to be a triple homicide, and subsequent suicide. Neighbors are in shock that the alleged shooter, Herbert Heim of Robin's Egg Lane in the Grassy Glen subdivision of Lysle, New Jersey, murdered his wife and two children before turning the gun on himself."

The scene cut to a previously recorded interview with a neighbor. Josie Abella, the caption read; a woman in her fifties with dyed hair in pink curlers and an alarmed expression on her face that might have been fossilized there. "Herb was such a quiet man," she said, mopping the corners of her eyes with a wadded Kleenex, mouth agape Edvard Munch-style. "But he loved those girls, you could tell. He might have kept to himself but he was a good father. Oh my word, I just can't believe this..."

Ben heard little else. The shock of it all was simply too much to bear. He wavered on his feet almost cartoonishly before collapsing back into the couch, spilling his beer and not caring, Woodward and Berstein quick to lap the puddle on the floor.

She went to him at once, on her knees as if begging, her fawn-colored eyes flashing with panic. "What, Ben? What is it? Please, Ben! What is it?"

When no answer came she took him by the shoulders and slowly, slack-jawed, he turned toward her.

"What is it?" She looked back at the TV: the face of Herb Heim flashed before them, his Buddy Holly glasses framing timid, almost innocent eyes. "Did you know this guy or something?"

He gulped hard. "No," he said, turning toward her.

Sydney saw the look on his face -- a horrid mixture of dumbstruck fright and sick fear -- and shrank back, scared. "No?" She wanted it to be true but somehow knew it wasn't, so she had to ask again. "You're sure, Ben? You're absolutely sure you didn't know this guy?"

A time passed; it could have been 30 seconds or thirty minutes -- either way it felt like a lifetime for them both,

"No, I didn't know him," he said finally, his voice raspy and weak, thinking of all of those messages...

"But..." And this last part he choked out like a terrified child: "But I think I was supposed to."

10

Saturday
11:59pm

Ben was still shaking when Sydney tucked the covers under his chin.

"You all right, big guy?" she asked in a voice that was an aching combination of distress and tenderness as she placed a cool compress across his forehead. Her face was the picture of concern amid his shadowy bedroom and he shivered, knowing that even the affectionate cadence of her voice couldn't warm him. And that likely meant that nothing on God's green earth could.

She'd led him from her apartment to his, pausing with him when he vomited again and again, murmuring words of comfort as they made their way across the street streaked with silver from the storm. Ben loved her for it, of course, but he still couldn't calm himself enough to take away the worry evident in her face.

He couldn't remember a time when he'd felt worse. His stomach was a cavern, assaulted by hatchet, systematically carved from the inside out. And forget about his head. It was housing an untamable ache of Guinness Book proportions at the moment.

And the fear.

His skin prickled at the recollection of seeing the name of the man who had been practically stalking him for the last few weeks in bold-print on the newscast, the recount of his crimes more sickening each time the words revisited. He'd murdered his wife and two daughters before killing himself...

Ben thought of those two little girls, imagining the fear in their eyes, their terrified screams, and the horror of the knowledge that the one man who was above all others supposed to protect them chasing them down, thirsting for their blood...

Sydney had tried her best to soothe him. "You've never met him, Ben. You don't know what he looks like. There could be a hundred men by the same name." But something gnawed at him in the way that only truth can, and he knew –- he *knew* –- this man, this murderer was the same one Millie had told him had called again and again and again.

Ben felt almost delirious. He began to convulse, bucking beneath the comforter as Sydney bolted into action. Wrapping her arms around him she said: "I really don't think you should be alone."

He felt her hands sweep his hair from his clammy forehead, the gentle rake of her fingernails across his brow, feeling the peaceful rise and fall of her chest, the softness of her skin against his own.

For a while -- who knew how long –- they stayed like that, with her arms tight around him like a mother's, rocking him ever-so-gently, willing him to find peace. And just when he was about to nod off, the booze finally catching up with him, he heard:

"You were too good for her, too, you know that?"

Her voice was the beat of a moth wing, barely more than a whisper, but that was the last thing he heard before tumbling backward into a shallow, jerky, nightmare-ridden sleep.

11

Sunday
12:19am

The man he was watching on the television was one of the most famous in all the history of the world and Bo Wrigley's attention was rapt just the same as if he'd been there himself, one of the mesmerized faces among that unfathomable crowd; as if he'd been old enough to witness his legacy at the height of its glory, had been able to feel the bone-shaking greatness live and in person. Nonetheless, years and oceans be damned, Bo felt the surge of the crowd from his hair roots on down; the power of that all-mighty swastika gleaming blood red from his bicep.

His father's old Windsor chair groaned beneath him as he leaned in closer and notched up the volume: The black-and-white program on the *History Channel* sprang to life in audio, now, as well.

From where the great man stood behind the podium -- gesturing wildly and shouting in a foreign tongue, the distinct rectangle of black stationed precisely beneath his nose -- he didn't seem crazy at all to Bo; in fact, just the opposite.

Completely absorbed, Bo licked his lips and felt the familiar dryness burn straight down his throat, the same one that came every so often, like a cornrow set afire. He smoothed his sweaty palms against his fatigues and leaned in closer, spellbound.

*Just look at all of those millions of people gathered there, inching into every available space of light and earth beneath that imperial balcony, packed closer than was naturally comfortable, admiring their fuhrer, each face shining with a special kind of brightness bathing in the sacredness of his presence...*Bo thought, moon-eyed and entranced, but not because of the speech being made -- (he didn't speak the language, after all) -- but simply by his bravery, so undeterred, so immovable.

Clearly Hitler had been misunderstood, no different than Bo himself, really, when he thought about it. A smile snaked its way across his cracked lips at the thought of this, at the idea of kinship.

Slowly the camera panned the masses and, despite the graininess of the footage, Bo's amazement was amplified by just how bright and glossy their eyes were; how much love was behind them...

The piercing ring of the phone interrupted his thoughts and he grumbled as he jabbed a thumb at the TV's mute button. He peered at the caller-ID and, though not surprised, was thoroughly annoyed nonetheless. "What's up, Dino-baby?" he asked before the caller had a chance to speak.

The Senator was not happy. "Don't you *'Dino baby'* me. Did you see the news? That crazy son-of-a-bitch went on a fucking killing spree. He --"

"Easy, easy there, Dino-baby," Bo chuckled, enjoying hearing the Senator squirm. "I saw it. And it's a good thing. If he's dead he's no longer a problem, right? And you can go on your merry way and win your little election with one less problem to worry about..."

"Don't you patronize me, Wrigley. Remember who feeds you," he spat, and Bo heard something like a trill of panic in his warning.

"Listen," Bo said with an exaggerated sigh, as if he were about to explain something complicated to a child. "Everything's fine. I got you your precious files back and let me tell you, it wasn't easy on such short notice."

He heard Bruni lick his lips. "But you got them?"

"*Yeah* I got them. I called you from the airport, remember? I got them and then I watched him. He's been with his little friend ever since."

"The reporter?"

"Yeah. The girl. Hot piece of ass, too."

"Is she still sniffing around the school?"

"Yeah, but don't worry about it. I got it covered."

The Senator laughed a thin, humorless laugh that seemed to echo on the line. "Don't worry about it," he mumbled, mocking. "Yeah well I *need* to worry about it."

"I said *I have it covered*. I'll have both of their places bugged as shit."

"Good. So what's Ben's story?"

Bo Wrigley chuckled. "Home in bed. Sick as a fuckin' dog," he laughed, "But home."

"Sick? Why sick?"

"He's been drinking like a banshee since he left his little girlfriend in Boston. *She* was a hot little thing too --" Bo said as he leaned back in his chair, eyes on the TV.

"Keep your goddamn dick in your pants, alright? We have a very serious situation here and --"

"Listen, everything's under control," Bo said, the images of Hitler reflecting in his gray eyes.

"So you say. Now about Heim. Have you been to his house?"

"Not since last month when I paid him a little visit. I didn't see shit then, and I doubt the cops'll find anything now. Guy was scared of his own fuckin' shadow. Last thing he was gonna do was risk getting caught. Just chill, my man," Bo said as he picked lint from his fatigues. "Everything's cool."

"Goddammit!" Bruni shouted, and Bo recoiled from the receiver. "Stop being so fucking cavalier! We're talking about my future here," he hissed. "We're talking about --"

"Save your lectures," Bo snapped back, eyes still focused on the Aryan army marching the streets of Berlin like robots, eyes vacant and wide like moon rocks. He could hear the Senator on the other end of the line struggling for composure. Dino Bruni didn't like it when other people were in control, but Bo Wrigley didn't care what the Senator liked.

"I want you to go back to the house. *Tonight.* I want you to --"

Now it was Bo's turn to get heated. "The place is swarming with cops! There's no way —"

"Listen to me now, and listen to me good. Those files you had to retrieve were email printouts. The originals are still on the hard drive. If the cops go through his computer they're going to find them. All of them. Everything! And then we're fucked. Do you hear me?" he all-but-screeched. "*Fucked.* It was one thing that Ben might see them but this is a whole 'nother story. Ben works for me. I could've made some shit up if he came around asking questions --"

"But he *didn't* see them. I assure you. I was on his ass the entire time he was in Boston."

The Senator snorted. "All fifteen minutes?"

"Yeah, I did my job," Bo said hotly, resenting any implication to the contrary. "And he didn't see them. I got them back for you. Had to bribe some dumbass nigger baggage handler, but I did it. The job's done as far as I'm concerned."

"The job is *not* done," the Senator said, just as hotly. "Don't you get it, Wrigley? The situation has detonated. I need you to go to Heim's house -- *tonight* -- and get the hard drive. Dismantle his email. I need you to obliterate the whole damn computer, if that's what it takes. I need you to --"

"And I need payment. I completed one job. This is another."

"Oh for Christ's sake, Wrigley, you know I'm good for it. Just get this taken care of."

"If I do this, I want more than my standard. You're asking me to go into a situation swarming with cops. Again, on short notice. And I --"

"Okay, okay." The Senator released a heavy sigh. "I'll give you a chunk of change tonight. That'll cover your time in Boston, tonight, and anything I need in the next couple weeks. But I'm gonna need you to do what I need you to do. No more talk about 'late notice' and all that bullshit. This is too fucking important."

"Fine. But I want double," Bo said as he watched the Hitler program being replaced by a program titled *The History of Hot-Air Balloons.* He snapped off the TV.

There was a pause then, and Wrigley could tell Bruni was about to protest, but thought better of it. He needed him, and they both knew it.

"Alright," Bruni grumbled. Bo Wrigley smiled in the dark, the absence of the television light making his apartment a cavern of shadows. Bruni had never been stingy before, and any prior incidents seemed pretty minor in comparison with this. This was huge. Doing a few jobs over the next couple weeks might set him up nicely for the rest of the year. He'd head down south to the compound where his Aryan brothers would be more than happy to have him stay for a couple months, where he could have his pick of the fresh meat brought in, the trailer trash girls who ran away from home and were eager to please the senior brethren. All that *and* he could avoid another shitty New Jersey winter.

"What do you need?"

"I need muscle. Heavy muscle."

"What about your boys? The Scottolinos?"

"I need untraceable muscle. Absolutely no ties to the area. And smart, too. There can be absolutely no fucks ups, you understand me? This has to be clean. The cleanest fuckin' job you've ever laid eyes on. You know anyone?"

"Yep."

"Good. You get that lined up, and then I need Campbell and the reporter watched. I need Jarvis, too."

"Jarvis?!"

"Yeah. Jig's acting so crazy I might need you to take him out all together."

Bo smirked, thinking of his Aryan brothers, the ones who got off on fucking up minorities just for fun.

"That it?"

Bruni grew quiet. "One more thing." His voice dipped. "I might need you to sniff around the prison. Make sure my brother's safe, being kept comfortable. Make sure he gets what he wants –- Percocet's, Roxy's, M & M's, whatever."

"I thought we already did that."

"Yeah well that was before he was denied bail. Plus I just got a report from the AG. Shit's worse down there than I thought. I need him to keep quiet on some stuff, and I don't want him to be tempted to..."

"Damn! You think your own brother's gonna turn on you?"

"I didn't say that," Bruni snapped. "It's just that the happier I can keep him, the better."

"Alright, alright. I hear you. That prison's no joke man. No joke."

"So I hear," Bruni muttered.

"Anyway. So that means we've got four matters then: Heim, Campbell and the reporter, Jarvis, and Iggy."

"Yeah but get on Heim tonight. Fuck the cops, alright?"

"Alright, Dino-baby. Consider it done. I'll be by in a few minutes for my cheese."

"And you'll do it? You'll go to Heim's tonight and get his computer? Be on call at least through the election? And I'll pay you double what you're used to."

"Double?" he laughed. "Hell yeah, I'll do it."

Bo Wrigley hung up the phone and began to whistle.

12

Sunday
10:09am

Ben sensed that a slow death would have been kinder than the way he felt at this moment. His head was a hostage in an unforgiving vice; his throat sore and scratchy from vomiting. Even though he lay in his own bed he was disoriented, so when he heard the footsteps in the kitchen, the rustling of pots and pans, he felt even more so.

He moved to get up from bed and regretted it immediately. His mind felt swollen and hallow, his mouth still hanging onto the taste of sick. His stomach convulsed in waves. Tsunami waves. He'd had had his share of hangovers over the years but this was ridiculous. He clawed through his memory and, after a moment, clarity broke though and he remembered it all: the newscast, the homicides, the messages from the murderer, and he released an involuntarily low moan.

Sydney appeared in the doorway, ever-pretty-as-a-picture but more evidently draped in concern. "How are you?"

He attempted a smile that emerged more like a grimace. "About as good as I probably look right now."

A faint smile. "You're pretty green."

"Yeah, well, I feel pretty green."

"Would food hurt or help?"

"Help, I think, but you don't cook."

"I can handle eggs," she insisted.

"*And* bacon?"

"And bacon," she smiled.

"Thanks but don't worry about it," he said, tossing the covers aside, "I need to get down to the airport. Gotta get my bag."

"So just coffee then?"

He smiled, grateful. "And some Advil. Or whatever. *Anything.* Just make sure it's a bunch, please. Like a handful."

"You got it." She said softly, but she didn't move. There was a long pause with her lingering at the doorway, hair still wet from the shower. "You okay, Ben? I mean, *really* okay?" she asked, and it seemed as though she were holding her breath. "Last night was pretty crazy."

"Yeah," he said as he rummaged through a drawer for clean socks and underwear, wishing that his head hurt less. "I need to find out who this Heim guy is."

"Do you want some help? I mean, in case you've forgotten, research is sort of my thing."

He stopped. Turned. Saw the look on her face and asked in surprise: "Really?"

"Sure, I don't mind."

"What about your story on the school?"

Folding her arms across her chest, she looked at him as though he were feeble-minded. "C'mon, Campbell. You serious? A guy who committed a triple homicide and suicide you seem to think is the same guy who's been calling you. Why wouldn't I help?" She shook her head. "My story can wait."

After a moment he grinned and tossed a pair of balled-up socks in her direction. "You rock, you know that?"

She snatched it from the air with one hand. Perfect catch. "I know," she smirked. "And *you* my friend will rock, as well, once you get your boss and Mayor Jasper and the Governor to agree to interviews with me." She tossed the socks back.

"Oh wait a second," he said, grabbing the white ball, glad that a good mood was quickly helping his hangover retreat. "I never said anything about the Governor. You need to call Chip for that one."

She threw her head back in exaggerated aggravation. "Oh Campbell, you suck."

"Sorry, Scoop. You know how the Governor and Bruni are always fighting. Right now's one of those times, and I doubt she'll jump at the chance to help me out. I'll get Bruni and Jasper, but then you're on your own, kiddo. But I have to tell you, this is probably about the best time to ask him for a favor."

"Why's that?"

"Chip just found out his wife is expecting. He's over the moon."

"Well that's great news!! Awww!" Her smile was billboard-big.

"Yeah, so, that'll help..."

"Well yeah, hopefully that'll help. But listen: I have to tell you, I really think this whole thing is going to be a misunderstanding. It's not exactly 'John Smith' but Herb Heim doesn't seem *that* unusual."

Ben started at the mention of the name, felt his skin grow cold.

She noticed. "Sorry."

The way she was looking at him with that earnest face scrunched intp worry made him feel a pang. But then a flash of memory sliced through, and he remembered with a cringe, leaning over her last night, ready to kiss her. Had she known? Realized? He thought of her hand on his chest *"Ben, I—"*

What? *Ben, I*...what?

She'd said the words and they hung in the air, but he was still thinking about her hand on his chest last night. To push him away or bring him closer, he didn't know. But he was determined to find out. Right after he figured out who this Herb Heim was, and why he had been so desperate to talk to him.

"Earth to Campbell?"

He turned to her and saw her leaning against the doorjamb, a wry smile on her lips.

He straightened himself. "Listen. You know as well as I do that there's no love lost between Bruni and the Governor. I'd help you if I could, but trust me. You're better off on your own. Chip'll be cool. That is something I *will* make sure of."

"Alright, alright," she said, conceding. "Fair enough. I'll help you but I really don't think the guy from last night is the same guy who's been calling, you know."

He looked at her and, whether it was because of his hangover or the Mona Lisa smile she was brandishing at the moment, he didn't know if she was saying that because she believed that, or because she just wanted to. One thing was clear, though: she didn't want him to worry.

"Well then," he said with a teasing grin. "You'll have no problem using your wily sources to come up with an answer, now will you, Scoop?"

She laughed and shook her head.

"Actually, I'm just kidding. I appreciate it, Syd, I really do. But you have your story to work on. All those interviews. And you have that guy coming over to look at the apartment. I'll just call Digger and see what he can come up with."

"You sure? 'Cause I really don't mind."

"No, it's cool. He'll be chomping at the bit to find out what happened with Kat, anyway. I'll make it worth his while." His smile was tight, fighting hard against the surge of anger that came with just the thought of her. "It's cool. Really."

"If you say so. But call me if you need anything, okay? You promise?"

"Yes, mom."

"No seriously. I'm sure there's a perfectly good explanation for all this, and I don't want you to be worried."

But he was. Worried as all hell. And full of a sick-tasting dread.

13

Sunday
10:33am

Bo Wrigley was a special ops vet who had volunteered for three tours in the Middle East before finally getting dishonorably discharged. For a time, nobody at home had been able to discern the official reasons behind it, but the answers quickly became clear once he returned. Docs at the VA diagnosed him with everything from Post Traumatic Stress Disorder to a variety of mental illnesses, but in the end he found that the specific label didn't matter. All that seemed to matter was that he *was* labeled, and as a result he was prevented from attaining a job of any significance. It was a thing he'd never gotten over. Still. All these years later. Hoping to find a career in law enforcement and failing miserably, he turned into a recluse. And a very hardened criminal.

"Couldn't pass the psych exam," Dino Bruni explained as he gripped the edge of the roof of the golf cart Sterling Sault was navigating along the asphalt path coursing through the foliage.

Sault snorted as he steered. "Big shocker there. "I coulda told you *that* much, Bruni. Guy's a fucking loon." He puffed on a Cuban "First time we stepped foot in that shithole of his. All that Nazi shit all over the place. And *I'm* German." Sault shook his head. Puffed.

"Crazy. Craziest guy I ever met." He laughed, a great big belly laugh, and slapped his hand against the steering wheel. "Fuckin' *nutjob*."

"What can I say? The guy does good work," Bruni shrugged as the cart slowed and he eased himself from shotgun. "Fuckin' *genius* when it comes to electronics, technology –- all that shit. Can't deny the guy's fuckin' *good*. You should've seen what he pulled off last night." In the bag he fumbled for his club, the one with the custom shaft and new grips, the sun searing against the back of his neck. "Not only that, but he's got a hell of shot. Must've been a sniper."

Big Bertha in hand, he poised himself before the tee, shifted his weight a few times and swung.

The ball soared –- a power fade –- moving left then right before landing in the heart of the fairway.

Sault took the Cuban from his mouth. "Nice shot, Bruni. That's a good two-sixty, two-sixty-five." He chomped down again and moved toward the tee.

Senator Bruni was a decent golfer, did well more often than not when he went out -- when his schedule would allow -- but he was no Sterling Sault.

President of Sault & Sault, he was a well-bred man who had his hand in more municipal, county, and state projects than anyone else in the tri-state area. He made millions upon millions by conducting business on fairways just like this one, with elected officials both more and less powerful than Dino Bruni. He had blondish hair, and what was left of it was maturing quite gracefully into a mane of distinguished silver; a man's man with a hearty laugh and quick wit; with the perfect amount of southern charm and dirty-joke proclivity that prevented him from seeming intimidating, despite his great wealth. He was a well-known prankster, with just enough prep-school pudge to make him seem approachable and teddy-bear-like, rather than the grudge-holding, slit-throat shark he was on every available occasion.

But his winning smile and sales strategy weren't needed today.

He and Dino went back. Way back. Selling himself to the well-connected Senator was a thing of the past; long-ago an agreement had been made: Bruni gave him every single project that came up –- the ones Sault wanted, anyway -- and the engineer funded the lion's share of the Senator's campaigns, in both legal and...Well, *creative* ways.

Some policy wonk somewhere had come up with the term "pay-to-play" to describe such an exchange, but Sterling Sault had a better term: Win-win.

He gripped and re-gripped his Taylor made Burner and swung. Bruni's shot was good, but his was great, landing twenty yards closer to the green.

Without a word, they resumed their seats in the cart and Sault pushed it into action. As they neared the balls, he ventured a look at Bruni, lowered his voice, and said: "Any word on that crazy fuck Heim?"

Bruni's face darkened. "Wrigley went over there last night and who knows how, but he got past a *battalion* of cops and got the little prick's hard drive. Made it over to the Statehouse, too, and got a hold of *that* hard drive, along with his personnel file, if you can believe it."

Sault's head snapped up. "You're kidding."

"Nope," Bruni said, puffed up and pleased. "Like I said, the guy's good."

"I'll say. Nobody knows where those files are even kept. And talk about a battalion of cops. The Governor's guys guard those files, don't they? Wrigley must've made himself invisible."

"Don't I know it."

Then the engineer snorted. "Can't fucking *believe* Heim off and killed his whole fucking family." Then he laughed. "Never knew that little pencil-neck had it in 'em."

"And the nerve to send us those emails. *Us*."

"From his work account, too." Sault said, shaking his head.

"Yeah. Well."

Bruni shifted uncomfortably in his seat, and Sault sensed there was more. "But?"

"But...I don't know." The Senator's face was as shadowy as a grotto. "Something just doesn't feel right."

"'Cause of Campbell?"

It was the Senator's turn to snort. "For fuck's sake, Sterling. *No*, it's not that. Fuckin' kid was only in Boston long enough to get dumped by that flashy little blonde. Had the emails in his bag -- *which* he checked at the curb -- so it wasn't like he could have spent the flight reading over them. He never even saw them -- we're sure of it -- but we've eliminated the possibility just the same. Turns out it was all a mistake, completely inadvertent, and probably my own fucking fault. Never should've had it in the office in the first place."

"So why did you?"

"I was supposed to meet with Jarvis and go over them later that night, compare notes and all that."

Sault was surprised. "He got the emails, too?"

"Yeah, and that's what worries me. He was pretty shaken up over it. A real mess."

They arrived at the next hole and Sault jammed the cart into PARK and turned to him, expression intense. "What do you mean 'a mess'?"

Bruni shrugged as they got out of the cart. "I met with him yesterday and he was like a lunatic," he said as he plucked a three-wood from the bag. "Acting all crazy. Thinks I'm gonna lose the election, is worried Iggy's gonna turn state's evidence in return for a lighter sentence. He begged me to meet with him and he cried like a bitch the whole time. I gotta tell you, Sterling. I'm nervous about this one."

"Fuckin' nigger," Sault said through gritted teeth, grinding his cigar. "I *knew* he'd become a problem at some point."

"What choice did we have? He was the only one who could get that thing zoned."

Sault scowled. "Every last coon on that worthless piece-of-shit City Council is more crooked than the next and you know it. We could've gotten the zoning, Dino. One way or another. We might've had to pay through the nose, but we could've gotten it."

"And then what? Then we'd have nine stupid jigs to contend with rather than just one?" Bruni spat, forgetting the golf game at hand, his blood pressure rising.

"I still think —"

Bruni held up a hand like a traffic cop, signaling an end to the discussion. "*Enough*, Sterling. We did the right thing."

Few people could get away with talking to the great engineer in such a manner, but Dino Bruni was one of them.

Sault's tone was quiet now, more subdued. "So what's he going to do then? Our good friend the Mayor?"

Bruni pursed his lips and threw his hands up –- exasperated -- as if a question of such importance was a vile imposition. "Fuck if I know." His concentration was on the tee as he made a few practice swings. "But we have him wired now." He eyed the fairway. "His office. House. You name it."

"You better get that church of his, too. He's tight as hell with that preacher what's-his-name. Fucking coons are thicker than thieves. If he was going to confess to anyone, it'd be him."

"Done," Bruni said as he hunkered down to prepare to swing. "Already taken care of. We got all of them, my friend. Jasper, Campbell..."

"The girl?" Sault interrupted.

"Not yet, but she's next."

"She still snooping around?"

"Yeah but it's not going well. Wouldn't be surprised if she jumped ship soon. You know as well as I do that if she's looking for a success story out of that place, she ain't gonna find it."

Sault was quiet during Bruni's backswing.

The Senator sliced. "Damn it!" he barked, and stalked back to the cart.

"Tough luck. Hey listen, Dino. I wouldn't worry about it. Get Wrigley to find out who she's been talking to and I'll throw a couple bucks their way, keep 'em quiet."

"But wouldn't that raise suspicion? I mean, they don't even know anything."

"Still. Better to be safe than sorry. Just have Wrigley find out what kind of questions she's asking and kindly pay them for their time." He clapped his hands together and smiled. "Done."

"You know, that's not a bad idea."

Sault slapped him on the back. "It's an excellent idea, and I'm full of them." They laughed. Bruni felt Sault's hand move to his shoulder, his grip tightening. "Now about your brother. What's the word?"

Bruni stiffened. He'd anticipated this of course, but still hadn't figured out how to answer it. What could he say? That he hadn't heard from Iggy yet and it worried him? Iggy turned to him for *everything*, always had. To say he was nervous that Jasper may be on to something was an understatement. Family or no, Iggy had always been a rat, willing to sell out anyone for anything as long as he benefitted. What was even more troublesome to Bruni was that Iggy was as dumb as a box of rocks and never had the foresight to look beyond the situation at hand.

"He's fine," Bruni replied, hoping his tone conveyed a breeziness he did not even remotely feel. "Going to visit him tomorrow."

"Good. Good," Sault said, releasing his grip, and Bruni exhaled more loudly than he wanted to. Sault didn't seem to notice as he went on: "And another thing. About Jasper. I'll have a talk with him."

"Think it'll make a difference?"

Sault laughed. "He's about to go into foreclosure, isn't he?"

Bruni chuckled, too. "*Oh* yeah."

"Then I don't foresee a problem."

"Just the same, I have Wrigley on it, too. In case a problem *does* crop up, Wrigley's going to handle it."

Sault paused and slowly turned to Bruni, wanting to make sure he understood exactly what was being said. He cleared his throat. "Handle it?"

"Yep. Without a trace, too. He's bringing in some outside people, so we're good." Then he added quickly: "But that's a last resort of course."

"Of course, of course. Last resort," Sault said quietly. "Sure."

Just then they heard the familiar buzz of another golf cart and they turned; a moment later a smiling, freckle-faced girl appeared from around the bend, driving the beverage cart.

"Gentlemen? Can I get you anything?" Her grin was genuine, if a bit chipmunky.

They took two airplane bottles of scotch each, and a pair of plastic tumblers filled with ice before climbing back into their cart. Sault tipped her handsomely and she left to bring relief to the next cluster of businessmen rejoicing the beauty of capitalism in the great outdoors.

They sat in their cart and sipped. Nobody was behind them on the course; they could take their time.

"Nice pair of tits on that one," Sault said as he puffed on his cigar.

"Compensates for that train-wreck-of-a-face, huh?" Bruni shot back, and they laughed.

"Well," Sault said, standing to take his shot, squinting against the harsh glare of the Indian summer day. "All look the same in the dark, now don't they?"

Dino Bruni sat back in the golf cart, a smile easing across his face. "Which ones? Coons or broads?"

A cloud moved across the sun like a hand spread across a mouth to discourage an ill-timed smirk.

"Both," Sault called over his shoulder, and they threw their heads back and laughed.

14

Sunday
11:20am

"It's about a hundred, hundred and ten years old. Center hall Colonial, as you can see. All the windows have been replaced so it's really energy efficient now..."

She continued on about the hardwood floors and crown molding and original light fixtures, but Bo Wrigley was more concerned with enjoying the delightful view from behind as she led him through his new apartment, smiling at his unbelievable luck.

"...As I'm sure you saw in the ad, the rent's thirteen hundred a month. I require first and last month's, as well as a security deposit..."

Sydney Langston was one of the prettier women he'd ever seen in person, much less spoken to.

"Trash days are Tuesday and Friday, and everyone is required to participate in recycling. House rules," she said with a shrug of her shoulders and a sweet smile. "I'm a bit of a tree hugger. I've written it into the lease..."

And of all the subjects he was supposed to tail, to spy upon over the years -- to stalk -– she was far and away the best. The most beautiful. Just look at those legs, that ass...

"The laundry's in the basement, along with storage facilities. If you want, I can show you those when we're done."

Oh the things he'd love to do to her...

She turned to him, a smile dancing across her face. "...And if you need anything, I live here, too, you know, so please don't hesitate to knock..."

Oh, I know, my dear. I know. Why that's why I'm here! It was hard to suppress his laughter. Bruni was going to *flip* at this development, that Bo would soon have 24-hour access to her. Bruni had only wanted her place bugged but Bo had a different plan, one that included installing video equipment, as well, that he could watch anytime he wanted, from anywhere. He thought of all the mite-sized cameras he'd place throughout: her bedroom, her bathroom, the shower...Just the thought of it sent lightning rods of excitement shooting through the veins of his cock.

"...And this is a fabulous neighborhood, lots of great restaurants and boutiques..."

After all, all work and no play makes Johnny a dull boy, now doesn't it? He mused, a smirk threading its way across his face. He'd know every movement, every breath. Soon enough he'd know her mind and body as well as his own...

"...So I guess that's it!" she chirped with a genial smile as she turned to look at him. "So you still interested?"

His heart was hammering, thrusting inside of him like a piston, like it used to do when he was in the service and getting ready to blow up whoever was the bad guy of the day, but instead of unleashing a battle cry, one that would both release adrenalin and generate more of it, he somehow managed a civilized reply:

"Am I interested? Oh yes, Miss Langston. Very much so."

15

Sunday
12:40pm

The crisp air conditioning of Bruni's campaign headquarters felt heavenly against his raging hangover, although it did little to quiet the sick feeling of trepidation percolating within. Ben picked his way around his desk, gingerly avoiding the stacks of unread newspapers -- both the headlines detailing Iggy's conviction and the ones about Heim -- knowing he would get no work done until he got to the bottom of it, but unable the digest all the gory details just yet.

His first call had been to Digger Vance. Longtime friend and political bloodhound, Digger was the best researcher Ben had ever known. The kind of guy you want on your team because God help the poor soul that made an enemy of him. Digger could find out anything about anybody at anytime, no matter how hard they tried to keep it buried. He was an absolute gem on The Hill; his skills desperately coveted and paid for handsomely. Digger wasn't his birth name, but it was the one that had stuck; he derived so much joy from finding out other people's secrets that Ben often told him if he ever got sick of politics, he'd make a mint working as a paparazzi for a Hollywood tabloid.

"Yo Campbell, what's up?"

"Hey Digger. How're things?"

"You know. Crazy as hell. Your opponent's sniffing around in ELEC. Just a heads up."

Great, Ben thought. *Just great.* ELEC was New Jersey's state-run Election Law Enforcement Committee, specializing in fundraising. *Just wait till the reporters get wind of this...*

But wait. He had more pressing concerns.

"Listen, I appreciate you keeping an eye on things for me, but that's not what I'm calling about."

"Oh no? Well then what pray tell brings you calling, Mr. Campbell?" Digger's interest was piqued, and as Ben began to explain he heard his friend scribbling notes furiously.

Ben relayed the whole sordid story, telling him the little he knew about Heim, and when he was done Digger let out a long whistle. "Wow, Campbell. That's one of the crazier stories I've heard in a while, I'll give you that. Let me see what I can come up with."

"Thanks, dude. I really appreciate it."

"Not a problem."

"And Digger? Do me a favor? Keep this on the down low, alright?"

"Man, this Heim character really has you shook, huh."

"You have no idea."

Ben's next call was to Sydney.

"What's up, Nurse Ratchet?"

"Very funny. How are you feeling?"

"Eh. I've been better." Now *that* was the understatement of the year. "You good?"

"Yeah, just on my way to an interview. You know, I really hate driving in Camden."

The thought of her there made Ben's skin prickle. "Be careful, Syd."

"No kidding," she mumbled, "The Badlands, no less."

"Jesus, Syd! Why didn't you call me? You shouldn't be going there by yourself. Do you want me to meet you there?"

"Relax. I'll be fine," she dismissed. "Listen, I have great news."

"What's that?"

"I just rented out that empty apartment in my building."

"Cool. To a big, strapping hunk of a man?"

"Not quite," she laughed. "He's a man, but definitely not a hunk, and definitely not for me."

He stretched back in his chair, crossed his feet on the desk and smiled at the ceiling. "Oh no? Why is that?"

"Oh don't worry," she said, and he could hear her smiling through the phone. "Just you wait. You'll see. He was like the Una-bomber or something. All decked out in fatigues."

Ben let out a low whistle. "Oooh. Don't you just *love* a man in uniform?"

"And *that* was the other thing. He whistled the entire time, and I don't even think he realized he was doing it. It was like it was, I don't know, *compulsive* or something. Thank heaven for thick walls."

Ben straightened up in his chair, putting his feet back on the floor. The plunk of them shook the hangover enough to remind him it was still there, making him wince a bit. "Did you do a background check?"

"Not yet," she said, breezily, "but I will."

"Syd," he said, his tone serious now. "You *gotta* be careful."

"I will, I will. Hey listen. That invitation still good for tonight?"

"Sunday dinner at Momma Campbell's? You betcha. She'll love to see you."

"Okay, great. You just saved me a trip to the grocery store."

"Glad to be of service. It'll be good to have you there for me, too, just in case Beth shows up."

"*Your sister?*" The shock in her voice was as subtle as a gong. "Why would *she* show up?"

"Your guess is as good as mine. Probably looking for money."

Sydney's voice was low. "Is she still...you know?"

"Messed up? Yeah. Totally. Completely. My mom told me last time she came around, she almost didn't want to let her in, she looked so bad."

"Your poor mom. Can you imagine? Thinking you might have to turn away your own daughter?"

"I know. Nightmare. But she has to think about Zoey, you know? Kid's only fourteen. Still impressionable. She can't see her mom looking like a strung-out junkie."

"Poor Zoey. I can't wait to see her."

Ben smiled. "She's always loved you."

"Well the feeling's mutual. She's a great kid."

Ben thought of his mother's message then, how she was worried over Zoe. He said a silent prayer that she was overreacting, and that Zoey wasn't headed down the same path as Beth.

Just then Marlena Torres entered and, in her customary clipped manner, strode toward him, stilettos clicking on the hardwood, sticking a document in front of him for him to sign.

"Hey listen, Syd. I gotta roll. See you tonight?"

"You got it."

They hung up.

"You didn't need to get off the phone, I just need your John Hancock," Marlena said, tossing her black mane over her shoulder.

"No, it's okay. What is this?"

"Expense report for next week's fundraiser."

"The one at Sault's?"

"You got it. Biggest one of the campaign."

"Yeah, well he's always been close with Dino," he muttered, scribbling his signature. "How much are you expecting to pull in?"

She offered a rare smile. "Tons."

He handed the report back. "Good," he said as she turned to go. "No wait. I want to ask you something."

"Jeez, you sound so serious, Ben." She looked at him, her exotic brown eyes narrowing before widening. "Is it serious?"

A ripple against his skin turned his flesh bristly, but he tried to keep his expression neutral. "No. Not serious, but..." *Yeah right. Triple homicide and suicide were no big deal, Campbell.* "...More like *important*, I guess."

Her brow wrinkled. "Oh-kay," she said slowly. "What is it?"

"You know a guy named Herb Heim?"

She thought for a moment, the faint creases in her otherwise smooth coffee-colored forehead deepening. "No, not that I can recall." He watched her search the recesses of her mind before turning and looking at him with conviction: "He's not a donor, if that's what you're wondering."

"I am. Can you just check against your lists?"

She rolled her eyes. "Ben." Her tone was like that of an old-school nun teaching unruly schoolboys. "I know our donors like the back of my hand. If he were in our database, I'd know."

"Alright then. A vendor then, maybe? Someone you dealt with at some point at one of the venues? A volunteer? If you don't mind, I'd appreciate it if you'd do some digging for me."

Marlena was one of the most efficient, organized, and, well...anal-retentive people he'd ever come across. "Well if I've had contact with him, I won't have to dig too far. Trust me."

Thinking of her reams of excel spreadsheets and detailed reports, he had to smile at that. "I trust you, Little Miss Moneybags."

Smiling, she feigned innocence. "I'm not all about money, you know."

"Hey. It's okay if you are. That *is* your job, my friend. And one you're damn good at, I might add." He picked up a memo from his in-box, the one detailing the weekend's take and waved it in the air: Marlena had raked in fifty-thousand dollars in two days, from low-dollar events, no less.

Her dark, almost-ebony eyes sparkled despite the pallid light radiating from the unforgiving fluorescent light above, as she curtsied.

He laughed. "Hey listen. Before I forget...I have a reliable source telling me that our dear friend Mr. J. Harrison Almond is looking into our fundraising efforts."

Marlena rolled her eyes. "Oh for Pete's sake. What's he looking for?"

"I don't know, but he's been poking around at ELEC so just make sure everything's on the up and up. Every I dotted and T crossed. You got me?"

"Of course." She was indignant. "It's just annoying, that's all. So you good? You need anything else?"

He smiled but it was forced; his mind was still wrapped around Heim and the inexplicable queasiness he felt welling within his galley and wandering upwards on a mission, threatening to reproduce his hastily eaten breakfast sandwich.

Since he'd arrived all he'd been doing was poring over the call log from the past two weeks.

HERB HEIM, the entry read. MONDAY: 11 TIMES. TUESDAY: 17 TIMES. BEN, PLEASE CALL THIS MAN BACK. HE SAYS IT'S URGENT. Millie's normally passive curvy penmanship was replaced with block letters and exclamation points, signs that she did not want to hear this man's name again.

Marlena leaned over his desk. "So what's this guy's story?"

Ben shrugged and pointed.

Marlena peered at the call log. Suddenly she recoiled, as if the log had reached out and stung her. "He called twenty-eight times in *two days*?" she asked, incredulous.

"Well he only left a handful of messages, but Millie said they got weirder and weirder so she did a quick check of the caller ID and saw his number pop up two dozen more times."

Ben could see Marlena combing through her memory: *Have I ever heard that name before?*

"Sorry," she said, finally. "It doesn't ring a bell. But I'll keep it in mind."

"Thanks."

"Have you tried calling him?"

Ben felt sick at the thought of the newscast last night. Clearly Marlena hadn't seen it, or read the paper today for that matter. *That's fundraisers for you*, he thought. But then he looked up and saw her watching him with such concern that he almost told her. *Almost*. But then his breakfast once again threatened to make an encore and he thought better of it.

"Nah, I haven't called," he said, hoping his tone came across as casual. "I'm afraid it'll be a stray cat situation."

She raised her eyebrows and smiled. "A *what?*"

"You know. Feed this guy once and I'll never get rid of 'em."

Laughing, she swatted him playfully with the document he had just signed for her. "You're crazy, Ben."

"No kidding," he muttered to himself. He was beginning to think he was losing his mind and, as he heard her footsteps making their way back down the hall, he heard the same thing echo again and again within them: Herb Heim. Herb Heim. Herb Heim...

After a time, he came to the conclusion that it was pointless to sit and look at this call log for a minute longer; clearly it wasn't going to solve anything. Any sane mind could see that. Plus, Digger was on the case now. And if there was anyone who could get water from a stone it was him.

He glanced at the clock. *How long had been sitting there like that? Just...obsessing.* He tried to put Heim out of his mind. "Time to get some work done," he said, pushing away from his desk, and headed outside to his car. He'd picked up his bag from the airport, but hadn't bothered to unpack it.

Pulling the duffle from the back of the Jeep, he was thinking he still had some time before dinner to go over the files he should've gone over in Boston, if not for Kat.

Kat.

Did he even care that she'd ended things? On some level he did, didn't he? They'd been together for nearly two years. He must feel *something*, right? But maybe that was just because of the shock of it. It was just that, well...it'd never before occurred to him that *she* might leave *him*. He'd always envisioned an end to the relationship –- of course he had, especially in the last six months -- but he'd always thought he'd be the one to do it. And it wasn't an ego thing. It was actually why the relationship had dragged as long as it had; He just couldn't figure out a way to end things without breaking her heart. In some ways, he figured, it made him a coward.

Fuck it. Maybe I am. This is what he was thinking as he unzipped his bag and found four bricks stacked where the files should be.

Bricks. Rough, red rectangles that stunned him, completely jarring him beyond comprehension, as though the Statue of Liberty had crumbled before his very eyes.

He stared down, a dumb, near-catatonic expression smeared across his face like mayonnaise on a windowpane. *Bricks*, was all he could think. *Bricks*.

He picked one up, as if he'd never before encountered such an unusual object. "What the..?" He wondered aloud, but his tone was more of bewilderment than anger.

Bricks. All his clothes were still there. *Bricks*. He checked the tag again: Ben Campbell, 223 Center Street, Piedmont, NJ...

Bricks.

A sudden jolt surged through him then, one that made him feel wobbly and sick and, for some odd reason, terrified; like a child certain something was beneath his bed, and the horrible nagging in his mind, his stomach, his psyche, as he knelt on the scratchy carpet and peeled the tail of the bedcover up and peered into the shadowy darkness below...

The trees spun around him: an out-of-control carousel unable –- or unwilling –- to stop.

Vertigo was something he'd heard of, but didn't quite know whether or not that was exactly what he was experiencing, and who had time to contemplate at a time like this? The earth was a mirage beneath him and he considered dropping to his knees to test its reality before the ground demanded he do so, bringing him down with a force beyond his control.

He hovered on all fours, the gravel beneath him digging into his palms, through his cargos and into his kneecaps. His head swayed. He felt like he was inside a torture chamber nobody else could see, wondering if this is what it felt like to truly go insane...

But then he came to. He spat a few times then, for no discernible reason, looked over his shoulders at the empty alley beyond.

Mistake.

At once he felt the hairs on his arms, the back of his neck come to attention like well-trained cadets eager for approval.

Something was not right. Not right *at all.*

Was he going crazy?

And just when he thought it wasn't possible for his situation to get any worse, it did: and he felt the sudden and sickly, creepy feeling that only arrived when one had the inexplicably concrete sensation that he was being watched.

16

Sunday

The smell of cannabis was so overwhelming it was as though the Jamaican countryside had been set on fire. As staggering as whiplash, Sydney had to brace herself lest she be knocked off the front stoop and back onto the sidewalk by its sheer bravado. The only thing that even came close to rivaling it was the stench of dog shit oozing toward her from the mangy scrap of backyard just beyond the chain-linked fence. Housing the source of the stink: menacing pit bulls pacing the dirt like panthers, eyeing Sydney with barely-hidden longing, making her bones rattle so violently she was worried it might signal something within them. Dogs could smell fear, couldn't they? In short order she pressed the doorbell again and rapped her knuckles against the splintery door harder than was necessary. *Come on...somebody answer...*

The door swung open and an onslaught of gangsta rap tidal-waved onto the street. A slight woman stood in the doorframe with twiggy arms crossed and an insolent tilt to her pointy chin. Sydney gave her the once-over: bare feet, fraying spandex shorts and a stained tee shirt, her eyes red and neck heavy with gold chains, a do-rag on her head and a spaced-out scowl on her scarred face; not a thing even remotely friendly about her.

Sydney's eyes danced, checking her notes against the number dangling by rusty nails on the outside of the house.

This couldn't be the right place, could it?

But then a voice bust through the haze of smoke: "You uh, Cindy?"

"Shanice Hopkins?" she asked in return, incredulous, and the woman nodded. It wasn't as though this was a sneak attack -- they'd spoken just yesterday, right before her interview with Marion Jefferson, and made an appointment for today. Shanice had called her by the wrong name then, too.

They stood for an awkward moment, just sizing each other up, before Shanice's jaundiced eyes seemed to regain focus and she remembered where she was. With a lazy nod she turned, calling, "C'mon in," over her bony shoulder.

This is just great, Sydney thought as she followed, suppressing a cough. *Hell of an interview this is going to be...*

According to her research, Shanice's son, Demetrius "T-Ray" Hopkins, had been an aspiring rap star and local celebrity on his way to Hollywood and beyond. Despite growing up severely underprivileged -- even by Camden standards -- he had stayed in school and had even taken Advanced Placement English classes four straight years at Sir Thomas More, all while juggling inquiries from record labels, promoters, industry music magazines, night clubs, and all that came along with breaking into the business. Considering how well-known he was, Sydney felt almost foolish for having never heard of him before beginning her research, but she had never gotten into rap. Apparently he was quite talented, his music wildly popular. But what she found most impressive was that it was not just about drive-by's and ho's. The lyrics she'd read showed thoughtful prose illuminating issues such as breaking the cycle of poverty and domestic violence, with no appreciation of the gang scene. If anything, his music exposed his proclivity for literature and language; it read like poetry.

Which was why this scene before her was so surprising. She'd gone from the bright of a beautiful day into a dank, crumbling row home that reeked of grease and weed -- a series of misshapen pilled blankets tacked to window frames intent on keeping the light out -- and felt like she'd entered another dimension altogether. The kind she was certain a brilliant mind like T-Ray's could have never thrived within.

Once her eyes adjusted to the feeble light, Sydney nearly gasped despite herself. Bodies were strewn about the living room like a battlefield of the defeated -- big, small, mostly young -- all draped in bandannas and stiff-brimmed baseball hats and apparel obviously chosen according to their gang affiliation -- their yellowed, druggie eyes clinging lifelessly to the TV, the 99-cent-meal commercial-of-the-moment captivating them. A few were sleeping, though one girl in the corner was laughing at nothing in particular -- an unnerving falsetto cackle -- her bugged-out eyes glinting in the blue TV light glow. Sydney looked closer and noticed two girls she was certain she recognized from the music videos she had viewed as part of her research. They had the same overt caricature sexuality about them -- big lips, big hips, big tits -- and were draped over one boy texting on the latest Apple invention -- a device her own boss used, one that she knew cost at least five-hundred bucks. On the floor another boy was slumped against the couch with a blunt stuck between his lips while a girl sitting behind him plaited his hair into cornrows, a shiny 57 Magnum sticking out of the waistband of his low-slung jeans.

Nobody even glanced her way.

T-Ray's mother, Shanice, perched herself on the arm of a Salvation Army couch situated cock-eyed in the center of the room, tottering unsteadily. "Turn this shit off!" she shouted to no one in particular, and a moment later, to Syndey's great relief, the deafening music ceased.

Shanice had been just fifteen when she'd given birth to T-Ray, making her a mere three years older than Sydney herself, who could no sooner see herself as a mother at fifteen than she could as a mother of an eighteen-year-old now.

While Shanice took a hearty pull from the bong, Sydney weighed her options. Though it was unlikely any information of any use would come from this interview, she wondered if she'd have to disclose that the subject was using drugs at the time? How would one even go about disclosing that? This was a vein of journalism that was well beyond her comfort zone. She wrote upbeat pieces with happy endings...

And that's when she reminded herself: this story, however unlikely it seemed now, still might have a fairy tale ending. It was a long shot, true. But optimism was her strong suit. And ultimately this shimmer of hopefulness was what persuaded her to stay and follow-through with the interview when everything else told her to leave.

Now that her eyes were accustomed to the grimness of the room, she saw a bean bag chair on the floor and moved to sit on it, subtly nudging aside the array of empty bottles of malt liquor scattered in her path, but stopped just short, stuttering in her steps, upon realizing a human was already curled upon it, snoring.

"Oh that's just Alfonse," Shanice said with a dismissive wave, as if that explained everything; smoke shooting through her nostrils like a cartoon dragon. "Don't mind him. He just sleepin' off a drunk."

Feeling excruciatingly awkward, Sydney continued to stand until Shanice shooed away the other lumps on the couch entranced by *The Maury Povich Show* on the forever-some-inch plasma in the otherwise empty room. They grumbled as they left, leaving behind -- to Sydney's growing horror -- a baby on the floor behind them. Tears pricked Sydney's eyes as she realized she hadn't even noticed the baby. Maybe a year old, he seemed content gnawing on a wadded up fast food wrapper, drooling as he grinned up at Sydney, his big brown eyes dancing. As Sydney sunk onto the couch she smiled back at the little cherub, but it wasn't easy. Whether it was the smoke itself or the idea of this adorable child being exposed to it, tears came forth that she felt powerless against.

When Shanice finally spoke, Sydney jerked. Not just because she'd begun to lose herself in thought, but by the sheer force and nature of it, especially coming from such a small being. "And take your damn baby wit you!" she blasted, and one of the teens came back, sucking her teeth in displeasure — a huge jelly donut of a girl, moving slowly, her belly already full with the next one on the way. In one arm she scooped up the baby; in the other, the bong.

When it came to Camden, few things ever surprised anyone. If you knew anything about ghetto or slum, it was exactly what you'd expect. And yet, even with Sydney's own personal experience with it, she still found herself taken aback, wanting to run, wishing she'd never even tried.

Alone at last, the two women sat regarding one another, the oooohs and ahhhhs of *Maury*'s audience bouncing in-between them. Shanice's eyes were formidable slits; a product of both the weed and an unmasked contempt for Sydney that was almost palpable and, despite the barrenness of the room, left Sydney feeling claustrophobic and encroached upon.

And one step closer to leaving.

Shanice seemed to be engaged in some sort of pursuit of power, itching for the upper hand, while Sydney wondered whether or not she should just chalk it up to a bad day and call the whole thing off. But before she could react at all, Shanice lit up a Newport, inhaled deeply, and blew it right in Sydney's face.

Ok, that's it. I've had just about enough...

But just when Sydney was ready to walk, Shanice spoke: "You wanted to talk about T-Ray, right? So talk."

Sydney's first impulse was always to try to build a bridge within an interview, and today was no different. She wanted to tell this woman -- a contemporary of hers no less -- that she was from here, too. She knew just how mean the streets of Camden could be; how unforgiving...

But what good would it do? A person like Shanice would never see the similarities they shared simply because she didn't want to. And maybe Sydney couldn't blame her. After all, that was a lifetime ago, and even if it hadn't been, it still didn't make her "one of them", and they both knew it.

Instead she decided to do what she did with any difficult interviewee; she reminded herself that this person was just a person. Shanice was somebody's friend, somebody's daughter. She used to be a little girl, and had the same fears and dreams as any other kid. She'd known the joy of giving birth, of becoming a mom.

And perhaps it was that last reminder that stuck the most; the thing that made a little of Sydney's own walls melt: this woman was somebody's mother.

But looking at Shanice Hopkins, the way she carried herself like a fist just looking for a fight, it took something extra in Sydney that day. She dug in deep, and began.

The smile came first. Easy, like molasses and trademark; the thing usually able to chip away at even the most stubborn of stones. "You must be so proud of your son."

She figured the weed might've had something to do with it, but she saw something in Shanice thaw a bit. And was that...was that a smile? "Yeah, he somethin' else ain't he."

"I'll say," Sydney said, looking around the room and nodding to the collection of posters on the walls: promotions for an upcoming concert or the release of a CD. And by anyone's standards T-Ray was stunningly handsome: silky mocha skin, electric green eyes, and a luminous smile that had likely melted hearts since his diaper days.

"Yep," Shanice said with something like gratification, her eyes bouncing from one to the next. "That's my baby, alright."

Just then the gangsta rap started up again, shrieking through the precarious rapport they'd built and Sydney nearly leapt from her skin then recoiled just as quickly when Shanice shouted: "Will you turn that shit off? Can't your dumbass see I got me some comp'ny?!"

Some grumbling came from the kitchen, but the volume was lowered.

But Sydney's relief was short-lived, because when she looked back at Shanice she saw that whatever headway she'd made had been erased in a moment and the door of her face was now slammed shut.

The woman was wound back up, harder than a diamond, and she knew that the interview was all but over.

Though she felt the biggest part of herself deflate, she mustered enough strength to try one last time to salvage this thing. "Demetrius excelled in English, didn't he?"

"Yeah."

"Do you think that helped his rap career?"

"Fuck if I know."

Sydney cleared her throat as she consulted her notes. "And he has a child, yes?" She asked, nodding toward the other room where the pregnant girl had taken the baby. "Was that him?"

"Naw," Shanice said, her voice raw with poison. "His baby ain't allowed here."

Hmm, wonder why? Sydney thought facetiously. She cleared her throat: "And the mother?"

"Who?" Shanice growled. "Diamonique?!"

"Yes," Sydney nodded, glancing at her notes. "Diamonique...um... Keyes?"

"That two-bit ho! The fuck you want to know about *her* for?"

Sydney cringed. "Are she and your son still together?"

"Look, I don't know whatchu came here for but I've had jus' 'bout enough a this shit!" Shanice was off the couch now, spindly legs planted like she was cocked and loaded and ready to fire on anything foolish enough to get caught within her crosshairs.

Sydney iced over, unable to move as fear rushed through her like a riptide, and before she knew it Shanice was towering over her, her body a mass of springs ready to snap at the first movement of her prey. "You wanna know about T-Ray?" she demanded, hand on her angled hip. "Well all you need to know is this! He was the best damn rapper the East Coast seen in a long time, and he was our ticket out! You hear me? Outta here! Yeah he had a baby young, but this is the muthafuckin' ghetto in case you ain't noticed, bitch! It ain't exactly unusual --"

"Listen, Shanice, I'm not here to judge, I'm just —"

"Then what you here for? Huh? *Huh*?! Bitch, what you need?!"

She was screeching now and as curious faces began to pop in the doorway, Sydney shrank back into the couch, her skin singeing with panic, suddenly wishing she'd taken Ben's advice to bring him along after all. Her hands were off her notebook, palms facing out, trying to show she meant no harm; that she was innocent of whatever crazy thing Shanice Hopkins had decided she was guilty of. "Shanice, *please*. I'm just doing a story on your son's school, that's all. Really. I'm truly sorry if I offended you somehow, I'm just trying to talk to all the students to see where they are now —"

Shanice sucked her teeth then and made a big production of rolling her eyes while Sydney braced herself. "Oh all's you want to know is *where is they now?*"

She was mocking her and Sydney knew it; still, she kept her cool. "Yes, that's all. I'm so sorry if I offended you." Still unsure why this woman has switched on a dime, she no longer cared, and was instead gathering her things fast, eyes darting toward the door.

"Bitch, please. You wanna know where T-Ray's at? Huh? Do you? Well he locked up, *ai'ight?!*" she all but screamed, "And don't nobody know when his sorry ass is coming home! Go ask that two-dollah ho of his! She the only one he talk to anyways!"

Even though Shanice was a good four or five inches shorter than she, Sydney found herself backing away, trying not to stumble, sure this lunatic might not let her live if she stayed. Those nasty, switch-blade-slit eyes of hers said as much.

"Yeah that's right!" Shanice shrieked, sending Sydney back further. "Not only did he not get me outta this shithole, he don't even call me no more! All he care about is that retarded baby of his an' that stupid-ass ho who had him! Shit, I wouldn't even be surprised if that ugly-ass thing ain't even his!"

Just then a figure appeared alongside Shanice, casting a long, thick shadow. He was as tall and wide as a grown man, but his face was a boy's, with half a head of cornrows and an eager hand on the glock stuck down his pants, his narrowed eyes like hollow points aimed right at Sydney.

Sydney's hand was on the doorknob now, slipping between her sweaty fingers, a five-alarm fire surging through her as fast as a rose-laden racehorse and just as she opened it and tripped backwards onto the stoop, letting a burst of daylight into the filthy row home, Shanice Hopkins crumbled to the ground before her –- now a heap of sorrow -- her do-rag askew and the gaggle of gangsters from inside stumbling toward her, toward the daylight.

"He was supposed to get me outta here, you hear me?!" she screamed, and the entire street turned to look.

The warmth of the day had drawn people outside –- waiting in line at the needle exchange on the corner, milling about in front of the Goodwill store at the end of the block -- and she tried not to notice the dozens of suspicious eyes pinned to her, witnessing Shanice's grief ricochet throughout the tenements.

"He was supposed to get us outta this hellhole!"

Taking the steps two at a time now, Sydney was on the sidewalk before she knew it, her breath a thread, her chest pulsing, her heart a throbbing time bomb within, thinking it would just be a matter of seconds before those cold-blooded pit bulls from the backyard were let loose and commanded to attack, their insatiable barking a ferocious drumbeat in her ears as she went running, running, running with hands over her ears, the cries of Shanice Hopkins slicing open her back, the wailing voice behind her competing with the wail of a car alarm –- and winning -- emitting a horrible sound like an animal caught in machinery:

"You hear me, you bitch?? He was supposed to get us outtta heeere!"

17

Sunday

Micki Bruni was a poor excuse for a wife.

She'd taken her vows on a whim and never looked back. As far as the perfunctory was concerned, she hadn't seen the inside of laundry room, dry-cleaner, car-wash, grocery store -- let alone cooked a meal -- since just after their honeymoon. In fact, no sooner had they unpacked their luggage than people were hired to do such things, as well as scrub stains from clothes, grow grass, burp babies, write thank-you notes, shine shoes, clip nails, decorate rooms, pay bills, empty trash, wash windows, wash floors, wash cars; apply band-aids and make beds and grilled cheeses for hungry children; iron, water plants, do homework, do the dishes -- do everything -- and, in particular, tend to the pet-store/puppy mill Chihuahuas she'd bought on impulse after learning of Hollywood's elite's scrawny, bug-eyed pride-and-joy.

Hiltons and Kardashians were idols of Micki's. They shared the same phony hair, expensive wardrobes and vapid personalities to prove it; they even spent money just as fast, but Micki Bruni was no heiress. Closest thing to celebrity the sassy Camden native would ever attain was getting knocked up by a funeral director's son who somehow went on to become a Garden State senator.

If there was anything wifely about the woman it was her role at her husband's elbow –- hair coiffed, sticky-pink artificially-pumped-up lips shimmering –- laughing at every last one of his jokes as they played to a crowd of sycophants munching on platefuls of catered food at one of his many fundraisers.

Micki had children, but she was no mother. After they were born she'd gamely bathed in the glow of gifts and attention, but soon grew tired of them once the camera flashes dissipated. It wasn't just their crying, either; that would've been too easy to blame. It was their constant requirements, their endless dependency. The way they acted as if she were the only goddamn human on the planet able to meet their various whims and wants. It was exhausting. Utterly fucking exhausting.

The terrible twos made a terrible situation worse, no matter how much her husband tried to intervene -- coming home and shedding his suit jacket as soon as he crossed the threshold, rolling up his sleeves as he jogged up the grand staircase, trotting to the nursery and working like the dickens to ease the burden of maternity –- But that was when he was home, and Dino Bruni wasn't home much. He was too busy clawing his way through the political ranks, and doing a damn good job of it.

Dino had obligations; had a family name to preserve, to prolong. He could stay home and be Mister Mom or he could step up to the plate and carry on the legacy his ancestors had toiled for so long to create. She knew that as far as he was concerned, there was no choice, and so he left the parenting to her. And, to Micki, it was a no-brainer: Hire someone and let them do it.

Once and while Dino might balk at her decision-making, but who was he to judge? When the boys were little, for instance, she'd refused to read to them, claiming they liked TV better. *Homework was boring –- she'd hated it as a kid; who could blame her for not going through all the bullshit a second time around?* Then they hit middle school and he became an Assemblyman in the Majority -– and motherhood fell to the wayside entirely. She now had an image to keep up, and life on the home front was all a bit too much for her. Some people were meant to be mothers, she reasoned, and she wasn't one of them. *What am I supposed to do? Sit around in sweats, knee-deep in diapers like some lazy slob, ironing shirts with a bunch of filthy kids whining for this, or for that? Please.* Her schedule was booked as it was. Nail appointments, massages, shopping for new clothes...or for new gardeners and maids. No sooner did she hire them than they quit on her, *the lazy fucks.*

"You believe this shit?" she griped to her sisters, a Capri ultra light stuck between her lips. She motioned toward the backyard. "The hell'd they sneak across the border for if they don't wanna work? Friggin' spics. Coulda fooled me they were poor, the way they lay around, sneakin' naps in their trucks, moochin' all day."

She turned toward the window, one of the many among the breakfast nook where she and her sisters were known to congregate, where a small man –- not even a man really, a boy, not much older than her youngest child –- was hunched over a trio of textbook azaleas, the back of his tee-shirt marked dark down the center with sweat, as if someone had taken a wet oar and slapped him along his spine. (Micki ignored this, as well as the dark half-moons beneath his armpits, his nimble fingers working fast despite the wretched heat) and instead rapped a bony knuckle against the glass, careful not to knock her diamonds in the process, causing the boy to get a fright. "Wake up, Paco!"

His name was not Paco -- not even close -- but he jumped back just the same, dropped his shears in the dirt and watched, his small mouth shocked into the shape of an egg. "You're in the land of opportunity now, baby! Better wake up and smell the coffee! Better start earnin' those pesos!"

And they laughed.

Her sisters, a trio of frizzy-haired chubby stumps who'd always envied the baby of the family, the one who had somehow skirted most of the knotty Italian genes and inherited the best of the German, were near-fixtures in the Bruni's McMansion. They'd grown up with the same alcoholic father and washwoman mother, but somehow they'd noticed from the beginning that baby Micki was different. Naturally thin with big blue eyes fanned by a harvest of thick honey-colored lashes to *die* for, topped off by a crown of fine blonde hair for the first thirteen years of her life until it began to grow mousy, and then they'd all chipped in to buy Miss Clairol to help the little beauty out.

It was her sister Patrizia –- the eldest -- who was responsible for her marriage. After all, she had come up with the idea to net Dino Bruni in the first place.

A star on the Varsity cheerleading team, Micki had been somersaulting and high kicking her way into Dino Bruni's heart from the sidelines of the Camden High football field, all while Patrizia watched on. And Patrizia was nothing if not an opportunist. She wasted no time in explaining to Micki what the Health teacher had left out, and a bewildered Micki had learned the (albeit a crude version) ins-and-outs of ovulation. Truth be told, she had been contemplating losing her virginity anyway, possibly before Homecoming, but Patrizia's interests lay in the long-term. After all, with ten years and three sisters between them, Patrizia already knew just how cruel the world could be.

"Get pregnant," she'd hissed into Micki's ears until it became embedded there. "He's a winner, that Dino Bruni. Look at his family! All that cash! It ain't like there's ain't never gonna be a need for coffins." Pointing to a calendar she'd said: "Here are the best days to do it..."

A string of nannies had raised her oldest: twin boys she decided she couldn't handle within a few weeks of their arrival home from the hospital. She tolerated their youth, just barely. (*Who the hell had time to keep track of all the Little League bullshit anyway?*) They were sent to St. Andrews Prep as boarders even before they'd grown pubic hair but, in her defense, she hopped in her Escalade and made the hour ride up to visit their dorm rooms to take them to lunch or dinner at least once a month. It didn't hurt that The Garden State Promenade -– replete with Fifth Avenue's finest this side of Hudson River -- was on the way. A new Prada handbag or pair of Jimmy Choos made the infrequent journeys seem more manageable.

The youngest was different. Now sixteen and a girl after her own heart, Maria-Lucia was a buxom, (sorta natural) blonde whom Micki had every intention of ensuring made the most of her looks while she still could.

"Don't be afraid to show a little skin," she would insist in the dressing room of some teenage mall monstrosity, shoving forth a hanger with a dangling piece of cloth pinned to it. When Maria-Lucia balked, Micki got mad: "What are you, a friggin' nun? Show a little T & A for Christ's sweet sake." Then: "You're just like your father, stubborn as a friggin' mule." And Maria-Lucia would roll her eyes, her acrylic French manicure texting away.

The only extracurricular activity that had ever interested Micki was cheerleading. After all, that was how had landed her husband -- her lifestyle -- and she had high hopes that her baby girl could make it to even greater heights.

Patrizia had summed it up best: "She's gonna make it BIG one day. Just look at her. She could have her own reality show."

It was a frequent topic of conversation among her sisters whose own kids were involved in relationships with people dabbling in various stages of criminal activity, or were the criminals themselves.

"From your lips to His ears," Micki would agree, crossing herself with the hand not occupied by a cigarette.

But Micki wasn't stupid, not by a long shot; especially when it came to her husband's career, and especially when it came to power. She kept close eye on his decision-making, the bills he was asked to sponsor, his staff. She monitored his email with the same vigilance as an SS soldier. She never missed a fundraiser. And though she knew her frequent phone calls to his district and campaign offices were met with the same eye-rolling, she ignored it, unless she caught it outright, which resulted in a tirade and subsequent urging her husband to fire the offender, despite his or her tenure.

She had just said goodbye to her sisters, all on their way home to put the finishing touches on their customary elaborate Sunday dinners, like all good Italian women, and now she was on a mission of her own. The phone had been ringing off the hook all day, and she was about to get to the bottom of it. Between collect calls from Iggy in jail to that irritating Jarvis Jasper, she'd barely had time to catch up on the latest gossip from her sisters. Then of course there was that little package that had arrived Thursday; the one with twenty thousand dollars in cash in it, and a simple note that read:

> Dino,
>   Thanks but no thanks.
> --H.H.

She'd hid the money and hadn't mentioned it, even though her first reaction was rage; thinking this was another mistress situation.

Only Patrizia had been able to calm her, reminding her that between the election and Iggy's trial Dino barely had time to sleep at all, let alone sleep around.

It had made sense at the time. And, she'd grudgingly admit, it still made sense now. But that didn't at all take away from her quest to get to the truth. It may not be hanky-panky but something was up, she just knew it, and she would be damned if someone was going to keep her in the dark about something in her own house.

Her marabou heels ticked against the marble foyer as she made her way to her husband's study. She found him, clippers in hand, back to her, carefully preening his collection of orchids, Raymond Scott's "Harlem Nocturne" whittling against the rich wood of the room.

Leaning against the doorjamb, Micki examined her manicure, feigning casualness as she gathered her thoughts. When she lifted her eyes, she was surprised by the bulge of emotion she felt looking at her husband's back, watching the serene yet methodical way he moved in his baby blue Thomas Pink shirt, pleated chinos, and tasseled Gucci loafers. It was the same emotion she had always while felt while watching her babies sleep. After the nannies had changed them and bathed them and scurried them into their pj's, she'd always felt the same pang of love, watching them breathe in soft, tranquil clumps, their bodies curled beneath the billowy duvet covers.

In that instant she felt love for her husband, but also something else. Something like pity. There was something about the sag of his shoulders, the air of worry circling him like a swarm of bees. It was an unusual sensation for her, and it made her shift uneasily in her own skin. Her brow creased despite the Botox. Dino wasn't himself these days...

After a moment she chalked it up to Dino having such a moron for a brother. If that dumb-ass Iggy's conviction cost Dino his re-election she might never forgive him. It was bad enough they'd spent a king's ransom on his trial. That alone was enough for her hold a grudge for years to come. Hell, she'd already declined all of his collect calls from the jail, and he hadn't even been sentenced yet...

She wondered about Dino, though. He was fiercely loyal — especially to his family — and, at this moment, she found this particular trait a liability rather than a good thing. But she was nothing if not cunning, and so rather than accuse, she decided she'd catch more flies with honey.

"Hiya handsome," she cooed.

If her husband was surprised by the intrusion, he didn't show it. He continued to clip the delicate flora, carefully tipping the watering can ever-so-slightly, back still turned to her, though she thought she detected a sigh before he said: "What's up, baby?"

"Oh nuthin'. Just wanted to check in on you. You've been awful quiet today. What happened? Have a bad game?"

She didn't mention the liquor she'd smelled on his breath earlier nor his unwillingness to join her at the afternoon football game to watch Maria-Lucia's performance leading the squad. She'd checked his schedule, too: after that round of golf with Sterling Sault, he was free for once. But she'd let it slide. Then she'd come home to find him sitting in his study; no music, no TV, not on a phone call, nothing. Just sitting there. Staring at nothing. And while it had given Micki the straight-up willies, Maria-Lucia had simply rolled her eyes and mumbled "weird", before heading upstairs and shutting her bedroom door behind her.

But Micki was worried. She frowned despite herself. Dino just didn't seem like Dino anymore.

"Everything was fine."

"Fine?"

He turned, rather stiffly she noted, and repeated: "Fine."

If he meant to put her at ease, he had failed. His eyes had a vacant, almost-ghostliness to them that made her look away.

But she was no coward. She looked back and concluded it was probably the scotch.

But still it was there. Something odd. *Off.* And then she thought of the denied collect calls and wondered if maybe Iggy was behind all this. *Yes*...she began to think slowly, *It had to be him. While she'd been out, he'd probably called and started his pissin' and moanin' about his bail getting denied, or about getting his conviction overturned and 'oh poor me, you gotta help me out' and gotten Dino all sad, or feeling guilty, or...or...just bent out of shape and* that *was why he was acting so strange...*

"Fine." She repeated, somewhat satisfied with her own deduction of the situation. And then she moved to leave. She meant to. Really, she did. But no sooner had she turned away then she turned back and before she could stop herself blurted: "This doesn't have to do with that no-good brother of yours, does it?"

"What?"

"This," she motioned with her arms, but it came across more as a flail. Though her actions might have been seen as clumsy and frustrated, her eyes bore into him as if she could extract the truth from him simply by staring hard enough. "*You.*"

"Me?" he asked, eyebrows arched, but he didn't really seem surprised. He just seemed tired.

"Yeah *you*. You're all...I don't know. Not yourself." Her eyes flicked toward the watering can in his hand and row of pristine flowers behind him and, for some reason she could not isolate, she softened. "What is it Dino, baby?" she asked, her voice gentle, as she moved toward him. "Is it the election?"

What happened next inspired in her as much surprise as it did anger.

Her husband actually recoiled –- not much, and likely imperceptible other to anyone but his wife –- but enough to make her look at him as if he were an intruder in the house, rather than its owner.

She stopped at once, and neither of them moved for a long, anticipatory moment. Then instinct took over and her hand flung to her hip and her neck cocked at an aggressive angle and she demanded: "What the *hell*, Dino?!"

Did she just see him shrink back? The great Dino Bruni?

No matter. The tirade swelling in her chest was about to break the levee. "You've been acting like a friggin' *nut* the past couple weeks, and you won't tell me *shit*. Are you screwin' around on me, is that it?"

(She was exaggerating. It hadn't been weeks, only days, but she had never been one for details. Or facts, for that matter.)

He seemed ready to laugh, but then caught himself. "Please, Micki. *You're* the freakin' nut. You think I have time to have an affair right now?" He slammed the watering can down on the great mahogany desk. She jumped as he roared: *"Do you?"*

She threw up her hands dramatically, as if greatly frustrated, as if she'd been pondering the state of their marriage endlessly, worrying through sleepless nights, when the thought had only just occurred a few days ago when the package from "H.H." arrived. She opened her mouth to ask about it but then thought better of it. She remembered what Patrizia had said, but more than that, she thought of how nicely that twenty thousand would fashion her fall wardrobe. Hell, if he was cheating with this "H.H." person she'd find out soon enough; no need to give away money over it.

Besides, if he was cheating she was entitled to that loot. She considered it "hush money" for keeping mum on the subject.

She lowered her voice. "Well what is it then? Your brother?"

He stiffened, but lowered his voice, too. "No."

Her eyes narrowed as if passing through a filthy alleyway, not wanting to touch a thing. "Have you talked to him?"

His face was cast downward, his neck too weary to rise to this –- or any -- occasion. "No. I...I haven't."

She let her anger dissipate a bit, wondering if he was upset that he hadn't heard from him. That maybe she should come clean and tell him that he'd called.

But then she concluded nothing good could come from it. *Let the stupid bastard stew for a while,* she decided. *Serves him right for wasting so much of their money. For getting caught in the first place like a two-bit cat burglar. For embarrassing the family. For jeopardizing the election...*

"So what is it? The election?"

He looked up, his face a roadmap: creased with age, crisscrossed with worry.

Her compassion, as fickle as his collection of hothouse flowers, began to grow at this. But it was only a second until it wilted and another thought blazed through her and riled her up and, as impulsive as ever, she pierced the peacefulness and asked: "It's that crazy-ass rooster, ain't it?"

"Who? Jasper?" In one swift movement he picked up the watering can and turned his back to her.

She rolled her eyes. "*Yeah* Jasper. He's called here two-dozen friggin' times today. He's the one who's makin' you all crazy, isn't he? He's the one who..." But he was no longer listening it seemed, and she flamed at his indifference. "Dino!" she screamed. "I'm talking to you!"

The Senator moved seamlessly from plant to plant, composed and impervious against her rage. "Hell if I know," he said quietly.

But then she stopped just as quickly as she'd started, the fury in her tone replaced by something pleading: a whine as unsettling as a tremor. "C'mon Dino. Level with me."

He laughed then; a hollow laugh, but hearty enough to be convincing to most. "There's nothing to level with you about, Mick. Trust me." He moved onto the next plant with a steady hand.

"I dunno. It's just weird." The tone of her voice reminded her of that of Maria-Lucia's complaining to her Calculus tutor. "What's he callin' so much for?"

When he didn't answer quickly enough, she grew annoyed and bored, and almost went to leave. He'd chase after her -- sooner or later, he always did. But something kept her lingering. Suddenly she felt as off-kilter as her husband seemed.

Dino moved, clasping leaves between his fingers as he did so, inspecting them and occasionally mumbling to himself.

It wasn't until she said *this* that he finally paused, and became rigid at once, as if a pool cue had replaced his spine:

"It doesn't have anything to do with the school, does it, Dino?"

The question loomed: offhand, yet heavy and cumbersome at the same time: a deflated hot-air balloon in the room, occupying the space between them, a great chasm separating them.

After a long drought of a moment, he turned to her, and she was startled by what she saw: the great Senator seemed withered, so unlike himself and more like a person trounced, one who hadn't give up, but had been given up *on*.

Her immediate thought: *Jesus, Mary and Joseph, he needs a day at the spa.*

His smile was taut across his face, and she knew the man well enough to know he was about to tell a lie. "No. It has nothing to do with the school. And it is no longer up for discussion."

She went to speak, but he held up a hand, stopping her.

"Do I make myself clear?"

She nodded despite the fact that she was stunned beyond comprehension.

He turned his back to her.

Mouth agape, she turned away and pulled her arms around her on instinct, feeling something like a draft move through the room, and looked outside: the trees were still, and the wistful night air pouring through the open windows of the study was calm and should have been soothing.

Still, she found she was shivering.

18

Sydney's Cabriolet shook as the hoopty bounced past her, the bass from its speakers shaking her from the inside out. Rattled from the meeting with Shanice Hopkins, her still-shaking hands struggled to light a Camel Light to calm her nerves. It was a disgusting habit -- one that both embarrassed her and infuriated Cody, her once-upon-a-time-fiancé -- but she didn't really care at the moment.

She was blocks away from Shanice now, from that stifling mausoleum of broken lives, but she was still in Camden, and though the interview had been over for an hour, that alone was enough to keep her tense.

Rolling down her window just enough to let the smoke snake outside, she sat back, so tempted to close her eyes and let a bit of the tension drift away, but knowing it was unwise to do so in a neighborhood like this, even in broad daylight.

Across the street the laughter from a cluster of young girls drew her attention and she watched as they played double-dutch in the scraggly vacant lot rife with aggressive weeds and wan deadened earth.

Despite her best intentions she let her mind wander and just like a bad habit it bee-lined straight to the thing she most wished it wouldn't:

her own days playing in Camden's abandoned lots, laughing in the face of poverty, too young to know better than to be cheerful...

Her childhood.

She thought of a birthday then -- her fourth? Fifth? -- But instead of remembering cake and ice cream, pretty pink streamers and bouncing balloons, she remembered a bright white cast and dark sunglasses: her Mom's broken wrist and black eye, courtesy of her Dad. And how, when she had gone to her mother to try and hug her, her Mom had shuddered; the almost tangible pain springing throughout the slight woman from even the softest of touches.

Tears leapt to her eyes then, just as they always did when the memories came. She'd always been grateful that they somehow knew better and managed to keep themselves at bay, but lately they'd been like landmines, cropping up at the most inconvenient times. She supposed this story had much to do with it, and it gave her pause. What exactly was she accomplishing with all of this anyway? It had been one failure after another. This was not the sort of thing her readers had come to know and like about her. They turned to her for the exact opposite. She stared hard at her collection of notes and research; both scattered on the back and front seats and organized neatly in her messenger bag. Maybe this was all a waste of time, like her boss said. Maybe Roger was right. Maybe...

And then she was thinking of her Mom again, lying in the funeral parlor, courtesy of dear old dad once again. Little Sydney had given the funeral man her most favorite doll ever -- a stuffed bunny inexplicably named Wilbur -- whom her mother was forever trying to wash and bleach and bring back to white again after Sydney inevitably dragged him all over creation. The funeral man's eyes were painfully kindhearted as he took it from her, gingerly, and Sydney remembered how, at first, his big hands had looked so hard and woody -- gnarled and inflexible, like an ancient tree -- but when she touched them she was surprised by how soft they were, as warm and powdery smooth as a just-baked doughnut. "Thank you, Mr. Bruni," she had said in her five-year-old squeak, and the gently-smiling man simply nodded, placing the ragged bunny carefully next to her mother's hands, already clasping a Rosary...

She choked back tears then, and when there was a sudden banging on the window, she jumped, unable to make out the person behind the fist, her tears mixing with smoke, an inch-long ash crumbling to her feet. Her heart thrashed in her chest like a fish on a dry dock, cold fear raking itself down her back, and it took several moments before her hands steadied enough to roll it down. Which she did, despite every warning she had ever heard.

"Oh I'm sorry!" a voice exclaimed, and somewhere inside of her Sydney registered that it was a girl, with a friendly tone like a jingle bell, and her terror retreated a bit. "But you're Sydney Langston, aren't you?" Before she could answer the peppy voice leapt in again: "I recognized you from the rally? When we named the school? You gave a speech?"

Sydney nodded dumbly, her own voice conspicuously M.I.A. went unnoticed by the grinning girl standing next to the idling car, her twinkly-white smile causing two deep and endearing dimples to pierce her cheeks: a face that could sell ice to Eskimos.

"You're early but I don't mind. I'm always early, too!" the girl giggled. "C'mon," she waved with a fine-boned hand, and Sydney followed without thinking.

To Sydney's great relief, Ebony Valdez was as vivacious in person as she had been in print, (in Sydney's notes), and her bedroom reflected every bright spec of color that seemed to dance around the girl like living effervescence. Sydney began to breathe normally again as she took in the warm wooden floors, the soft cotton of the lemon-yellow curtains. The walls were painted in heart-lifting lavender, the sheen of them catching the light from the bay of windows hovering above the window seat: a plush lime green velvet cushion beneath it, a well-worn copy of an open book pressed down in order to save the page. Sydney noticed the title, *A Tree Grows in Brooklyn*, and she had to smile. It was one of her favorites, too.

One of Sir Thomas More Tech's success stories, Ebony was just the gust of fresh air that Sydney was desperate for after Marion Jefferson and Cyrus and Cedric Ashe and T-Ray all of the other crushing stories of failure she'd encountered that had nearly sucked the life from her. Though it had been hours ago, she could still hardly shake the cries of Shanice Hopkins from her ears: those hopeless, jaundiced eyes. Those wails of anguish.

The smells of roast pork, beans and rice, and heavenly flan wafted from the kitchen, bringing Sydney back to the moment. Ebony was in college now, determined to become a lawyer, and came from a good family: a rare breed in these parts.

As she plopped with a bounce onto her pink-and-white polka-dotted bedspread covered by a collection of stuffed animals, Ebony's big brown eyes sparkled. "This is so amazing! I have, like, a celebrity in my room!" she all-but squealed, and Sydney suppressed a blush.

"Well I wouldn't go *that* far..."

"No I mean like, you *are*. What's it like to be so well known? You're totally like Jennifer Aniston an' shit!"

A red sheepishness crawled up her neck. "Oh please! I'm not famous *at all*..." she insisted, but was cut-off once again.

"Well you are here in Camden, girl!" Ebony said, bouncing, a plush *Ariel* doll clutched in her spindly yet muscular arms, her yellow sparkle nail polish catching streamers of afternoon light pouring through the windows like curls of butter.

Smiling, Sydney jostled her notes into position and straightened her spine against the back of the desk chair Ebony had pulled out for her. Flattery embarrassed her; it was time to get to work. "Okay, so you ready?"

"Ready!" Ebony grinned.

"Great. Okay then," she began gently, "tell me about Sir Thomas More Tech."

This first question launched the girl into a ten-minute monologue, spaced only by sparse, bated breath, her giggles and dimples punctuating the text Sydney scrambled to capture in her longhand.

"...Getting accepted there was huge, you know? 'Cause they had so many applicants, only the best got in." She stopped then, blushing. "Sorry! That sounded so conceited, didn't it?"

"It's okay," Sydney smiled. "You're right. Your school was comprised of the best of the best."

"Well," the girl replied, a shadow crossing her face, "In Camden that's not exactly tough to be."

The weight of the statement, the truth of it, stabbed at Sydney. "Good is good, Ebony, no matter where you are, or where you're from," Sydney insisted, more fiercely than she'd anticipated, and the girl shrank back a bit in surprise. Then, more gently: "You should be proud of yourself." And Ebony smiled widely at this, gratitude emanating from her like a sweet perfume.

Sydney resumed her questioning. "So you were captain of the debate team. What was that like?"

"Well, it was a happy accident, really," Ebony said as she poked out a long, thin leg from beneath her, motioning toward a collection of faint, cream-colored scars webbing her knee. "I went to cheer camp -- got a scholarship and everything! -- And ended up blowing out my knee, summer before sophomore year. It was such a bummer. I was on-track to be head cheerleader, but you know. You get lemons, you gotta make lemonade."

"So why debate?"

Ebony shrugged. "Miz Havernash suggested it. My guidance counselor. I wasn't allowed to put any weight on my knee at all, for so long...There was no alternative physical activity...And I told her I wanted to be a lawyer 'cause they help people, ya know? And she said I'd made an impression on a teacher or two for being a good arguer..."

Sydney smirked and raised her eyebrows. "For being persuasive?"

The dimples deepened, the velvety eyes alight. "Exactly!" And Sydney had no doubt.

But then, thinking of the Ashe brothers, of T-Ray and Sherrod Jefferson, she said: "Just a few more questions, if that's okay."

"Sure," Ebony smiled, and Sydney felt herself smiling too, grateful for the hopeful girl, for the hope she lent to Sydney, allowing her to believe that there were reasons to have faith in a faithless place.

"Can you tell me about your classmates? Do you keep in touch with any of them?"

"Well," she began slowly, "I tried to get everyone together, you know, for like a reunion? But it's so weird. I could barely get in touch with anyone!"

At this Sydney perked up, her pen stuttering in her hand. *Tell me about it,* she thought with a roll of her eyes, thinking of all of the dead ends she'd run into in pursuit of an interview. "What about your friends?"

She shrugged, wrapping her arms around Ariel a bit tighter. "My friends, they all...I don't know. Some of them are fine, but most of them...I don't know. It's like they turned into zombies or something."

Sydney felt her spine harden. "Zombies?"

"Yeah, they're like...I don't know. They're there, but they're *not* there at the same time." A silence fell over the girl then as she shrugged. "If that makes any sense."

"It does," Sydney nodded, although she wasn't sure that was entirely true even as she said it. "What do you think happened to them?"

"Well I've heard stuff, you know. Through the grapevine or whatever. And I've seen a few of them." She stopped when she said this -- remembering -- and released an involuntary shudder. "Like Malik Jordan..."

"Voted best looking?" Sydney's smile was mischievous.

"Oh God, and was he!" Ebony gushed. "Ooooh girl! I had such a crush on that boy!" But then her eyes grew soft and sad. "I saw him this spring, right around Easter. It was pouring rain...cold as hell. He was in line at the shelter on 17th and Grant. I'd never seen someone who...who..." she gulped, "Who was my age and you know, looked so old. He's homeless now, hooked on crack. He looked like an old man. Lost all his teeth. He was just so..." she sighed, looked at Sydney. "It was just really sad, you know?"

Sydney swallowed the lump in her throat and nodded.

"Some of the school's brightest stars are...are just so messed up. Girls I cheered with...a lot of them are, you know..." Shame tainted her face then, and Sydney's heart went out to her.

"It's okay," she said softly. "I know what they've become."

"But they weren't like that! Deshandra Carmichael? Our Valedictorian? Working in *porn*?" she shook her head, unable to believe. "And Ashanti Prince? Probably the nicest girl in our grade –- no, our whole school! President of the Future Business leaders of America! Now look at her."

Sydney remembered her encounter with Ashanti, waiting for her to finish her number at Gurlz Gurlz Gurlz on Admiral Wilson Boulevard. Sydney shuddered remembering the dank stink of the place, the way the men paced like hungry, dangerous animals, the revulsion she'd felt when the smarmy manager had approached her and asked if she was there for try-outs.

Ashanti had come off the stage and waved Sydney over to a table away from the DJ booth, where they could actually hear each other.

Ashanti was friendly if weary, and more forthcoming than some of the others, but Sydney's discomfort kept her from concentrating, until finally she couldn't take it anymore and said: "Ashanti, are you sure you wouldn't be more comfortable in...In...I don't know, different clothes?"

Ashanti had looked down then, at her naked body, and disgrace made a brief flight across her face before she looked back up, her eyes deadened, and said: "Bein' naked ain't nothin' to me no more."

Thinking of the girl's GPA at Sir Thomas More, Sydney had reached across the table then and grabbed her hand. "What are you doing here, Ashanti? You don't belong here."

"The hell I don't." She took a hard drag of her cigarette then. "First time my momma caught me an' my step-daddy, she told me I was a ho. I was seven years old; I didn't want to lay down with no man.

But she called me a ho then, and said that's all I'll ever be." Smoke snaked from her mouth, hiding her eyes. "Guess she was right."

Thinking of this, Sydney looked at Ebony. "Do you think it has to do with their parents?"

Ebony's eyebrows stitched together in confusion. "Their parents?"

"Yeah. I mean, do you think that some of your classmates would have made it like you have if they had parents like yours? Or do you think they would have joined gangs or gotten hooked on drugs or sold their bodies anyway?"

Ebony's soft eyes flickered with tears as her gaze switched from clinging to Sydney to clinging to the sunlight spilling into the room. Sydney's eyes followed, landing on the window box outside beneath the bay of windows, a crowd of bright red blooming geraniums clustered in them, their petals poised like seductive lips. Just as Ebony Valdez was a bright spot amongst Camden's plight, so was this house; neat, well cared for, its owners proud and determined to do the best they could with what they had...

Thinking of this almost made Sydney feel worse, a jumble of emotions brawling within, wishing this family could get out of Camden, wondering why they hadn't already, feeling guilty because she had, knowing that they probably would if they could...

"Ebony? You okay?"

When she shook her head, the tears fell.

"It's okay," Sydney said, moving toward the girl on instinct. "I'm sorry. I didn't mean to..."

They were quiet for a while as Sydney sat with her arm around the girl, letting her quiet sobs fall against her shoulder.

"This is an awful place. Camden. It's hell on earth, isn't it?" Ebony asked, but the question didn't warrant a response.

19

As stealth as a Boa, Bo Wrigley moved through the dim apartment as efficiently as one could without the luxury of electricity or familiarity. The former was a matter of necessity; the latter was what was of concern: he'd been in and out of the reporter's home enough by now to know its nuances, yet and still, he found himself stubbing toes, banging shins.

He was irritated as he worked, his fingers moving nimbly but his heart beating fast; hearing the sounds of the old woman's television permeating from next door, sweat inching down his brow, worried about the arrival of the reporter, not knowing when she'd return.

Normally he'd never be such a mass of nerves, but this was new territory he was venturing into, after all. And just the thought of seeing Sydney Langston's beautiful body…of having it all to himself, captured on film no less –- his to use, to take pleasure in, to get pleasure from at any time –- was enough to send him into fits of unfathomable joy.

He fixed the last of dozens of the miniscule cameras into place; it's total dimension no bigger than the head of a pin. This one went into the shower head; this one, just for him, as a special gratuity for a job well done.

And he smiled.

An hour later he was just another anonymous passenger in Coach, settling in for the five-hour direct flight to Louisiana, where his Aryan brotherhood awaited him.

20

Sydney's progress thus far:

La'Kisha Bailey: GPA 1.8. Basketball Dance Troupe (co-captain). Art Club. Voted "Class Flirt". Student at Castle's Cosmetology School (Philadelphia), set to graduate on time, plans to be a manicurist. Works part-time at Ida Isley's Dance Studio on Route 38.

Alejandro Baptiste: GPA 3.3. Color Guard. Voted "Class Clown". Patient at County Psych Hospital (no history of mental illness).

Deshandra Carmichael: GPA 4.1 (weighted to include advanced placement classes) Valedictorian. Marching Band (Flute). Black Student Union. Voted "Most Likely to Succeed". Working in porn.

Maria Guittierez: GPA 2.2. Choir. Remedial math. Nanny for "Nannies for Hire" (reputable firm). Annual income: $56,000. Plans to open her own daycare facility one day.

Mailk Jordan: GPA 2.7. Track star (Hurdles). School newspaper columnist. Voted "Best Looking". Crack head.

Yoshiro Kim: GPA 4.0. Asian American Club. Knowledge Bowl. Mock Trial. Student at Temple University, current GPA 3.8.

Sara Knotts: GPA 2.9. Cross-country. Environmental Club. Voted "Most Reliable". Volunteer at St. Mary's Assisted Living. Planned to become a nurse, like her mother and aunts. Prostitute.

Nia Otero: GPA 3.0. Head Cheerleader. Peer Helper. Voted "Most School Spirit". Unemployed, on welfare.

Satiri Patel: GPA 3.6. French Club. Marching Band (clarinet). Habitat for Humanity volunteer on weekends. Voted "Most Likely to Make a Difference". Rejected by Peace Corps. Whereabouts Unknown.

Ashanti Prince: GPA 3.2. Cheerleader (Football, Basketball). Member F.B.L.A (Future Business Leaders of America). Voted "Friendliest". Stripper at Gurlz Gurlz Gurlz on Admiral Wilson Boulevard.

DeAndre Quan: GPA 2.1, Basketball star. Voted "Most Athletic". Point Guard for Duke.

Hassan Simmons: GPA 3.7. Track star (Long Jump). National Honor Society. Voted "Best Smile". Survived two drug overdoses. Working at Desi's Car Wash on Rte. 70.

Ebony Valdez: GPA 3.9. Debate Team. Black Student Union. Spanish Club. Former cheerleader (retired due to injured knee). Rutgers, Pre-law.

Amir Watts: GPA 1.7. Film Club. Voted "Best Dressed". Owner of a hair salon. Annual Income: $77,900.

Toshi Williams: GPA 2.8. Air Force Junior ROTC Program. French Club. Drama Club. Voted "Best All-Around". Killed by friendly fire in Iraq, though military reports insinuate it looked suspiciously like a suicide, with witnesses claiming she was "spaced out" and "like a zombie". However, autopsy toxicology reports show no traces of illegal substances in her system.

21

5:45pm

When Ben and Sydney got out of the car at 6115 Green Street, an endearing dappled lane tucked away in the suburban enclave of Piedmont, the first thing they saw was Zoey, clad in head-to-toe black despite the heat of the day, swinging alone on the porch swing, her legs –- skinny and pale and still growing –- dangling, the raked-white toes of her clunky merlot-colored Doc Martens scraping against the concrete porch. Her hair –- once a willowy mass of soft fawn –- was now heart-stopping black and worming its way into a viper's nest of filthy Dred locks. Sydney felt her heart drop and, as she snuck a look at Ben, she knew he felt it, too -- likely ten-fold.

Zoey looked up when the car's doors closed in unison.

Ben and Sydney exchanged a brief look of dismay before he put on a cheerful face and called: "Hey! Small fry!" Then he made the goofiest face Sydney had seed in a long time, and she bowed her head to hide her smile. "Is it Halloween already?" He checked his watch dramatically, then he shook his head and lamented, "Aw, man, I hate to break this to you, Zoe-master, but that calendar of yours is broke as a joke!"

Rolling her eyes in typical teen-fashion, Zoey replied: "Oh c'mon, Uncle Ben." But a smile was lurking in there -- somewhere –- and Sydney felt a nugget of hope.

"You might need to call someone; couldn't tell you who, though. Some pumpkins maybe. A ghost or two. Your fellow ghouls of the night. Just as a courtesy, you know? To let them know the big night's still a couple months off, and ya'll can lay off on your costumes for the time being."

Sydney, too, saw the heavy black eyeliner, the macabre pasty foundation and blood-red lipstick. The Bardot-black ensemble. Sydney had to admit that compared to the adorable fourteen-year-old she had seen just six months before, Zoey *had* morphed into a bit of a side-show act, and no amount of Ben's warnings beforehand could have prepared her for it. Though she hated to be cruel, Sydney took one look at her and had to agree: Zoey *did* look like she was wearing a costume, and a rather off-putting one at that. Nonetheless, she quickly gave Ben a look before stepping in: "*Yeah*, Uncle *Ben*. Give it a rest. *I* think you look awesome, Zoe."

Zoey hugged her tight while Ben ruffled her hair (as best he could, gnarled mess that it was) and tickled her twice, before the trio went into the house and through the short hallway -- cozy and rife with framed family pictures Ben could name from memory -- to the kitchen, bursting with smells.

A sunshine yellow apron over her turquoise hospital scrubs, Susan Campbell was moving trays of something or other but stopped at once when she saw them, her face blooming into a smile bright enough to rival the lights of Broadway. "Oh you're here!" she exclaimed.

First she hugged Ben, fierce as a Momma bear, then Sydney, clasping both of her hands and standing back to exclaim: "My word, Sydney Langston. Just when I think you can't possibly get any more gorgeous, you go ahead and do!"

Blushing, Sydney mumbled a hasty: "Thanks." Ben smiled at her; it was rare that a woman as beautiful as Sydney didn't seem to know it, nor enjoy having it acknowledged. But, then again, that was Sydney.

"How is that sweet Nana Jean of yours?"

"Oh she's *wonderful*, same as always. I called her on my way over. She was getting ready for a date."

"Oh I love it!" Susan laughed. "Isn't she a pip?"

Sydney joined her. "I know. She's got a better love life than I do."

Ben forced himself to ignore this last comment and instead opened the oven to peek inside. "Mmm. Roast chicken. My favorite."

Susan Campbell swatted him with a dishtowel and shooed him into the breakfast nook. "Sit, sit. Tell me all about your campaign. How is it going? I've been trying to read the papers, sweetie, but I've been getting double shifts lately, and I've just been too pooped. You understand, don't you?"

Of course he did. Ben's mother had been a neo-natal intensive care nurse for nearly twenty years and loved her work, despite how difficult it could be at times. But ever since Ben's father passed away, she seemed more drained by the day-to-day than ever before. Ben knew her work was taxing but he also knew it wasn't just work that was exhausting her, either. He looked at her now, at the dark circles and the crow's feet fanning her eyes as she smiled, and he was glad to be back, away from DC. Closer to her. Home. Able to help.

He thought of the bricks then. Of Herb Heim. But then saw her face streaked with worry and feigned airiness.

"Well Ma, I hate to break it to you but you're not missing much. We're getting crushed in the press at the moment."

"But it was his brother that got in trouble, not him, right?" Susan asked.

"I know but the press is using it anyway. Trying to make him seem unethical. Guilty by association. Not only that, but they're going over everything with a fine-tooth comb. And now the opponent we thought was a non-entity is making noise. Snooping around in our fundraising, which of course is public record, but probably trying to catch us on a technicality or something and get the press on *that*."

A timer went off, and Susan rushed toward the kitchen.

"Can I do anything to help?" Sydney wanted to know. Then she spied a plastic bag on the corner, the green stalks peeking out, and snatched it. "C'mon, Zoe. Let's go peel some corn."

Susan smiled as the pair made their way to the old picnic bench in the backyard, a place where she remembered happier times.

She and Ben watched as the girls sat opposite each other, legs straddled over the weathered wood, talking and peeling the husks away before Ben turned to her. "So Ma. The message I got from Millie said you wanted me here today to talk to me about something..."

His mother looked wistful, standing at the sink and wringing her hands in a damp dishcloth as she watched Zoey laughing, her braces glinting in the late afternoon light.

"How is she?" he asked, and it wasn't until a few moments passed and she still hadn't answered that Ben realized he was holding his breath. "Mom?"

Susan Campbell sighed then, exhaling what seemed like a mountain of grief. "Which one?"

He knew what she meant: mother or daughter. Beth or Zoe.

"Either. Both." Then he looked out the window and saw the same sight she did: the child trying to play dress-up; the kid-adrift, a freshman trying to find her niche in high school...Who couldn't relate? "Zoe."

Susan squared her weary shoulders and, without taking her eyes from the picnic table said: "I wanted you to come here today because... well...Your boss. His kids are at Saint Andrews, aren't they?"

Ben was surprised she knew this. "They are, yes."

"And your boss is on the Board, no?"

"Jeez, Ma. You've really done your homework...what's this all about?"

Susan turned from the sink then and, in that instant, Ben saw and felt the enormous burden that had been placed atop his mother in the past year: the pain of suddenly losing her husband to a heart attack, the pain of losing her daughter to dope, the pain of losing baby after baby -- other people's children she came to love as much as her own -- as an occupational hazard; the pain of having to take custody of her grandchild and navigate her through life, worried now that this might not be "just a stage", that the all-black wardrobe and ridiculous face paint meant she was headed down a dark road. Or worse: already there.

Her face was defeated. "Zoey's fallen in with a bad crowd."

"No kidding," Ben said, almost to himself.

"Can you talk to him about getting Zoey in? To Saint Andrews? Senator Bruni? She probably doesn't have the grades at this point, but..."

"But it's only September! The school year started...what? A couple of weeks ago? And she's already..."

She shook her head warily. "It happened this summer. I don't know how, but it did. I was working so much, and I just didn't think..."

Ben's heart began to beat faster, guilt plaguing him and beginning to spread like a bad rash. He'd been preoccupied with the campaign, with Kat, and his selfishness suddenly astounded him. "Mom, it's not your fault. You can't blame yourself. Don't worry—"

She turned to him, fiercely now. "She has to get away from these kids. She just has to. If she doesn't, I just don't know what'll happen..." Her voice cracked then; broke.

"But what about the money? St. Andrews probably costs fifteen, twenty thousand a *semester*, Ma..."

She held up a hand, palm towards him; she'd already thought of that. *Of course she had,* he thought. *She's probably been thinking about this since...*

"She's already been suspended, Ben. Twice. This last time for a week."

"Christ, for what?"

"Skipping school the first time, drinking on school grounds this last time."

"Jesus," Ben exhaled, knowing they were both thinking the same thing: this is exactly how Beth started out.

"She was dead-drunk at ten thirty in the morning. Threw up the whole afternoon."

Through the window he watched his niece gabbing to Sydney; she was so skinny, so young. How much could it even take to get her drunk? Two beers? Three?

"She didn't even apologize. Didn't seem sorry in the least. Said it was 'her life', that she was old enough to make her own decisions."

Ben looked at his mother then. Recent-widow. Hard working nurse in a high-stress field. Playing "Mom" when her mom days were clearly over; trying to shield her granddaughter from her own daughter, the one she'd raised and never once imagined would be trading tricks for hits on the pipe. The pain -- the sheer weight of it, of so much resting on the already-bowed shoulders of a woman who should be enjoying her twilight years just like all of her friends -- travelling to great American landmarks in RV's and spending winters in warm spots -- but was instead tethered to a new and different form of motherhood, without the relief of having a husband to shoulder it with.

Ben closed his eyes and willed away the headache now growing and gaining considerable strength.

If he had been a different type of man he might have worried about his career first; that he was already planning to ask Bruni for a huge favor -- a cushy job in the Governor's mansion, one that paid six-figures and demanded only a minimal amount of his time -- in return for sending him back to the Legislature for another term. He might of thought of Kat, and the failed proposal, and how the only way to get her to say yes, to get her old man's approval, was by having said job. He might have come up with some reason to put off such a request, might have suggested they wait until the end of the semester and then re-evaluate, or some other such stall tactic.

But, for all his faults, Ben Campbell was a good guy -- some might even argue perhaps to his detriment -- and he was *not* about to let his mother down. "Of course I will, Ma," he said finally. "I'll do anything I can."

The kitchen's blue-and-white gingham curtains billowed lazily, rising and falling against the open window, reminiscent of ocean waves curling over themselves.

Susan turned to her son, her soft face a creased Asian fan: regimented, though thin and pained by even the slightest touch of too much pressure, like it might crumble or tear in a sharp wind. "Bethy's shooting up in her neck now," she said, and Ben felt sucker-punched.

"Oh, Ma." *Just when he thought it couldn't get any worse...*

His mother's voice sounded strangled. "She can't find any other veins anymore...They've all collapsed..."

"What about her feet? I thought she was doing it in her feet..." Ben was talking –- fast, though his heart was racing faster –- fear and shock swirling about him. Anger that his sister was putting her family through this, that Beth was such a poor excuse for a mother, daughter, sister; fearful that his only sibling might end up dead at age thirty-four; shock that she'd sunk to a new low, but not surprised because she was always sinking to new lows.

But most of all he felt positively sick, felt the kitchen spinning all around him. *Her neck?* He knew that was an addict's last resort; it could cause paralysis. And that was *with* a clean needle...

His mother shook her head, hanging low; her face sagging sad like a Bassett Hound's.

"Please. Ben. I hate to put anymore on your plate but..."

But he heard little else. His eyes were on Zoe as she gabbed away with Syd, animated and laughing, like the kid she was supposed to be. He rose and went to his mother, who both visibly relaxed and strengthened within his arms. "You got it, Ma," He said, his embrace growing fiercer. "You got it. It'll be okay, Ma. I promise." He felt her shoulders shake with sobs and pulled her tighter.

Just then the backdoor squeaked open and there was Zoey with Sydney right behind. Sensing something serious was taking place Sydney met Ben's eyes and quickly steered an oblivious Zoey into the family room, letting Susan continue to cry for just a moment longer. Letting Ben comfort her.

After a time Susan declared: "Alright gang. Let's eat outside." Tears discreetly wiped away and face as bright as always, she squeezed Ben's hand one last time before moving toward the oven.

Around the picnic table they all agreed that the fleet of summer mosquitoes seemed to be gone for good. The sky was baby blue with perfect pink clouds resting upon it, illuminated by a sunset that seemed intent on making sure the world knew just how perfect September could be.

Looking at Zoe working across an ear of corn typewriter-style, her calves –- pale and thin and somewhat scabby -- swinging from the faded red picnic bench, her pinkish cheeks dimpling with the odd smile -- it was actually easy to get past the harsh, jagged charcoal streaks across her eyelids, the way it reminded Ben of the color of the shadow of a painful bruise. And how it reminded him of the last time he'd seen Beth. She'd had matching shiners and had a fat, blood-crusted lip.

Zoe looked like a young Beth and Ben felt sick.

It was so grotesque the way his sister seemed determined to destroy herself. How she'd shown up high as hell at their father's deathbed; had skipped the funeral altogether. How she seemed hell-bent on making bad things worse.

His mother looked at him then, wringing her hands over and over again in her napkin. Her eyes were red-rimmed and gaping, but her smile was hopeful. Happy even. And Ben knew he had no other choice but to go to Bruni.

22

7:18pm

Tick tock, tick tock, tick tock.

Every second was as unforgiving as a guillotine as Dino Bruni considered his fate.

Always a pragmatist, he went over everything, beginning with the good things first:

#1   Ben hadn't seen anything from the papers he'd inadvertently taken from Bruni's desk before he'd left for Boston; not Heim's emails, nothing. Wrigley had paid off a luggage handler and removed them, replacing them with who knew what –- but, no matter, it was a done deal. An added bonus was that the girl wouldn't marry him and thus he could remain focused solely on the re-election. Wrigley had him and both his girls under surveillance, and they'd have to be goddamn clairvoyants to be any the wiser, Wrigley was so damn good.

#2   Heim was dead, something of his own doing, and nobody could say otherwise, no matter how many times Bruni and Sault had considered doing it themselves. Bo Wrigley had gotten the hard drive from his home and office, as well as destroyed his Statehouse personnel file.   Probably overkill, but it was done. And a happy bonus was that Heim had taken out his whole family, too –- now there was no need to worry about whether or not he'd told his wife anything; she was soon to be six feet under, too. And even if he had told her anything, and she had gone on to repeat the news, it'd be considered hearsay, plain and simple, if they ever found themselves in a court of law.

He regarded the bottle of single malt before him and filled the empty crystal snifter next to it. He took a long, deep pull –- not his first of the night, not even close -- and the anticipated burn arrived with a warm welcome.

But…(and there was *always* a 'but', now wasn't there?)…There was some bad news, too.

#1   Iggy hadn't called him, not once. His own brother, the same one that'd been nothing less than a remora of the worst kind for the majority of his life, needing advice and hand-holding at every turn, was now mum, not asking for anything for once, and it was highly disconcerting.

#2   On the other hand, he couldn't get Jarvis to shut the fuck up. Fucking guy was acting like a cat on a hot tin roof. No assurance was strong enough, no warning threatening enough. However, after tonight it might all be different; Sault was going over there and everyone knew how persuasive Sault could be. Dino held a good thought for this one. If not, he would be on the phone with Wrigley in a heartbeat, and that son-of-a-bitch Jasper would be dead before sundown.

#3   Then there was the wildcard of the evening: Micki. She'd always been a snoop, but only when it suited her whims, spending the bulk of her time wrapped up in herself and out of his business, which was just fine. Plus he'd always been able to handle her. Always. But he didn't like the way she had looked at him tonight, not at all. Usually she had no filter and whatever she was thinking just came right out of her mouth; do not pass "Go", do not collect $200, just right the fuck out. But not tonight. It was like she was holding out on him about something and he didn't like it one bit. And the last thing he needed was to have Wrigley tail his own wife. Such a request would make him feel small; like he couldn't handle his own business. And nothing could be further from the truth.

The breeze coming through the ring of open windows in his home office was lilting and gentle, and he closed his eyes against it, falling back against his chair and letting the scotch sink in.

He'd take care of everything. One way or another, it would all work out. Even if it took a fucking bloodbath, he'd get his way.

He always did.

23

7:19pm

After dinner Zoey had grudgingly gone upstairs to do homework and Susan, still in her scrubs, was drinking coffee and poking at the remnants of apple crisp with her son and one of his oldest friends, and she couldn't remember a recent time when she felt more content.

"It's just so good to have you here," Susan said, reaching across the table and clasping their hands. "Both of you."

"Thank you so much," Sydney beamed. "Everything was wonderful."

The majority of dinner conversation had centered on the mundane, and now that Zoe was out of earshot, Ben wanted to really talk. "So enough about us. How are things with you? How's work?"

"Oh you don't want to hear about that." Susan said, waving him away. When they didn't begin with a new topic she looked at them. "Or do you?"

Ben knew how much his mother loved her work, and it was the first time it occurred to him that, with his Dad gone, she had nobody to come home and talk about it with. She'd never expose Zoey to the kind of horror she saw on a regular basis. "Of course, Mom."

"Well," she said, unsure if she should reveal the whole truth or keep it "sunny-side-up", as she'd always liked to call it. She saw their faces and decided on the former. She sighed. "It's been a tough week." She ran a hand through her hair, and Ben noticed new streaks of gray that hadn't been there when he'd returned from DC, just six months ago.

He cleared his throat. "Yeah?" He could tell she was eager to unload, so he sat back to let her.

"Yeah," she continued, and she pressed her hands together. "Well. For one. There's the quintuplets. I'm sure you've heard about them?" She looked up.

"The Mondano five?" Ben chuckled. "Of course, Ma. We haven't been living in a cave."

She laughed, too. "Well they're doing great. *Just great.* And I'm *so* glad. Their parents are such dolls. With all they've been through with fertility treatments and the like...and of course she was on bed-rest through the latter of her pregnancy... but everyone –- all of them -- are doing so well at this point that they should be leaving soon. Things will certainly be quieter without them, without the press and all, but of course the end-goal is always to have them return home safely."

"That's awesome, Mom."

Sydney nodded, smiling broadly. "Really, it is."

Susan Campbell sighed then, and both Ben and Sydney looked into their coffee mugs, knowing what to come would be sad. "But that's the good news. There are the others, of course. Like the poor Hopkins baby. Nobody knows what's wrong with him and believe me when I tell you that they've had every expert in to take a look at him. He's just so small, but he's not premature, which is weird; and his brain activity is downright bizarre. His mother's young, and she's prone to these...I don't know...*outbursts*. Who could blame her? Her baby's in the NICU with this myriad of issues and nobody knows why, so nobody can *tell* her why. But what's worse is that nobody seems to be able to handle her, or want to even try, and so it's this vicious cycle: Nobody has any answers, so she explodes, and nobody wants to be around her so she can't get any answers, and so on and so on. She's taken a shine to me for some reason, and I finally just said to her: 'Listen, Diamonique. You've got to —"

Sydney's head shot up. "Wait a sec. Are you talking about Diamonique Keyes? From Camden?"

Susan looked puzzled. "Yes, that's who I'm---Why? Do you know her?"

Sydney blushed then as she fumbled her hands around the base of her coffee mug. "Well, not *personally*, not yet, but I'm working on this story about the first class of Sir Thomas More Tech. You know. The charter school—"

"The Senator's school!" Susan said brightly.

"Yes," Sydney said, eying Ben. "Bruni's school, and I have a bunch of interviews on my agenda, and she's one of them. According to the yearbook, she was voted 'Most Popular', and while I'd like to interview every single person in the class, it's a human interest piece so I'm trying to pick out a handful of people and, you know, kinda see 'where are they now?'."

Susan's face went from lively to dark in an instant. "Well, I hate to be the bearer of bad tidings but..." she sighed, profoundly. "The poor girl's in hell at the moment. This sweet little baby of hers...Well. I just don't know how *anyone* could handle it, let alone a nineteen-year-old single mother."

"Do you know anything about the father?"

"Just that he's in jail."

"Surprise, surprise," Ben muttered, and both women glared at him. He looked up from his rumbling phone. "Sorry, but I gotta take this," he said, "We have a photo op on Tuesday. Trying to get some good press for a change," and let the door close behind him as he made his way to the backyard.

They turned back to their conversation and were animated as they talked on, until finally Ben came back in and said: "I hate to end this, Ma, I really do, but I need to get back to some folks. If you knew how many messages I have..."

Susan walked them out the car and, just after she hugged her and before she climbed in, Sydney asked: "Susan, would you mind if I came by during your shift? I'd love to meet Diamonique and I -"

Susan patted her arm. "Of course, love. Ben knows my schedule. You come by anytime you want. Your story sounds great."

"Thank you so much," Sydney said and hugged her again before she settled in next to Ben, who called out: "Love you, Ma!"

"You, too, my precious baby boy!" she called back, and Ben was smiling as he could still see his mother –- standing on the patch of movie-stub sized lawn, waving goodbye well after he'd moved onto the next block, and the next, and the next.

24

8:49pm

No sooner had Bo Wrigley stepped out of the stale air of the plane and into the sultry Louisiana eve than the sweat started streaming; thick worm-like lines snaking from forehead to neck and down the spine, and no matter how many times he leaned forward and to the side, his faded fatigues stuck to the vinyl driver's seat of the rental the whole way there.

The ruthless humidity pressed-in all around, the songs of cicadas rising like smoke from the dusty banks straddling the road. The moon: a lone fang dangling among nothingness. The road darker than any sane notions of possible, and he cursed that damn Avis woman for the fiftieth time as he leaned forward and peered into the black. He'd ordered an SUV but had somehow ended up with *this* piece of shit, and was now concerned his little putt-putt might careen off into the muddy waters at any turn, and rightly so.

He reminded himself to be patient: not just because the drive was long and tedious, but also because it was easy for a Northerner to forget just how much slower things moved in this part of the country. He'd made the mistake before, of letting his eagerness get the better of him, of being too pushy. Or, as Jesse Timms liked to call it: "too fuckin Yank". And if there was one man in this world who resented the hell out of being rushed, who moved *at his own goddamn pace, thank you very much,* it was Timms.

Whistling like a frantic kettle the whole way, Bo passed the riverboat casinos lit up like Christmas, the smoky BBQ joints and dusty RV parks; the fan boats tethered to rickety docks, the ancient seed & feeds. He passed tractor supply companies, Conoco's, little white churches, and more places claiming to have the Delta's best craw daddies and etouffe than he cared to count. Scraggly, top-heavy pines whipped by, reflecting in the bayous on either side of the vacant road; the curly-cue-sounding French names flying past in rapid succession like sheet music until his tired eyes blurred them into one long, indecipherable word.

The can of Red Bull balanced between his knees was warm by now but he drank it anyway. Although, in the past, trips down to Jesse Timms country had been purely for pleasure, this one was strictly for business. And he had to bring his "A" game, without a doubt, because Timms was a hard sell and Timms didn't fuck around. True, they'd been friends since Week One of Black Op's Basic Training, but there was no room for sentimentality in Timms' world, and he wasn't about to make any for *anybody*.

By the time the road narrowed to dirt and the untamed brush began to intrude further and further into the car's path, Bo was jumpy. The twang of country music had long ago given way to the unsettling cries of a fanatical evangelist preacher shrieking through the tinny fuzz of the car radio, giving him bad jolt, making his mind play tricks on him just as his eyes had been doing, making him wonder if the crazy preacher was talking only to him.

Moonlight didn't seem to stretch this far into the bayous and he was getting sorry his cell wouldn't work out here. Initially he'd been glad for this; Lord knew Bruni would be punching redial every ten, demanding an update, and he had no desire to look like someone's lackey in front of Timms. His phone would be confiscated upon arrival of course, whereupon Timms' own lackeys would be monitoring the incoming calls and reporting to their leader like clockwork, suspicious little soldiers that they were. That he'd trained them to be.

But it was darker than Bo Wrigley thought possible, darker than the outer edges of space, darker than was naturally comfortable, and he was beginning to wonder if maybe he'd missed the turn. It wouldn't be the first time. Though he understood the reasoning behind having the compound way the fuck out here in the boondocks where a person could wander for weeks without seeing another soul, it didn't make the place any less creepy. And Bo Wrigley had been in a lot of creepy places.

He slowed the compact and pulled it to the side of the road, gravel sputtering and coughing behind.

At that same moment something -- a deer? -- Darted from the black and streaked in front of the headlights of the rental, arresting his heart in his chest. His arms and legs flailed in reaction, his knees and elbows locking into steel as he slammed his breaks so hard the seatbelt cut into his throat, choking him. The world blurred around him, swirling black against mottled gray, and when he lifted his head and the dust had finally settled, his heart was still jack-hammering as he felt a rush of pure terror blaze across his eyes when he saw just how close he was to the edge of the embankment to the blue-black bayou, a flash of yellow gator eyes from down below, content and lying in wait. He'd been close to death so many times before but this was different. Back then he'd been a marine, and he'd had a load of guys behind him, watching his back. But now he was on his own, out here in this godforsaken abandoned land. Would anyone have ever found him? Would anyone have even bothered to look?

Coughing hard, he rubbed his throat, tilting the rearview mirror to see just how bad the damage was. *Ahhh. He'd seen worse.* He turned it back and pressed his hands against his tired eyes, rubbing his face, hoping to quiet the jitters hopping along his skin, up his neck, long enough to engage the GPS. He drained the rest of the Red Bull, waiting for a satellite somewhere –- anywhere -- to locate his position but, just as he'd figured, it was a lost cause...

By design the compound was damn near impossible to find. And that was for those who actually *knew* what they were looking for in the first place. Timms, of course, wanted it this way: A headquarters impossible to infiltrate; an organization so tight there had never been a defector; an operation as covert as a corpse, so underground that somehow Timms had never been arrested, had never even gotten so much as a jaywalking ticket: a monumental feat, you'd have to admit, no matter what your politics.

Of course it would be ludicrous to think the FBI and CIA and Homeland Security and their ilk didn't know who Jesse Timms was; they did. Oh boy, they did. He was Public Enemy Number One as far as hate crimes went, suspected of orchestrating the bombings of hundreds of abortion clinics, synagogues, and Baptist churches over the years. Even the home of a Supreme Court judge. But he'd never been caught, and they wanted him, bad. They just could never get close enough to actually *find* him.

Once he'd calmed his nerves Bo checked the mileage on the speedometer, confirming he still had ten miles to go. Just like cell phones, written directions to the compound were strictly forbidden. He'd made that mistake once and never again, although one time, years ago, after a two-year stretch without being able to sneak away from Jersey, from Bruni, for even one visit, he'd written them in pencil on a small piece of paper and swallowed it just before he'd reached the outskirts.

But that was unnecessary tonight. He'd been here just this past spring, and his bearings were all coming back to him now. He slowed down as he made his way to turn off the semi-beaten path, gravel crunching under the tires of the shitty little compact he'd had to settle for. Well, at least it was American. Last thing he needed was a sermon on *that*. He loved Timms like a brother, but his tendency to lecture anyone -- his own peers included -- rubbed Wrigley raw at times.

And then, all of a sudden, there was white: glaring, heart-arresting bright white lights so all-encompassing he had a hard time catching his breath.

What in the world...?
But then he knew.
After a few moments longer than was considered comfortable by anyone's standards the hand-held flood lights were lowered, revealing a semi-circle of no-nonsense guards poised like statues: guns cocked, loaded, and hungry as hell to rise to the occasion.

"State your business." A baritone demanded before he'd had time to adjust to the new level of bright.

"Here for Jesse Timms," he stuttered, his eyes pinched into slits, sounding more unsure of himself than he wanted it to, as he rolled down the manual window at a furious pace.

The guard was skeptical to say the least and moved in closer, close enough for Bo to see his shaved head and white tank top; his tapestry of Nazi tattoos, and barely shave-able baby face.

And his AK-47.

The guard in charge was eighteen if he was a day, and Bo saw him motion to someone in the dark, far past his line of sight. All he could make out in the murky moonlight was the glinting chain of a succession of eager-looking Colt M-4 carbines amid the bloodcurdling fangs of a pack of snarling German Shepherds trained to kill -- all fixed on him.

"He expecting you?" His tone and face told the world he didn't believe a goddamn word coming out of anyone's mouth besides Timms'.

Bo swallowed hard. "Yes. I'm an old friend. Bo Wrigley," he said, a bit vexed at this third degree he was getting. *Didn't they have some sort of list of approved visitors?* But then, when he thought about it, he guessed not. They were out here in the middle of nowhere for a reason: they didn't want any fucking visitors.

The guards –- a goddamn brigade of them now –- surrounded his car, spitting tobacco juice as they stared him down, rifles pointed, lit up in the muggy night by his headlights like apparitions.

But then someone –- the person, or people, beyond in the dark -- must've given approval because the head guard consulted his bluetooth for only a moment before nodding his authorization. "Alright

Mr. Wrigley." There were no smiles, no offers of apology for any inconvenience. "Junior here'll ride with you up to the main house."

"Oh that won't be necessary. I know where I'm going. But thanks."

Thick as cinderblock, the guard was about as yielding as one. He jerked his head toward a kid who may have been chubby but was so light on his feet that he was in Bo's rental and pulling him out of it before he'd even breathed again, his anger at being manhandled by these kids growing by the second. Security had always been at a premium at the compound but this was ridiculous.

But then he remembered. It was a conversation he and Timms had had sometime in the spring when Bo had come down for a little R & R, needing to get away from yet another of those god-awful Jersey winter/springs when everything is shaggy-dog-wet and chill-bone cold. He'd needed a reprieve before Bruni's primary campaign got off the ground, some good old-fashioned southern hospitality to do a body good. Sunshine and swimming holes. Hot barbeque and cold beers and catching fish from the dock. *And well,* he'd thought, *a little underage pussy never hurt anybody, now did it?*

"You think shit's tight now? Boy, just you wait," Timms had said. "Federal government's shady as hell as it is. And now they got a no-good nigger runnin' shit?" Timms spat tobacco as he slugged on his High Life, his voice veering from its normal, unnervingly even tone to reveal incredulousness that could have been construed as having a hint of panic if Bo hadn't known the man better. "No tellin' what they'll try an' do to shut us down. They'll take any ol' reason to come lock our asses up, like we some kind of common criminals."

He remembered it now, precisely. End of April. The 20th to be exact. Jesse Timms' conversations were never interrupted, but he'd made an exception this one time, on this day, when a gaggle of his girls had come in then –- young, skinny, trailer park girls with dark roots showing through bleached blonde, daisy duke cutoffs and big dopey smiles –- the prettiest of them all, Jesse's bitch-of-the-moment carrying a home-baked sheet cake and presenting it to Jesse like a sacrificial first born, the giant swastika made out of precise trails of chocolate chips. They'd all sung happy birthday then, and the one-time brief interruption was allowed in favor of honoring Hitler's birthday a la mode.

Just then his thoughts were interrupted as a wide gate swung open to reveal a waiting Humvee and before he knew it, the chubby kid was guiding him by the elbow. He didn't need to glance over his shoulder to know that his rental was being taken somewhere to be rifled through, his bags searched –- anything suspicious disposed of, never to be seen again –- and his vehicle impounded until his departure.

But even if all went well –- and that was a big "if" -- when his departure would be was anyone's guess.

25

9:04pm

Poppy the maid would have been livid to have been beckoned at such an hour for anything, let alone to serve things to folks who could've easily gotten it their own damn selves, when she should have been out of her uniform and into her jammies by now -- her aching, diabetic feet propped on a pillow, one hand in a bag of pork rinds, the other on the remote, waiting for the latest re-rerun of *Dr. Phil* to illuminate the miniscule screen of her bedroom television -- but she was even more so because it was for *him*.

Using her hip to open the swinging door separating the butler's pantry from the dining room, a freshly polished silver tray balanced on her open palms, her temper was calmed by thoughts of what her friend LaShay Dupree had told her. How when she'd regaled her with a re-enactment of the scene between Bruni and Jarvis underneath the bridge, LaShay had educated her with all kinds of juicy knowledge of the wrong-doings of Camden's politicians past -- of how these elected suits lied and robbed just as readily as the thugs on the street. How they preached one thing then summoned their underlings to do another. Of how they clawed and rose to the top so they could lecture the masses like preachers, evoking legislation like scripture...And how they all eventually got caught and sent away, like the criminals they were. LaShay had woven a tale so dramatic and sensational Poppy had sat as rapt as if she were watching her daytime soaps, each tale of deception and demise more outlandish than the last.

LaShay had offered even more, too: salacious inferences of what that smarmy Senator and her brother-in-law had been so heated about that day, about the recent articles in the papers that Poppy never bothered to read, and the reasons why Bruni might've been motivated to treat Jarvis like his little bitch.

"They up to no good," LaShay had said simply, leaning back beneath the drier at Lettie's Hair Salon, letting the pink curlers work their magic.

"You think so?" Poppy had wanted to know, her voice carrying over the noise of the driers, well into the recesses of Lettie's.

"Chile, please," LaShay had said with a satisfied smirk. "I *know* so."

It was enough to make her so happy she might've skipped into the living room like Sally-go-lucky and done a little tap dance with the tray resting on her head, but then that snooty-ass engineer had had the nerve to laugh when she'd asked him what "neat" meant. *Who the hell ever heard of a damn drink bein' neat?* She'd felt like screaming, hand on hip, neck zigzagging, attitude punctuated by the sucking of her teeth. *Damn! The only difference her kinda folks knew about drinks was hot and cold. He think he better than everyone 'cause his name all over ev'ry building an' billboard in town, but he got a whole 'nother thing comin'...*

But instead, here she was, poised to serve both the Mayor and that rude-ass cracker his drink, "neat" and all, without even a simple word of thanks.

She was used to being ignored, and this night was no different. No matter what the preacher said on Sunday –- no matter how good it might make her feel at the time to hear how the meek inherited the earth –- Monday would come and she'd be right back to being invisible, rich folk moving past her like she was nothing more than a shadow, only bothering to pause long enough to let her knew what they needed, and that they needed it fast.

For an example she need not look any further than her own sister. Henrietta had been her best friend at one time; the two had grown up just a few years apart, and Poppy felt she had always treated Henrietta as good as any sister could. She'd made it a mission to dote on her, even, and was happy to do so. At a certain point –- she guessed it to be around the time she quit school –- Henrietta's beauty became the topic of many discussions. "There's just somethin' 'bout that girl," people around the way would say about Henny, shaking their heads as if they just couldn't quite wrap their minds around something as strange as one sister being so beautiful and the other so homely.

Henrietta's light skin and straight hair was the envy of their little Georgian community; not only that, but she somehow managed to be slim without being skinny, and curvy without the promise of chunk. Everything Poppy was not.

Little Henny had bloomed into an exquisite young woman and despite the many suitors lined up around the block, she'd gone on to marry a Yankee: the man named Jarvis from some foreign northern city who would one day become Mayor. For a while she'd stayed the same, and though Poppy couldn't quite put her finger on *when* her sister had changed, it almost didn't matter because all that did was that Poppy was certain that she *had*.

Things only got worse when Horace left, and poor Poppy had never seen it coming. To her credit, Henrietta had stepped in to take care of her older sister in her time of need, flying down to Georgia and staying for a whole week, bringing her mince pies and letting her cry over her runaway husband till the wells ran dry. Horace had gone to Reno one day and never came home. So the story went, he'd hit it big at craps and found a peppy little cocktail waitress only-too-happy to help him spend it. Two months later he'd come home, broker than when he'd left –- his whisky-slinging harlot long gone -- and Poppy had almost taken him back.

Almost.

But she hadn't even the chance to think about it because before she knew it Henrietta had swooped in, scooping her up and insisting that she come live at the Mayor's big mansion on a beautiful river in New Jersey. "But what about *my* house?" Poppy had wanted to know, and hated the way her sister looked around the place, as if the walls were contagious. It might've been little, but it was clean. Well. Sort of.

"We'll just sell it," she'd said, patting Poppy's hand, as if it were the easiest thing in the world. "Don't you worry none."

But no sooner had she moved away from the only home she had ever known and into the big house on The Banks than Jarvis put her to work. "Need to earn your keep," he'd said to her, handing her a mop, as if by ripping her away from her snug southern home and bringing her here to live alongside them in some godforsaken urban jungle he was doing her some kind of favor or something.

Next thing she knew she'd gotten into trouble with that church's damn bingo and that hellhole Atlantic City (and all them damn credit cards) and before she could blink an eye he had her in a uniform, running her ragged, acting as if she was lower than the ground he walked on, as if that had been his plan all along.

So, despite what the preacher said, Poppy only felt good as long as the sermon lasted; then it was right back to being invisible old Poppy who never seemed to get things quite right.

She set the steaming porcelain cup of tea and its accompanying saucer in front of the Mayor and wanted to roll her eyes at how ridiculous it was for a grown-ass man to be sipping out of such a dainty thing, but then the engineer grabbed the tumbler of scotch from her hands before she could set it on the coaster, surprising her, and she forgot about her nasty brother-in-law at once.

"Easy, easy," the engineer reprimanded as he eased the glass from her hand, looking to her like he might actually lick the dining room table if she were to spill a drop. "*I'll* take that."

Poppy rolled her eyes. "G'night, gentlemen," she said, her tone perfectly clear and respectable, belying her emotions.

But they'd already moved on. Neither man's gaze met hers, let alone held it, and so she shuffled off as they continued to talk, and continued to ignore her. Their conversation fell against her back as she left, but Poppy felt her ears perk at the words. She might've been just a maid, but she knew scandal when she heard it and so, as soon as she made her way across the threshold into the shadowy pantry, she decided *Dr. Phil* could wait.

"—Jasper," said the calm, lilly-white voice. It was a voice Poppy knew well: the kind used to giving orders and having them followed without question. Long ago LaShay had filled her in about the engineer, too.

"One of the richest men in allllll of Jersey," she'd said, and Poppy's eyes had bulged to the size of beanbags, unable to comprehend such an incredible thing. And, although she didn't quite grasp what exactly an engineer was, or what they did, it almost didn't matter, because the only thing she could ever think of when she saw the man on one of his billboards or riding around Camden in his Malbach, being driven around like it was the most natural thing in the world, all she could think about was the way he looked at Jarvis as though he were dumber than dirt, and for that reason alone, she was mystified by the man.

"Listen, Jarvis, you need to understand that—"

"I don't need to understand shit!" A fist pounded the dining room table and Poppy jumped in her orthopedics amid the dark of the pantry. "This thing is outta control, and it's gettin' closer to home, in case your cracker-ass ain't noticed!"

Poppy's eyes protruded in the dark. *Cracker-ass? Cracker? Ass?* Did Jarvis *really* just refer to the great engineer as a...a...*cracker?* She placed the back of her hand against her forehead...

Well, maybe not faint -- too dramatic -- but swoon, perhaps. She leaned forward instead, straining her neck and her ears; worried she might miss a single syllable.

"—Jarvis, *listen*. Please. Heim was crazy as hell; out of his mind, even. It has nothing to do with us."

"No?" He was downright snotty in his skepticism, and Poppy felt anticipation running through her like electricity, punctuating itself with her widened eyes and a giddy smile upon her face.

"No." The voice was firm, confident.

"Well I don't believe you."

Poppy felt her chest grow tight, and realized that she was indeed holding her breath. She let it escape in small, incremental tufts while sneaking peeks between the swinging door and the jamb, where an inch-or-so gap let dim light pour forth. She pictured the Mayor and imagined how, on an ordinary night, she might have made their drinks and retreated through the kitchen and up the back steps to the corridor that led to her small bedroom...

But not tonight.

Poppy held still and listened.

Listened and held still.

It wasn't easy; the walls of the old house were as thick as a tomb's. But each time she heard something that caught her curiosity, she reeled it in like a catfish from the pole, socked it away and demanded her mind to commit it to memory. She may not have been the smartest girl on the block but she wasn't the dumbest, either, and from the little she had gleaned already from LaShay and that little meeting under the bridge, she already knew that Jarvis was in a whole mess of trouble. That Senator had been mad as hell, and now he'd sent his crony to talk to Jarvis and finish his dirty work.

This is better *than Dr. Phil,* she thought with a smirk. After all, they were talking about Camden, and if she couldn't connect the dots about what they were talking about, LaShay certainly could.

Much to her dismay they had lowered their voices, and now all the straining in the world couldn't help her hear. Briefly she considered her options and, not one to beat around the bush, she decided to venture bravery and creaked open the swinging pantry door just a touch -- just enough to let a thin column of light pour forth -- just an itsy bitsy smidge to let her hear and see anything she needed to.

And just in time to see the engineer hand Jarvis a sweet-smelling stack of crisp new money as thick as a brick.

His hands were clasped behind his head as he lay, covers tucked under his chin, Henrietta snoring softly by his side, the smell of her jasmine lotion mixing nicely with each whir of the oscillating fan in the corner and wafting past.

But Jarvis could not relax; he lay rigid as a corpse, dread pricking at him like fire ants, sweat slithering past his temples and pooling on the linens beneath.

What Sault had said had made sense: Any credibility Heim might have had evaporated the second he decided to play Rambo and shoot up his nearest and dearest.

"He proved once and for all he was a fucking lunatic, and no jury would ever be able to get past the fact that he annihilated his own family. We're talking a mass execution here. C'mon Jarvis. Use your head. You're smarter than that."

This was true, and Jarvis had felt his apprehension toward Heim melting a bit as Sault continued to talk and the healthy glasses of scotch continued to soothe.

"But what about Iggy?" he'd asked, interrupting Sault and sending an impatient grimace across the engineer's tanned face. *This is what had been troubling him most*, and just the thought of their exchange by the bridge and how Bruni had done nothing to assuage his fears -- belittled him, even -- was enough to resurrect the sleeping anger in Jarvis. He'd sat up in his chair then, intent on getting some real answers.

Sault smiled warmly -- as Cheshire a smile as Jarvis had ever seen -- waving a pair of Cubans produced from his shirt pocket and nodding toward the terrace. Jarvis rose and followed in silence, as if he were a guest in his own home.

The gentle lapping of the Delaware below waltzing with the dainty breeze of the summer night was enough to fool anyone into thinking they were in a place of peace. But before the tips of their cigars had even turned amber the wail of police sirens carved through the dark, sending him shuddering despite himself.

"Little too close for comfort, eh Jarvis?" Sault mused with a chuckle, and the condescension in his voice evoking an irritated Jarvis to the point of insubordination.

"Yeah well it ain't exactly *utopia*," Jarvis retorted, knowing the choice of words would sting.

Though Sault coughed a bit, it was muffled enough to come across as dignified, and he recovered as quickly as if it had never come to pass.

Ignoring Jasper's little dig, he leaned his elbows on the terrace rail and toked his stogie, smiling serenely as though he'd never seen a sight so pretty and didn't know when he might again, so he'd better soak it in while he could.

Jarvis had to hand it to him, the man was good -- but Jarvis wasn't buying any of it. Not anymore. "I *said*," he continued, feeling bold: "What about Iggy?"

Sault smiled then. He'd been waiting for this, you could tell. He took his time answering, savoring his cigar and gazing over Camden as if it were a Hawaiian sunset.

"The Bruni family is tight, Jarvis," he said finally. "Always has been, always will be. And nobody knows his own brother better than Dino. Trust me when I tell you that Dino has been taking care of Iggy his entire life, and Iggy knows he needs him. We have nothing to worry about."

This made sense, but still he pressed on.

"So Dino has seen him then?"

Sault's smile faded.

"Listen Jarvis. You have a lot on your mind. Perhaps I can help ease a bit of that burden."

That hefty dose of cash had been persuasive as well. But Jarvis still felt ill at ease, although the smartest part of himself told him he better not voice his concern again. He'd said his piece, and any further suspicion should be well guarded. These were dangerous men he was dealing with, and only a fool with a death wish would be remiss.

26

10:29pm

As his key jingled in the lock of his apartment, he heard his landline ringing inside.

"I'm coming," he mumbled as he kicked past a Fed Ex box and opened the door, flicked on the switch, and snatched it from its cradle.

He hadn't realized how tired he was till he flopped onto the couch and heard Digger Vance's voice coming through the line.

"Campbell, what's up? I've been making myself acquainted with your friend Mr. Heim."

Dear God, he thought. *Do I even want to know?*

"Yeah?"

"Yep, and I gotta tell you...guy's clean as a whistle."

Ben sat up at this, disbelieving. "Really?" He had been expecting the worst; or at least something bad. Not, well...*nothing* at all.

"Yep. Just some government drone who's worked for your Department of Environmental Protection since he graduated. Came from a normal family, has hardly caused a ripple his whole life. Regular Joe Blow. Barely ever gotten a parking ticket, guy's so clean."

Ben slumped, speechless.

"You still there, Campbell?"

"Yeah, yeah. Sorry. I'm still here," he said, running a hand through his mass of floppy curls. "I just can't believe it, that's all. This guy's been friggin' stalking me for weeks. It *had* to be for a reason."

"Well, not necessarily. Not if he was just some nut. Which, if you recall from the other night, he *is*. He had no notable domestic issues, wife was some dopey small town girl turned secretary at a local yokel real estate firm -– also clean as can be -- two little girls on the honor roll. And yet he murdered them. So yeah, I'd say you could chalk up the phone calls to pure nuttiness, plain and simple."

"But still."

"Listen dude, I'm stumped myself. I mean, unless you've got some shithole environmental wasteland you've cleaned up and need approval to turn into an industrial park or something, I have no idea why you'd ever even be in contact with this guy."

Ben sat up at this. "What do you mean?"

"I mean that's what he did for the State. He was the one in charge of keeping records of the brownfields and Superfund sites that got recycled into useful land. He was just your typical pencil-pushing bureaucrat. Nothing more, nothing less. I'm sorry I couldn't help you more, but listen Campbell; I'd just let it go. You've got enough on your plate to worry about, with the election, and the trial and everything..." He lowered his voice then. "And I'm sorry to hear about Kat."

"She told you?"

"Yeah. It sucks man. I'm sorry. But you know, it's not a lost cause. If Bruni wins and you land in on your feet, snag a job in a good spot... you never know. Her old man might come around."

Ben felt himself tense. "Listen dude, thanks for the help but I gotta go."

"Alright man. Look, if you need anything else --"

"Thanks, but I'm cool." And he hung up, pissed as hell. He hated the idea of his life being gossip fodder.

But at just the mention of her name, all he wanted was to do was talk to her. For too long now he couldn't stop thinking about the bricks in his luggage, and the unearthly feeling of being watched. And, despite what Digger said, he couldn't (wouldn't?) believe there wasn't more to the Heim thing. It just didn't make any sense. None at all. And Kat had always been a reliable voice of reason, especially when it came to politics. Surely she'd have some valuable insight into this. He could almost hear her voice, switching from languid/casual to the clipped, no-nonsense tone she adopted the moment "business" was introduced into the conversation: a trait he doubted she'd ever noticed about herself, but had always been one he'd marveled at; admired even.

Oh Kat, he thought with a great sigh of...what? Regret? Resentment? Relief? The latter two didn't even seem possible, not now. Forget the Old Man and the condescending way she criticized his career decisions –- those things weren't even on the radar at the moment. All he could think of was the buttery way her skin felt just out of the shower, and the way she sounded when she laughed and how it was something like music. He imagined that pert little nose he'd kissed a hundred times, and how he'd never seen her toes bare: every single day of the two years he'd known her they'd always been painted. These details seemed critical right now. Evidence, somehow, that he knew her better than anyone. Certainly more than Tad Ernst. Possibly even better than her own father.

But nothing mattered more at the moment than knowing everything was going to be okay; than feeling her arms around him and hearing her say it.

That J. Harrison Almond wouldn't find anything unsavory in their fundraising reports.

That the press would move on from Iggy's trial.

That there was a perfectly reasonable explanation as to why a perfectly insane stranger had been contacting him for weeks and weeks, and why there had been bricks in his bag.

That Bruni would be able to get Zoey into St. Andrews and away from that bad crowd.

That Zoey would be okay. That his Mom would.

And Beth. His poor, lost sister. He needed to hear someone who loved him tell him that they'd find her before she was lost forever. That she'd be okay.

That they all would.

※

The Senator answered on the first ring, as if he'd been expecting him.

"Oh Campbell, it's you," he said, and Ben realized he was expecting someone to call, but it certainly wasn't him.

"I'm sorry to call so late but I needed to ask you something."

"Everything good?" Bruni asked, distracted. Ben was used to this question; Bruni always asked it when he was in a hurry, and there was only one answer he was looking for.

"Yes, everything's fine. I uh," he cleared his throat, "just need a favor is all."

"Talk to me."

And Ben did. The healthy snifter of scotch had lent itself to Ben giving more detail to Bruni than he normally would have, but it didn't seem to faze the Senator in the least.

When Ben was done telling his story, Bruni replied: "That's a shame," his voice laced with gravity. "I had a brother involved with drugs and...Well...it's a helpless feeling. Nearly put my mother in an early grave."

"So anything you can do...I would be grateful. I really would be."

"Consider it done."

"Really?"

"Really."

"That's great, Dino. I almost don't even know what to say."

Dino laughed: a rarity. "How about you thank me?"

Ben laughed, too. "Thank you, Dino. Thank you so much."

When all was said and done, the entire conversation took less than seven minutes, and when he hung up, Ben felt almost foolish for getting so worked up about asking for help. Hell, this was Dino Bruni he was dealing with. They were tight. And family meant everything to Bruni. *Of course* he understood. Ben poured himself another drink and called his mother to tell her the good news.

27

Monday
12:11am

Sterling Sault was not happy.

His cell was off, his slippered feet propped upon Italian leather, his wine glass full: typical indications of a relaxing night at home. But the screw smeared across his face told another story.

Melissa was curled on the couch, her attention focused on the Late Night Movie channel; Julia Roberts playing the part of hooker-with-a-heart-of-gold: a notion he found so ludicrous it only confirmed to him that his latest girlfriend might just be the dumbest one yet, which was no easy feat. She laughed as Julia soaked in a bubble bath and bee-bopped to *Prince*, and Sterling felt himself cringe. "You mind?"

Melissa looked as though she'd been slapped; startled more than pained, her eyebrows and pert mouth surprised into a childish pout. He nodded toward the remote. "Volume."

"Sorry." Like a surly teenager she rolled her eyes.

A moment later he saw her hand sneak to the remote and turn it back up. As if he wouldn't notice. As if he was as stupid as she.

He rose and made his way down the hall, her calling after him: "Where you goin', honey? Hey honey bear?"

But he ignored her. She was irritating him. He supposed it was his own fault; he had picked her, after all.

But he had a short fuse tonight. Shorter than usual.

These people were driving him nuts. *Fucking politicians. If only they'd relax.* Everything was fine. Everything was *fucking fine.* Ever since he'd left his house, Jasper and his whining had been ringing incessantly in his ears. The worries about Iggy. The election. Heim. And it was making him crazy.

He took to a chaise lounge on the veranda and fired up a Cuban. Ever since his last divorce he'd made a penthouse in Center City Philadelphia his home, and now as he stretched out, the lights of the cityscape mingling with the starry night, he had a hard time remembering why he'd ever lived anywhere else.

Melissa appeared in the doorway. "Can I get you anything?"

He considered his wine: Plump Jack, usually a favorite, but tonight a paltry comfort after such an exhausting exchange with Jasper. He tossed the remains into the row of landscaping bordering the spacious veranda. "Scotch on the rocks, babe. And make it a healthy one."

September was languid all around him and he felt a shift of burden dispel with each shake of the trees' leaves in the balmy breeze. He looked up. Soon enough red then brown would replace the green, and campaign season would be in full swing, as well as all the headaches that came along with it. Last thing he needed was pointless drama created by paranoid politicians, on top of all the other fundraising and ass-kissing he'd need to do in order to secure his projects and status among the decision-makers who could make the difference of a few extra million in his bank account.

He puffed his cigar. *Fucking Jasper. Had his panties in a bunch and now they had to talk him off the ledge.*

There was no proof so there was anything to worry about. None whatsoever. In fact, Sterling would have been more worried if Heim *hadn't* killed his wife. Then there might be a chance someone would know. But at least he'd had the sense to take her out as well, and the chances decreased significantly that anyone knew of their little arrangement.

They'd also averted another crisis: Bruni's campaign manager had picked up those emails, but he'd never seen them. Wrigley had taken care of that. And now Bo had wired everything -- Campbell's apartment, car, office. Same with his little reporter friend. He hadn't gotten to their cell phones yet, but it was only a matter of time; Wrigley was good. Who else could have sneaked past all those cops and gotten Heim's hard drive and personnel file? They were in the clear. Now if he could only get them all to calm down.

Plus he had other things to worry about. Sault & Sault was the lead firm on several multi-million dollar projects from here to Harrisburg to Manhattan to Baltimore: everything from bridges to schools to courthouses to jails. Getting Bruni re-elected was a priority, but he was just one of a hundred politicians Sterling Sault needed in office. True, he was an old friend, but Sterling couldn't spend all of time preoccupied with this issue, babysitting the pair of them. His foot was coming down. Right after the fundraiser. Which reminded him...

He drew his phone from his slacks.

His assistant sounded groggy when she answered, and it was then that he realized it was well after midnight.

"Sarah?"

"Um, oh sorry," fumbling, "Um Yes, Mr. Sault?"

"Where are we on the event for Dino Bruni?"

There was a muffled sound, something like a moan, and he imagined her sitting up and turning on the lamp in her tidy bedroom, her husband beside her cringing as he rolled away from the light.

"Um..." He heard the shuffling of papers. "Everything's fine, Mr. Sault. I have everything under control. Will you be in the office tomorrow?"

"For a little while."

"Well I'll have a full status report on your desk first thing."

"Good. See you then."

Jabbed thumb, end call.

He always did a big event for Bruni, right here at the house, which was always well attended and well run. Sarah and the girls from the office always did a great job -- best caterers, best invitations, best people invited, with the deepest pockets -- despite the fact that they technically weren't supposed to do anything by way of fundraising for political candidates, but that was of little concern to Sault.

What mattered to him were two things and two things only: making money and carrying on his family's legacy, which was perhaps why he and Bruni got along so well: they certainly had the same priorities.

Suddenly Melissa appeared, startling him. As she handed him his drink she planted a kiss on top of his head; he nodded his thanks before taking a long and vein-warming sip. "Just bring out the bottle, babe." It was going to be one of those nights.

Sault & Sault had been in the engineering business since his great-grandfather founded it over a hundred years before. Like all the other great Sault men before him, Sterling had gone to St. Andrews Prep and Lehigh University before going on to run the family business, putting the Sault name on every building and project he could get his hands on. He'd grown the business, too; not just maintained it. Grown it bigger than his father had even, which of course was always the goal of every son, wasn't it? Now he could boast seventeen offices in five states, the majority of which were concentrated within a ninety-mile radius of Philadelphia. But more than that, though, he had done the Sault name proud.

Well, except for that divorce. That was pretty nasty, *and* public.

Ever since he'd decided to keep things simple: girlfriends only whom he told from the word "go" that marriage was out of the question. He'd be damned before he let go of one more thin dime in another divorce. After Ava he'd vowed he'd *never* lose that kind of money again. No, he would jump off the closest bridge before *that* ever happened again.

And forget children, he told them, one and all. The kids he had barely spoke to him as it was.

He had Melissa now, his sixth or seventh in a string of gorgeous (if dimwitted) young and nubile blondes. He had become a cliché, but if it bothered him, you'd never know it.

As if on cue, she materialized beside him, a worried expression stamped across her baby-face. "Is everything okay?"

"Yeah, fine," he said looking up at her. She was wearing an old monogrammed oxford of his and it hit her at mid-thigh, the starchy pale blue a sultry contrast against her bronzed legs.

"You sure?" Her concern was so sweet and stupid at the same time it made him smirk.

His eyes travelled from her thighs to her face and as his smile grew, the worry in her face vanished; a big toothy grin capable of giving Miss Julia Roberts herself a run for her money bloomed. "Is there anything I can do for you?"

He set his glass aside and patted the cushion of the chaise, and she sat next to him, leaning close, letting the oxford fall open just far enough for him to see her perfect apple breasts bobbing, waiting to be taken.

"Actually, there is something..." he said and, after placing his cigar between his grinning teeth, began to undo his belt buckle.

Her face curved into a mischievous grin as she sank to her knees and began to rub the bulge beneath his chinos. While she went to work, Sault leaned back, forgetting Bruni and Jasper and even that little prick Heim, and closed his eyes, puffing away, smiling.

But just as things began to get interesting his cell bleated, breaching the quiet of the night, and he wanted to hurl it from the rooftop.

"Oh Christ," he groaned when he saw it was Bruni. "Sorry babe but I gotta take this," he grumbled as he cleared his throat.

"How was it?" Bruni demanded as soon as he answered.

"Jarvis? Total shit show."

"Oh great."

"I know," Sterling replied, his voice on the edge of non-committal as he watched Melissa work her way down his legs, her ears showcasing four-carat studs he'd just given her just because it was Tuesday and she did shit like this — like THIS – and he was barely able to breathe watching her long blonde mane spilling across his stomach but was still able to report: "He was a mess, just like you said. Total fucking mess."

"So he's still scared? Even after I talked with him?"

"Shitless. Actually, paranoid is more like it. I don't think there's any talking him off this ledge."

"Fuck," Dino muttered.

"Listen, I don't want to make a bad situation worse, but I think you should know that he didn't even want the money."

"He *what?!*" Bruni all-but screeched.

Sault grimaced. "Yeah, he's off the reservation, Dino. He took it, but there was a hesitancy that I..." *God*, he thought, watching her, *She is simply incredible.* And then it was evident: He either needed to stop her or to stop Bruni from talking. There was just no way he could do both...

"Look, what it comes down to is this: I don't think we have any other choice but to..."

"But he's going into foreclosure! You said so yourself."

Now Sault was getting irritated. Dino's voice was getting bitch-like and he didn't like it one bit. This was exactly the kind of thing he didn't need. He thought of Jasper then, and the way he'd almost seemed offended by the money, and his blood began to boil. He'd just given him fifty thousand reasons to keep quiet; to keep his cool, and the dumbass *still* couldn't be considered anything but a loose cannon. How much longer could he put up with this? He thought of the election then, and as he watched Melissa in the pale moonlight it seemed worlds away. He had a myriad of things to take care of by then. Did he really need this hassle? Of taking care of politicians who were like children? Who were so difficult to appease, who took ages to mollify? Christ, it was like herding kittens. Who needed that?

"Goddammit..." Bruni was muttering.

"Look, Dino," he said from around his cigar, but just then Melissa hit a sweet spot and all at once his next thoughts evaporated. For a moment he lost himself.

"Sault? You there?"

"Yeah, yeah. I'm here."

"What are you suggesting?"

"Let's make things easy for once, alright?" he said, his voice growing soft on him as he felt himself slip away into another dimension, to a place where there was only pleasure, and everything else was blotted out completely.

"And?"

Farther and farther he felt himself slipping, and just before he was lost completely, he said: "Just take the fucking nigger out."

28

1:01am

Beneath the waxen light of the moon, a barefoot Sydney paced the threadbare rugs of her apartment. Down below, the restaurants and boutiques of Center Street had long bid adieu, and with every creak of the floorboards she felt her aloneness.

In a fit of frustration she'd thrown aside her covers and begrudgingly flipped on the lights, knowing it was useless to wait for sleep that wasn't going to come. Her mind was a Ferris wheel, returning back over everything it knew, pausing to allow theories to exit and retreat, picking up new ones with the same predictable regularity.

She'd never felt the need for a formal dining room, and had thus made it her office, situated squarely in the center of her home, which was fitting considering how profoundly her work dominated her life.

On the wall she had taped and arranged a mass of notes, news clippings, and documents all regarding Sir Thomas More Tech. The "wallpaper" fetched from end to end of the room, and as she paced she paused, looking at it, wishing the answer would just jump out at her already.

She picked up the phone: two voicemails, one from Cody. But the first was from Nana Jean, excited and chattering about her date that evening. "We went to Pinsetters and I bowled a two-ten!" she giggled. "Oh and Marv was just a peach about it. We went to DelMicio's after for the early bird and he bragged about it to anyone who'd listen!" Sydney smiled. She couldn't imagine there was anyone lovelier, more full of life than her Nana...

But then she grew melancholy, her smile fading. How was it possible that a woman in her seventies had a more active dating life than she? She thought of Cody then and glanced at the clock. It was only nine in Arizona. She had made a point to distance herself from him; not in the physical sense of course -- that was already taken care of. But by only answering every third or fourth of his emails, and none of his calls. It had just been too hard. She didn't know what she wanted, after all. So wasn't this the fair thing to do?

But something in her had weakened. If she thought about it long enough, hard enough, she was sure it could be attributed to this project. All these kids in Camden who'd already started life well behind the rest of the pack; who'd been given a shot at a state-of-the-art facility meant to raise them up, and they still hadn't been able to shine. It was enough to make her cry. And suddenly she wanted him, though she didn't know if it was really Cody she wanted, or if she just wanted *someone*.

"Hey," she heard herself saying into the phone the moment he picked up.

His voice was a supernova lit by surprise. "There's my girl!" She closed her eyes against the warm familiarity of his voice, hugging it. "I was just thinking about you."

And she felt herself succumb. "I've been thinking about you, too," she said. And, after, a few moments of pleasantries, of hearing about Arizona and the new coach and how pumped he was for the season, he asked her about her work, and she let it all pour forth. The interviews, the sad stories. The blasted dead ends and loose ends that just didn't make sense. The way something felt wrong about the school, the uneasy feeling that was growing stronger by the day.

And just one story below, in the empty apartment Bo Wrigley had rented from her, the tapes rolled on, the video detailing every step she took and the microphones recording every single word pouring from her pretty little lips.

29

1:03am

It was amazing how good a nice cold beer could taste after a long day. Dealing with Bruni before he'd left, plus the flight delays and a never-ending drive through the unforgiving pitch-black countryside in a crappy car -- not to mention that run-in with the deer -- had shaken him up. Now, as Bo sat alongside his old buddy Timms, tucking into his fourth or fifth, it all seemed like years passed.

"This is hittin' the spot, man," he said, draining his longneck. "Hell of a day."

Jesse Timms nodded, his attention on the lake below -- or perhaps on his sharpshooters stationed intermittently around the banks and yonder, armed to the gills and bloodthirsty for trespassers. "Boy, you don't have to tell me. Fuckin' airlines. All run by them money-grubbin' Jews." He spat muddy-colored juice into the dirt. "All of 'em. They'd ship us like cattle if they could." He leaned back and scratched his chest, his taut, tanned muscles riddled with Aryan tattoos.

"Yeah it's good to be here. And the girls don't hurt, either," Bo added with a giddy beer-fueled chuckle, and Timms almost smiled before unloading another healthy wad of juice.

The heat of the south had Timms's girls clad in all-things-skimpy and Bo enjoyed the view as they giggled and fussed over him. "Damn, this is the life. You really got it made here. My hat's off, man."

Jesse Timms had a harem. He called them "broken dolls". They came to him from all over: as far west as Texarkana, and as far south as the Hillbilly Riviera. Girls broken by those entrusted with their care, desperate with what he called "daddy complexes", eager to please his army of soldiers -- but nobody more than their leader.

Timms was at war with the world, and the way he figured, if the U.S. military was smart they'd take a chapter from his book, avoiding a whole lot of trouble by supplying a harem to their fighters rather than letting them "tangle with foreign stank". That way the bloodlines were "kept clean", he told Bo, and the soldiers were kept disease-free and happy.

And, according to Timms, happy soldiers were good soldiers. Loyal soldiers. For proof of that, Bo need not look further than Timms' overturn rate; there simply wasn't one. Even if they didn't know it themselves, these social delinquents and lost-soul malcontents who'd run away or simply "aged-out" of the foster care system came to him in droves, looking for love, guidance, parenting, partying. But most of all, they came looking for something to belong to.

"And once I give it to them, they're mine forever."

The dusty yard was draped in the kind of humidity one craves after long, cold winters but, after a time, either comes to loathe or love. Bo took in a deep breath and exhaled just as grandly; the warmth of the whisky and the beer and the night was an elixir he was powerless against. He sank into a chair that one of Timms' girls had pulled for him as if he were royalty.

"So," Timms began slowly, his eyes burning through the brackish night, making sure Bo knew he saw him clear as day. Bo felt uncomfortable but knew it wasn't personal; Timms just had that way about him. "Tell me what kinda havoc you been wreakin' up north."

He'd anticipated this question, of course. But, short of lying, he knew his answer would likely disappoint. Timms might've been his closest friend from his marine days, but he had standards so high nobody could reach them. Bo made a lot of money working for the go-to guy of some of the most powerful men in New Jersey, but that was something Timms would likely scoff at. He was of the mind that if you weren't part of the solution -- fighting for white power each and every day; hell: every *minute* -- then you were just another piss-ant part of the problem.

"Well," Bo said, clearing his throat, his eyes focused on the glassy lake before them. "I'm glad you asked."

The whole way here he'd wrestled with how to broach the subject. Knowing Timms as he did, knowing how much he despised the government and all it stood for, knowing he could care less about party lines -- believing that they were all pansies pandering to the minorities, destroying the very fabric of the nation one policy-cloaked reparation at a time -- it would be a hard sell to convince him as to why he should help Bruni. Lord knew if he ever saw his voting record, all that money he'd pumped into Camden –- an urban mecca of everything Timms despised –- Timms might have half a mind to take him out back and shoot him himself. To hell with his underlings –- this was a job he'd enjoy personally.

Now, with the booze coursing through him giving him much needed courage, Bo decided to exclude all the periphery information. About Bruni and his brother. About Sault and Heim. About the bricks in the kid's luggage, the cameras in the reporter's apartment: All of it. He skipped any detail that might sidetrack Timms, any fact that might give him reason to get mad. Because of all the fucking lunatics of the world you didn't want to enrage, Jesse Wayne Timms was at the top of the list.

So Bo took a sip of the whisky in his right hand and chased it with the beer in his left, and fast-forwarded to the brass tacks; to the only kind of detail that would not only interest Timms, but would also motivate him. "There's a fuckin' nigger causing trouble and we need a little help keeping him quiet."

With a long, slow slug of his beer, Timms considered this.

Bo took this as a signal to continue. "I would do it myself, of course," he said quickly, knowing Timms not only expected this but would respect nothing less than such an admission. "But I'm already knee-deep in this shit, and my boss wants untraceable help. Guy's paranoid, and getting worse by the day." Then, by way of explanation he said: "This coon's a bit of a big wig around our way."

"Cash?"

"Of course."

Timms nodded as the insects serenaded them from somewhere within the black of the night.

Then, after a time, Timms unfurled a dangerous smile -- his otherwise boyish grin yellowed by the tarnish of tobacco juice -- cocked his bottle of beer to toast, turned to Bo and said: "Consider it done."

"No shit?"

"No shit. *Hau weg den Scheiss*." They clinked their bottles together. "Here's to one less nigger in the world."

Wild hyena laughter was curdling through the bayous, and it took more than a while for Bo to realize it was his.

The harem was fanned around him and Timms; a halo of young girls giggling and dancing before them –- performing, actually, as if they were kings -- as *Sweet Home Alabama* blasted from the speakers into the dark of the night.

Bo was disappointed when Timms motioned for a minion to cut the music –- he could've watched those girls bounce around for hours –- but was decidedly less so when he heard Timms' announcement: "We gonna have ourselves a little contest."

The girls were giddy with anticipation.

"A dance contest?" One chirped excitedly.

A smile snaked across Timms' face. "No, baby girl. A different kind."

"What?" "What?" They all wanted to know, their eager eyes glimmering in the moonlight.

"A dick-sucking contest."

Bo sat up at this.

The girls blushed and tittered into one another's shoulders, whispering and giggling as they waited for further instruction.

"What does the winner get?" a well-shaped sixteen-year-old asked, hand cocked on her hip, sexy smile on her lips.

Timms grabbed her around the waist. "Winner gets to sleep with me tonight."

Overjoyed, she jumped up as he released her, clapping and squealing along with the others, delight trilling through the tall pines.

"And the loser?" a faceless voice asked from the back, and Bo found himself thinking: *Good question, sweetheart...* Because with Timms, there was just no telling...

Timms pulled hard on his beer and looked thoughtfully at the night sky. Eventually, without tearing his eyes away he said: "A bullet to the brain." Then he slapped his palms on his thighs and, as if on command, raunchy hard core ghetto rap began to play, drowning out the nervous laughter, and the girls formed two lines: one in front of Timms, the other in front of Bo, dropping to their knees as soon as it was their turn.

Bo was spent by girl number four, and as he lay back in his chair waiting for Timms to be done he thought: *That's it. I'm done with Jersey. I'm done with Bruni.* This *is what life's all about.*

But then he smelled it and felt it before he even heard it. The gunpowder in the air first, then the warm, wet liquid pooling at his feet.

When he looked down, his breath evaporated. *Timms was serious?* His booze-stained brain just couldn't believe it. But his eyes were all he needed to know the truth, for there before him Timms was tucking away his silencer, and there -- right at his feet -- was a girl with blood gushing from her temple, knocked to the ground, her knobby knees still bent, small mouth still open; a girl no more than twelve or thirteen, if she was a day.

30

Monday
10:20am

The gilded dome of the Statehouse gleamed against the cerulean sky, a rare coin of beauty suspended above a lackluster cityscape and, as Ben made his way along the highway, his mind a jumble of thoughts, it was the only thing keeping him focused.

The bricks in his suitcase still had him puzzled, annoyed, and -- if he were being honest -- frightened. The airline had been no help whatsoever; he had neither the time nor the inclination to fill out a report, detailing his loss. It was just a bunch of files, after all, of no value to anyone but him. And that was what was so baffling: who would bother to not only steal them but replace them with bricks? The rational part of himself told him that thief had obviously chosen his bag by accident, and would be in for a rude awakening once they realized their mistake. Still, it bugged him.

Then there were the endless stream of wretched headlines slamming Bruni's brother, and the Senator himself. He hated how their opponent had smelled blood in the water and used it as an opportunity to strike. Just an hour ago, at a well-attended press conference, J. Harrison Almond blasted the Bruni brothers as if they were one in the same, calling their lack of ethics appalling, using the dismal economic state of affairs in New Jersey as a spring board to rile the masses, talking about how while millions of Jerseyans struggled to make ends meet, the Bruni brothers thought they were above the law and could make money in whichever way they chose -- legal or not.

It was a brutal assault, and completely unexpected which made it so much worse. A complete novice to the political game and in way over his head, Almond had seemed like such a non-entity for so long, it was maddening to know that he was now so emboldened as to take public swipes at Dino Bruni. The sheer gall of it was bad enough, but what was worse was that a lot of what he said could easily be taken to heart. Their poll numbers would take a hit, no doubt. His speech was good, and his answers-under-fire even better.

Ben felt sick about it, but reminded himself it was just one press conference, and it was still early. The election wasn't for another fifty days -- a *lifetime* in campaign politics. They could recover. There was still time. But Bruni was nervous and his jitters were nearly tangible -- a state Ben had never before seen him in.

And, of course there was Heim. Digger had done nothing to allay his fears whatsoever. Which was why he now found himself hurdling toward the state capitol at well past the speed limit, thinking that maybe seeing Heim's office might give him a bit of insight into the man, and why he'd been dead-set on talking to Ben.

But Chip had shot down this idea at once. "It's been cleared out. Nothing left whatsoever, not even a paper clip. It's like he never existed."

And for some reason, this was what was haunting Ben more than anything.

"I could get in a lot of shit for this. You know that, right, Campbell?"

Chip Wesley's lanky strides paced the gleaming halls of the Statehouse, Ben at his side.

"I know, dude. And I appreciate it, so much."

"Yeah, well."

Chip was annoyed and Ben wanted to remind him that he'd offered to do anything to help. But he didn't want to ignite Chip's legendary temper so instead he turned to his friend and laid it on thick. "You have no idea, man. Honestly. I owe you, big time. You cash in anytime, you hear me?"

"Yeah, well...you can do two things for me."

"What's that?"

"Make sure your boss quits pissing off my boss, for one. And two: win this fucking election."

"Done," he quipped, and waited to see a smile eek across Chip's face.

But a smile was not in the cards. Instead, Chip stopped mid-stride before turning to him, his face as solemn as a tombstone. "A month ago, I might have believed you, Campbell. But now you're in one hell of a dogfight, my friend. And I'd be lying if I said I'd bet on you."

The State Troopers standing guard examined their credentials with such excruciating care that Ben felt himself growing antsy. Even after they let them pass, the troopers' gazes still lingered, suspicious.

Once inside the bowels housing the State House personnel archives, Ben followed as Chip coursed through the maze, stunned by the rows of mountainous files meticulously kept, sure they needed to leave a trail of breadcrumbs in order to find their way back out.

"Here we are," he said eventually, releasing a sigh. "Finally."

"Thanks man," Ben replied, focusing on the letter "H" headlining the section of annals, watching as Chip stepped aside and addressed his phone, signaling his work was done here and Ben was on his own.

After about twenty minutes, an aggravated Chip tore himself away from his inbox and addressed him: "You find it yet, or what? I've got things to do."

But Ben hadn't.

No matter how many times he'd gone over the alphabetical succession of files, he had not found Herb Heim's. He felt like a complete idiot, but it was the truth. He threw his hands up and said, "Dude, I'm telling you. I'm sorry to hold you up but I can't find this thing to save my life."

After a dozen or so minutes of checking himself, Chip began to shake his head. "This is impossible, Campbell. *Impossible.* Every fucking person that ever worked here is in these files. Everyone! And this guy Heim worked here for what? Twenty years? It's impossible..."

"I don't understand..." Ben began, but then he did. And he felt that same feeling all over again, the one that made him dizzy with fear, his skin crawling like some sick kind of disease, sure he was being watched.

31

11:14am

*L*egacy.
That was the word pinballing through his mind as Dino Bruni weaved his way through the Sunday drivers on Route 70, eager to use every last minute of visitors' hours to assess the situation with his brother. It bothered him to no end that two full days had gone by without so much as a word from Iggy –- it just wasn't like him. Iggy was like Dino's shadow, always had been, turning to his big brother more than any grown man should, especially in times of crisis. Dino couldn't imagine anything scarier for a wuss like Iggy than jail, yet he hadn't heard a thing. He'd expected tears, relentless calls begging for forgiveness, for money, for Dino to help find him a way out...But no; there had been nothing. Dino was so concerned he almost ventured a call to the Warden, but thought better of it at the last minute. No need to get him involved in a family affair.

And family. What of it? What of his family, and its legacy? Everyone knew Iggy wasn't exactly the sharpest tool in the shed, but getting busted for a crime as stupid as running a chop shop –- something people have done successfully for years -- was almost beyond comprehension. Dino thought of his father then (God rest his soul), and what he would say about this. Getting arrested and sent to jail on face value alone wouldn't perturb the old man –- the neighborhood was full of former convicts, particularly Mafioso, that shared more than a few Sunday dinners with the Bruni clan. Dino had countless memories of passing platters of peppers and sausage and Mom's macaroni around the dining room table of the house on Hinton Ave., sitting captivated by the stories the gangsters told, all while charming Mom and Nonna with enough compliments on their cooking to last them a week. They were friends of Dino's father; trusted brethren. No, jail alone wouldn't have caused much of a stir. But with nothing else to back it up -- no accomplishments, no reputation, no good name to leave behind -- that was the unforgiveable thing.

And Dino could understand why, especially after A.J.

That was what angered him more than anything -- how Iggy could have done something so dumb, without so much of a thought as to the family's name, their legacy. Having one son as a colossal disappointment was plenty for any family, but because A.J.'s demise was so scandalous, so shameful for people as conservative and old school as the Bruni's, they'd filled their quota for years to come, and Iggy should have been sensitive to that.

Alfredo, Jr. -- A.J. -- had been every Italian father's dream: a first born son to carry on the family name, the family business; handsome and athletic, the apple of his father's eye. Three years younger, Dino remembered his brother being his hero, in awe of the way girls swooned at his big brown eyes; the way nobody in the neighborhood -- in all of Camden! -- Could hit one of his knuckleballs, not even all those Jackie Robinson wannabes from the other side of the tracks.

But around the time Dino was ten or so, he noticed tension in the house where there had been none before. Hushed whispers between his mom and her sisters as they gossiped in the kitchen, shooing him away when they caught him eavesdropping. His mom crying, his dad growing red in the face and slamming the door behind him when he left the house, always after some type of run-in with A.J.

Then the taunts started. With almost crystalline clarity Dino could remember the very first time he heard the word queer. It was Joey DelVecchio, a neighborhood punk that had never been of much consequence to Dino, who began leading the chorus singing schoolyard songs about A.J., and the visuals the singing inspired had made Dino physically ill.

But not ill enough to prevent him from giving DelVecchio the beating of his life. In fact, that day launched Dino's career as a force to be reckoned with, bloodying noses and accruing detentions all in the name of defending A.J.'s honor, continuing to fight long after everyone knew the truth, that his brother in fact *was* a queer. Defending him because that's what family did.

Even though it was an embarrassment, considering the times, it wasn't all that unusual. Everyone knew a queer or two but everyone had the good sense not to speak of it. No, it wasn't until the seventies came along and the free love of the sixties gave way to rampant drug use, granting A.J. the permission to not only have sex with whomever he chose but to also get high while doing so. He chose heroin or, depending how you look at it, heroin chose him. Either way, his fate was sealed.

Dino remembered his mother's tear-stained cheeks every time she returned home from confession, and how Nonna's church attendance went from every morning to twice a day, the way her gnarled fingers would work the rosary beads with a vigilante's discipline as she murmured in Italian. It was excruciating for everyone involved, but Dino's Dad was hit the hardest. It pained Dino to see his father in such turmoil, how it reduced him from a pillar of the community to a man to be pitied. It could have -- probably *should* have been the death of him -- but A.J.'s death came sooner. Found beside a dumpster in an anonymous back alley of Philadelphia's gay district, a needle in his arm, A.J. was quietly buried in a private ceremony just a few days later, Nonna's knotted hands still working those beads long after the casket had been lowered into the frozen January earth, and the small huddle of mourners had thinned to nothing.

He died in 1982. The official verdict was natural causes, but there was nothing natural about it. It was just that by way of Dino's father's position as the most well known mortician in the area, he and the coroner were tight, and favors between friends were passed easily.

No matter how much misery his firstborn had dragged him through, Alfredo Sr. couldn't bear the thought of his son's last impression upon the world being one steeped in such disgrace. The legacy he'd left. The heavy burden of shame. Dino found it a blessing that his Dad died before the *real* truth every surfaced, that while a drug overdose had ultimately taken A.J. out by the knees -- a tragedy by any standards -- it was actually a true act of mercy when you thought about it, considering he had been dying of AIDS for at least a year or more, slowly being eaten away from the inside out.

The Camden County Jail was exactly as you might imagine: a marrow-chilling, archaic institution cloaked in the drabbest of hues, grudgingly offering only the most minimal of state-sanctioned solutions to meet the most basic of human needs.

The Senator felt himself both grow red and indignant as he was padded down like a common criminal -- his temper nearly exploding as his crotch and buttocks were intruded upon -- until a corrections officer -- a captain or something or other -- nodded at his rubber-gloved subordinate that the Senator was free to pass. Bruni snatched his belongings from the tray on the metal detector's conveyor belt: car keys, phone -- and stalked away, put out by being subjected to such practices as if he were some kind of crook.

"Good morning, Senator," The Assistant Warden said with a genial smile, but it brought with it no placation. The walls were a sickly hue, the glare of the intense light making even the healthiest of skin look as pallid as the dead. He felt the stares of the admitting C.O.'s: a ghoulish experience like no other, knowing they were the same eyes that had seen the depths of how low humanity could sink, of how depleted a man could become. Thinking of how they were so often responsible for encouraging such a plunge, rejoicing in stepping on necks to keep good men down. He thought of Iggy then, wondering if they were giving him a hard time, knowing they probably were, and he felt his blood pressure rise. So when one asked, "Beautiful weather we're having isn't it, Senator?" he didn't so much as offer them a nod.

As he followed without question Bruni felt his stomach roll over itself at the thought of his brother following without question, marching like an ant with all the other ants, rigged together in a series of manacles, hearing nothing but the sound of chains clinking, echoing off of the suffocating corridors, falling on deaf ears. How many reports had he received over the years regarding the state of the state's jails, never once giving thought to the people behind the statistics? Making decisions that would affect their lives profoundly; all with the same offhand consideration he gave when ordering lunch. *He'd never make that mistake again,* he thought with a grimace.

The Assistant Warden was a jittery man who seemed dangerously easy to rattle -- a scary attribute, given his position -- and as Bruni felt his way through his thoughts like a hand in the dark, he kept the conversation to a minimum -- "yes", "no", "none of your business" -- despite the jumpy man's insistent attempts at otherwise.

As they snaked through the innards of the institution, his imagination running amok at where his brother was spending his days, and worse -- his nights -- he found himself regretting so much, and it was a feeling as repulsive to him as it was foreign. Iggy had always been a dumbass, but he was never a *bad* kid. This latest stunt was something that deserved reprimand, sure -- but to be caged like an animal? Held here with the dregs of what the filthy streets of Camden had to offer? Please. There had to be a better way. Some kind of compromise.

Didn't there?

After realizing that Bruni was ignoring the majority of his questions, the A.W. finally got the message and excused himself, leaving Bruni alone.

He shook out a handkerchief and swiped the stiff, unforgiving plastic of the ancient chair, and took his seat on the free man's side of the glass.

As he waited Bruni lost himself in the influx of emails on his phone, vaguely thinking of the AG's report and how the proposed solution to all of the prepaid cell phones infiltrating the jail was to use technology against itself and encapsulate the jail in a veil of sorts, preventing the ability for any cell phones or PDAs from receiving transmission once on the jail grounds. He had been asked to sponsor such a bill but in all of the drama of the past weeks, it had slipped his mind.

But now it made him wonder about something. Consider. Perhaps Iggy hadn't gotten in touch for good reason. Perhaps there wasn't enough privacy and he felt he wouldn't be able to speak freely with Dino. Maybe Dino should look into one of those pre-paid cells himself. They seemed to be working like a charm for every other prisoner, why not Iggy? Wrigley could have it slipped to Iggy, no problem. *Yes*, he thought with a burst of optimism. *Maybe that was the answer.*

But just then a door opened with a jarring racket and Bruni's head snapped up, expecting to see Iggy shuffle through accompanied by a blank-faced officer, looking gaunter than usual, his normally thick five o'clock shadow a mere silhouette of itself.

Instead he saw a squat, jacked, Hispanic C.O. looking almost apologetic. "I'm sorry Senator, but Inmate Bruni has declined any visitors today."

"Excuse me?" he said, fumbling to tear himself away from his emails. "What did you say?"

Clearing his throat, the guard spoke louder. "I said I'm sorry, but your brother doesn't want any visitors today."

"He *what?*" Bruni was starting to get the gist now, and his anger was growing the way a volcano did, building up at the base and steadily rising.

"I'm sorry," the guard repeated.

"Did you tell him it was *me??*"

"Yes, sir. I did. But the inmates have rights, too."

"*Rights?*" Bruni all-but spat.

"Yes sir. They have the right to refuse visitors if they so choose. I'm sorry."

The fury inside Bruni was whirling so frantically he could no longer keep his hands steady, his phone falling to the floor, tumbling, somersaulting –- almost in slow motion –- until he gained control over it. He stared at the C.O., disbelieving.

"I'm sorry," he said again, and despite the fact that he was deeply apologetic and it was not even his fault in the first place, Bruni found himself furious –- his rage brinking on the insane. His blood was at a boil now, and as he felt the veins in his neck bulge against his collar he did the only thing that came naturally and flung the phone against the wall with an extraordinary smash, making the C.O. flinch, the device exploding into a thousand shards and a million little pieces.

32

12:33pm

"More sweet tea?" Nana Jean called through the kitchen curtains.

Sydney rose from the Adirondack chair, sunk her bare feet into the lush grass, and shook her head 'no'.

Nana Jean's house was a bright and airy Cape Cod with gingerbread trim painted so sweetly it looked good enough to eat. Sydney had nothing but the fondest memories of growing up here, just a few blocks away from the Campbell's. The old tire swing was still hanging from that ancient maple. Sydney went to it and tugged on the fraying rope, sure it wouldn't hold her anymore, but loving the heartening recollections that came along with feeling the smooth sunbaked rubber. She could almost see herself soaring until the world became a swirl of blue skies and green grass and white clouds, her stomach aching from laughter, her hair wild behind her like a flag in the wind, Ben behind her on the ground, pushing her higher and higher.

The back screen door slammed and she went back to her chair, alongside Nana, their bare feet sharing the same worn wooden ottoman, Nana Jean's toes painted *Rich Girl Red,* and Sydney smiled despite herself.

"Hot date tonight?"

Nana Jean laughed, her melodic Texas accent gilding the afternoon breeze. "Oh yes ma'am. And you will just *love* him. He's a keeper, this one."

Sydney loved hearing about her dates. For a woman of her age, you'd think she'd be relegated to daytime TV bus trips to bingo halls. But not her Nana Jean. "Oh yeah? Where did you meet him?"

"Line dancing down at Prospectors. And boy, can the man dance! I told him that first night, 'Dancin' with you is like walkin' on air', and it's the truth! Plus he likes my cooking, and as we all know, that's no easy feat."

Sydney knew what was coming next, and she braced herself.

"Speaking of. How is that dear boy Cody Briggs doing?"

Sydney cringed. "Oh Nana. I don't want to talk about it."

"I know you don't, darlin', which is exactly why you need to."

Sydney unloaded a heavy sigh and looked out at the sprawling landscape, carefully avoiding her grandmother's baby blues. "Look. It's just that I can't see myself in his lifestyle is all. It's just too much flash, too little privacy. And all the groupies. They're like piranhas. And you know as well as I do that Cody is a good guy --"

"He sure is."

"— But he's still human. So he'll say 'no' to a thousand girls, and then there'll be that one...and they're on the road...and no one has to know...and he's lonely...and I just couldn't rest my head every night wondering if this was the one night he said 'yes'."

The statement swung in the air between them like an abandoned hammock, as Nana watched her granddaughter's face with sympathy.

"And then I think to myself: There's six billion people in the world, so roughly half of them must be men. So how is it that there's only *one* right person for each of us? One soul mate? Maybe some people are right for us at certain times in our life, and some people at others. And that's when I get confused, because then I think of the people who have always been there for me, who have always loved me, and I wonder if I'm a fool for resisting them, for not taking a chance...I don't know, I—" she stopped abruptly, almost as if she just realized she was speaking to someone else and not just out loud.

Nana Jean smiled a knowing smile. "You're thinking about Ben."

Sydney blushed deep crimson, but did not say another word.

"He's always loved you, you know."

"Oh please," she waved her off, but it wasn't convincing in the least, and Nana Jean wasn't buying it.

"Never say never. That's all I'm going to say."

"Alright, alright," she said. "Speaking of never, did I tell you about Roger?"

"Your boss?"

"Yeah."

"No, darlin'."

"I couldn't believe it myself, but he and Ellie are divorcing."

"Oh no!"

"Yep. Married thirty years."

"Well," Nana Jean said, plucking her words as carefully as if they were for a bouquet. "One never knows what goes on between closed doors. Just remember that, dear. That's why it's safest never to judge."

"I know. I'm just sad for him, is all. He spends all his time working now; wanders around the office all hours of the night like a ghost. I wish there was some way to help him..."

Nana patted her arm and a warm silence passed between them.

"Gosh, I love it out here," Sydney said softly, gesturing to the emerald lawn bordered by bursts of the wild and unruly garden. "It's like your own slice of heaven. I don't know how you do it. I can't even keep a cactus alive."

"It's a work in progress, dear. It doesn't always work out the way I planned, but it still turns out pretty most of the time."

Sydney smiled a lazy, lopsided smile. "A little like life, eh?"

Nana Jean smiled her Mona Lisa smile, a twinkle in her brilliant blue eyes. "No, *a lot* like life, darlin'."

An Indian summer breeze shook the leaves and sent the scent of roses wrapping around them as they watched the bees and butterflies do their dance from plant to plant.

"Goodness gracious, Sydney Jean. Don't you look just like your Mama. Pretty as the day is long."

Sydney smiled, but it was long and slow and sad. "And see, that's another thing. Mama thought she loved Daddy, and look what happened to her."

"Don't you dare go down that road, missy, you hear me? Your mama's mistakes ain't no reason to be scared to love. She picked the wrong man and she knew it, and I knew it, which is why she ran away from me and hid all those years. Hid you from me, too. People called us estranged but that wasn't it at all. Your mama knew she was doing the wrong thing and she was too proud to come home. I would've taken her in, and she knew it. I would've spared her any lectures, too, 'cause she sure didn't need to hear any, not with all them black eyes and bruises and broken bones; they told her everything she needed to know about the bastard she'd married."

"God I miss her."

"Me too, darlin'. Every single day."

A butterfly landed between them on the ottoman, and Nana reached out to brush Sydney's hair from her face. "I understand that you're scared, darlin', really I do," Nana Jean began. "Love is a scary thing. But the worst decisions we ever make in this life are the ones governed by fear."

Sydney turned to her and reached out her hand, willing the tears pricking her eyes to stay put.

"I know. You're right. It's just easier said than done sometimes."

"But it doesn't have to be."

They sat in silence for a moment, just clasping hands and regarding one another, and before Sydney knew it, the tears started to fall.

"Aw jeez," she said, laughing. "Look what you made me do! Now I'm going to have a bright red nose and puffy eyes…Good thing you're the one who has the date tonight and not me."

"Cold cucumber slices will fix those puffy eyes in no time," Nana said as she wiped them away.

Sydney looked up at her face, close now. Nana Jean was seventy-five but hardly looked a day over sixty. "How do you do it, Nana? How do you stay looking so good? I sure hope I have your genes."

"Live your life to the fullest and the rest will follow and fall right into place. You'll see."

Sydney's smile was coy. "Aren't you going to lecture me about smoking and sun block and all that?"

"Goodness no. The doctors can say what they want but I think having a good man to love, an honest day's work, and good friends to unwind with is all a body needs to be happy and healthy. If you feel young, if you give love and get love, you'll look young."

"That's it? That's your secret?"

"Well that," she lowered her voice to a conspiratorial whisper. "And a little nip of bourbon every now and again never hurt nobody!"

When their laughter faded, Sydney became earnest. "I feel like I've aged ten years in the last two weeks."

"Why's that, darlin'?"

"Oh this story I'm working on. It's a nightmare. So depressing. I think I might just hang it up."

Nana was surprised by this. "But you never quit half way through a story."

"I know, but this time it's different."

After Sydney explained her progress thus far, Nana Jean's face was as sober and regretful as her own.

"That's such a shame."

"I know, and I just can't seem to find any sort of silver lining. I feel like I'd be letting down my readers if I let the magazine print this. I just feel like they'd be so disappointed. This isn't what they've come to expect from me."

"No, it's not. That's certainly true. But do you think it's a story that needs to be told nonetheless? I mean, even if it's not your usual fare?"

Sydney threw her arms up. "I don't know. I'm just so frustrated. It's just so hard listening to these stories. One after another, each one worse than the last." She thought of Ebony Valdez then. (*This place is hell on earth, isn't it?*) "Even the good ones are still sad."

Nana took her hand once again and Sydney closed her eyes against the soft touch.

"Well darlin'. Maybe that's why you need to tell it."

She opened her eyes in surprise. "What do you mean?"

The old woman's smile was tender: "Sometimes the most important stories are the ones hardest to tell."

33

12:45pm

Migraines were like mafioso the way they snuck up, silently, taking you out by your knees before you could even breathe your name. Jarvis didn't know any hit men personally, but over the years he'd heard enough stories about the Scottolino brothers to know that movies like *The Godfather* and *Goodfellas* weren't just the product of some overly ambitious Hollywood imaginations –- that shit was real.

But migraines he knew, and this one was a mother. The lights were dim in the parlor, and Poppy the maid had been placing cool compresses on his forehead every thirty minutes for who knew how long, but it refused to retreat. He'd vomited at least three times and felt as weak as a soldier down, his blood draining and staining the battlefield. By the time Henrietta came home, he was about to wave the white flag.

"Aw baby," she said, dropping her handbag in the hallway and rushing to his side, the smell of jasmine pirouetting all around. His eyes fluttered open and he winced against the miniscule spits of light sneaking through the slats of the Plantation blinds, splitting through his skull like coffin nails. "It's a bad one, ain't it?"

His face gave the only answer she needed.

"'Member what the doctor said?"

Yeah he remembered all right. But someone forgot to tell mister know-it-all, M.D., that when folks are in pain, the last thing they want to hear is how it's all in their head. Man, he could've knocked that fool out.

Six years ago, when the Senator had first approached him with his plan, Jarvis had spent countless sleepless nights with his head in an unforgiving vice, until finally Henrietta had had enough and sent him to a specialist.

Jarvis remembered him as distinct as day; the bifocals perched on the thin nose, the diminutive hand and nasally voice. "Outside of physical illness or dietary lack -- neither of which you suffer from -- there are three sources of migraines: Guilt, anger, and allergy."

"Say what?" he'd demanded, incredulous.

Undeterred, Doc went on: "Our tests have ruled out the third cause, so your best bet is to find a good therapist to get to the root of your issues."

Issues, Jarvis had thought with a snort, thinking of the Scottolino Brothers and how menacing they could be when they were dead-set on getting what they wanted. *You have no idea, Doc.*

"I'm still not following."

"Whatever it is you're feeling guilty about, or angry about -- or both -- has manifested itself physically. *That* is the cause of your migraines. And it's something I can't help you with."

Goddamn witch doctor, Jarvis had mumbled as he pulled his Caddy from the lot and spun his wheels before lurching into traffic. *I paid a fifty-dollar co-pay for that snake oil??*

Needless to say, he'd never gone back.

But now, as he lay here in the dark, his nerves alight with soul-souring anger, leaden guilt, and electrifying fear, he wondered if there might be some truth to what the doctor had said after all.

Sault had been over the night before, and left a fifty thousand dollar gift behind. But as desperate as Jarvis could be for money at times, the idea of it no longer held any interest, no matter how many outstanding bills he might have. In Heim's last email he'd alluded to sending back some of the money Bruni had been paying him off with, and Jarvis could understand that now. The need to sever the ties, to tell Bruni and Sault to take their money and shove it up their asses once and for all, to spit in their faces and scream from the rooftops: *I can't be bought!*

But damn! The notion of Heim murdering his whole family over this business gave Jarvis the creeps like nothing else. No matter how scary this situation had gotten, how Heim could have done such a thing was beyond him.

But then again, maybe while Jarvis' guilt was eating at his mind, causing him this debilitating pain, Heim's guilt had swallowed him whole.

"Jarvis baby," Henrietta said as she closed the parlor doors gently behind her. With nimble fingers she took his hand in hers. He exhaled and felt himself sink a little deeper into the couch. "I think you oughtta go talk to the Reverend. I've known you thirty years an' I know this ain't just a migraine." He felt like crying at this, loving his wife for understanding, feeling a relief so strong that he almost broke down right then and told her the thing he should have told her five years ago: the whole sordid truth, from beginning to end, come what may.

But before he could, she went on: "Whatever's botherin' you baby is more than a migraine, and only the Lord can help you."

And that was it. She was right. And Jarvis knew what he had to do.

Reverend Morehouse was beyond pleased to see the name his secretary had entered onto his calendar: Jarvis Jasper, 2pm; her loopy cursive written in red, indicating high importance.

While not the closest of friends in the traditional sense, the pair had a long and genial history of understanding one another's needs and fulfilling them with the utmost discretion. Morehouse was a man of God, of course, but the church couldn't run on faith alone. Right or wrong, money was an earthly necessity, and the preacher wasn't about to let his flock go hungry.

Usually they met at the Mayor's home, not in the offices of the church, but the Reverend figured time must be of the essence, easily conjuring an image of a scenario where the good Mayor might need his help right away, and that suited him just fine. He was more than willing to help. "You scratch my back and I'll scratch yours," they'd often said with a deep and knowing laugh.

Yes, he'd be happy to help the Mayor, to give him a good scratch.

And, after reviewing the treasurer's most recent report of the church's finances, he'd be just as happy to let the good Mayor know that he was itchy, as well.

34

12:46pm

Ben's head was beyond muddled. From the moment they'd realized Heim's personnel file was missing to the moment he'd seen Chip Wesley's face drain of all color, every one of his recent fears had been confirmed: something horrible and strange was going on all around him, and someone bad was likely behind it. The bricks. The missing files. Not to mention the triple homicide/suicide from the man who'd practically stalked him just before he'd committed it.

But for the life of him Ben couldn't imagine who was at the root of it all, or why.

It was a gorgeous day; not boiling hot for once, and the breeze was almost orgasmic it brought such relief. Ben decided to ignore the stack of newspapers he read religiously every morning to the one place that never failed to clear his mind: the Philadelphia Art Museum. He settled in at the top of the steps -- the same ones *Rocky* made famous -- tucked away by a fountain, and closed his eyes against the morning sun. He was being frivolous; he had about five million things to do, but instead of addressing even one, he moved to turn off his cell when it rumbled in his hand.

Kat.

"Hey," he said, not sure what tone he wanted to take until he spoke. How were you supposed to react to the person who just turned down your marriage proposal?

"Ben." She said, almost breathless. "Thank God I got you."

He straightened his spine. *Thank God, eh? What happened to 'maybe my dad is right?' huh? What the hell happened to Tad Ernst?*

But no. Somehow he found his mojo. "What's up?" he asked, heart pumping, his tone laced with an ambivalence he did not feel.

"Oh Ben. This is...this is um, really difficult. And I hate to do this over the phone but..."

He felt a chill run wild at the same time his cheeks flushed. She sounded so unlike herself, so unsure...so un-Kat. He couldn't imagine what was next.

He heard weeping on the other end of the line and began to panic. Kat never cried. Ever. He leaned forward, elbows on his knees, the cell pressed to his ear, his face twisted in concern, his veil officially off now; his heart a ticking bomb. "Oh Ben..."

"What is it, babe? Is everything okay?"

At once his thoughts leapt to that prick Ernst, imagining every possible horrible thing he might have done to her. And just as he'd imagined all summer long in various improbable scenarios, he pictured himself pummeling that son-of-a-bitch blue blood, of ripping him out of a chair by his pretentious, flipped-up collar and making the little pansy shit his monogrammed drawers.

"What did he do to you?" he hissed.

"What? Wait —- who?"

He jumped to his feet. "What did that asshole *do?*"

His voice was so loud, so intense, that innocent bystanders waiting to view the famous works inside the museum looked on with worry, pulling their children close to them, eyes darting nervously for a security guard.

"What are you talking about, Ben? Who—"

"Ernst! *What did he do,* Kat? Don't protect him—"

Then she did something odd. No, it was more than odd -- it was the thing he expected least.

She laughed.

"Oh good God, Ben! Tad? He...oh God no...*Please*. He would *never--*"

"Then what? What is it?" He was still standing, gripping the phone with a wrestler's wrath, the city spilling all around him.

Her laughter evaporated into silence. He could hear her breathing.

"Oh Ben," she said, her voice heavier than he had ever heard. "I'm pregnant."

35

12:47pm

"And this is our computer lab. It's one of three. Each floor has one. We have Macs, scanners, LCD monitors, webcams for interacting with students abroad, docking stations that allow students with special privileges to take laptops home. All the latest software. Everything is top of the line, as you can see."

Dr. Jermaine Seymour was proud of his school, and Sydney smiled at him -- her host for the day -- as he closed the door of the last of the very impressive classrooms and continued to lead her through the corridors of Sir Thomas More High Tech where he reigned as Headmaster.

"And you've been here since the beginning?" she asked as they rounded the corner toward the cafeteria.

A wide smile flowered. "Since Day One."

"And this campus cost taxpayers three hundred million, is that right?"

She felt the man stiffen, almost stutter in his steps, but when he turned to her the satisfied smile was still plastered across his face, almost unnervingly so. "Three hundred *and twenty* million."

Adding to her notes, she nodded. She took a deep breath, wanting to ask a thousand questions, but wanting to keep her hand close to her chest more. She didn't know why; perhaps it was something in the chilliness in his vibe or the disapproving droop of his eyes that tipped her off, but her inclination toward silence was motivated by something almost primal. So she listened to that inner voice and kept quiet.

His intonation, while steady, had an edge of defiance in it that had left her feeling intimidated since they'd first met an hour earlier. Or maybe not intimidated exactly, but certainly uncomfortable. "Small price to pay for an education, wouldn't you say? For a chance at a bright future?"

But before she could answer a group of students rounded the corner, pausing in their laughter when they saw their principal. "Hey Dr. S!" one called, and they all followed suit.

"Headed to lunch?" he called back.

The tallest of them turned: "You know it! It's pizza day!" And they all laughed.

He turned to Sydney with a peacock smirk. "All organic ingredients. Whole-wheat crust. We use only locally grown vegetables from a co-op in Salem County."

She smiled. "The Garden state."

"That's right," he chuckled. "The Garden State. Are you hungry? Would you like to try some?"

"Thank you, it sounds delicious. But I had a big breakfast."

"Very well then. In any event, it's something that we thought to be important. Feed the body as well as the mind." He clasped his hands together in front of him then, consulting his watch, he said: "So. I think that about covers it. Is there anything else you'd like to see?"

"No, I think that's all. It's been a great day, and I really can't thank you enough for the tour."

"The pleasure was all mine."

Then they were shaking hands and she was on her way to her car, the glass doors swinging behind her, the Headmaster's piercing eyes on her every step of the way.

It was the whistle that got her attention. When the shrillness of it pierced the air, it arrested her in her tracks. Her eyes swung to her left, to the football field, two hundred yards or more from the parking lot. For reasons unknown even to her, she turned away from her Cabriolet and bee-lined toward the great expanse of green.

The stadium was just like the rest of the campus: modern, well planned, and breathtakingly beautiful. An architect's dream, it hovered on the horizon like a mirage, sunshine shimmering on the Delaware River in the backdrop, the daylight dancing against it like the bevels of a jewel, illuminating the striking Philadelphia skyline beyond. She stood for a moment, soaking it all in. It was a sight so impressive it simultaneously made you both forget that you were in Camden, and reminded you what three hundred and twenty million dollars could buy.

The bleachers were wide, long, and comfortable: a far cry from the splintery boards she'd watched countless games from at her own high school. And although they were turned off at the moment, the lights towering from above allowed her to feel the rush of adrenaline of watching the Big Friday Night Game, a feeling she still got every time she went to watch Cody play.

She tucked into a bleacher about halfway from the top. All alone, she thought of him then, and of their conversation two nights before.

"I can't live without you, Syd. I really can't." He'd never been so candid with her. So vulnerable. It made her want to run all two thousand miles to him in Arizona. Hold him tight. Never let go.

Down below the football team was taking a break. Laughter was admonished by one of the coaches as the next drill was being set up. Trainers hauled thick fireman-style hoses to fill the bright orange coolers, while the overheated players stood in line for the water fountains, unable to wait. Helmets were removed, water ingested – by the bucketful it seemed. Sweat poured from them like mountain streams.

She thought about what Nana Jean had said, how the worst mistakes were made in the name of fear. How love was scary but worth the risk.

Still...she didn't know. When it came to love lives, Ben was right: she had everyone's figured out but her own.

And what of Ben? At times she felt a connection with him that went beyond chemistry. But then there was Kat. He'd proposed to her for goodness sake; it wasn't as though she were just a passing fancy. But that made her wonder, too. They were so blatantly wrong for each other...

Sydney had spent the better part of two years wondering what he could possibly see in her.

As she gazed below at the lush, jade field, her thoughts switched to Cody. To his offer. ("Come out here, Syd. You'd love Arizona, really. Be in the sun. I miss you, Syd. Come be with me.") She thought of it and what it meant to her, and how she felt about it. It was true, she loved him, but could she really expect to spend the rest of her life waiting for the other shoe to drop and still be happy? That was no way to live.

And maybe he'd regret it, too. That was certainly a very real possibility. Maybe he'd regret being tied down. It gave her a sick feeling, thinking of that one girl he just couldn't say no to, whomever she might be. She felt tears begin to leak from her eyes. Groupies were as ever-present as roaches -- they'd been here long before she, and would be here long after. How strong of a man would he have to be to turn away from those screaming, admiring fans who would do anything for him? How could a man go from being worshipped by the masses to coming home to a tired wife and hearing about a broken dishwasher or dirty diapers or piles of laundry and still be happy? She didn't know if he could, and that was what worried her.

Was she scared? Or a fool? *Probably both*, she thought with a mirthless chuckle. And so what if she did take him up on his offer, pushing aside all of her fears, only to be hurt, just like she'd anticipated all along? Then they would be right back at square one with no trust, no sacred foundation to stand upon. And to make it worse, they might've exchanged vows by then. Had a child even.

No, she couldn't live like that. Well, maybe she *could*, but she *wouldn't*.

Still, the tug toward him was undeniable.

At the far end zone the cheerleaders were stretching, gearing up for an afternoon of tumbling and tricks. On the visitor's side: the color guard marching in step, their R.O.T.C counterparts watching from the sidelines, clad in heavy ornate uniforms, probably ready to pass out from the heat.

As Sydney watched she couldn't help but think of Cyrus and Cedric Ashe. This had been their playground, where they'd broken all those records and chased their big dreams, the ones that were supposed to have taken them to the NFL. Then she remembered: she had asked Cody about them the other night, if he'd ever heard of them.

"The Ashe brothers?" he'd said. "Hell yeah, I've heard of them. They were supposed to set the League on fire. Shame what happened to them."

Her ears perked at this. "What do you mean?"

"They got into some kind of accident, didn't they?"

She'd scrambled through her notes then, spread before her on the bed in a wide fan. "Accident?" she'd asked, brow wrinkled, cradling the phone between her shoulder and cheek. "I don't think so…"

"Well maybe it wasn't an accident, I don't know. I guess I always just assumed so because it was a brain injury –-"

"Brain injury? Hold on a sec, where is that pen…?"

He cleared his throat then, uncomfortable all of a sudden. "Look Syd, this is off-the-record, okay? I don't even know if I'm supposed to know about this, or if it's even true. All I know is what I heard."

"Jeez, it's not like I'm going to quote you or anything, Cody."

"I know, I know. I just don't want to –-" he sighed then. "Fine. I'll tell you. But like I said, this is just what I heard." He took a deep breath and let it go in a whistle like a deflating balloon. "So apparently they had good SAT scores, right?"

"Not great but yeah."

"But good enough, right? You only need something like a 720 at University of Florida. So anyway, they did pretty well on the SATs, they had decent enough grades in school. Again, nothing to brag about but who cares, right? They were well on their way. So they were all set to go to camp, and when they showed up in Gainesville, word is that they were like zombies."

"Zombies?" She felt faint; the room beginning to tilt around her like funhouse mirrors.

Zombies. Ebony Valdez had used that same term to describe some of her classmates. Marion Jefferson had, too.

What is this? Sydney thought to herself. *A Stephen King novel?*

He laughed nervously. "I know it sounds crazy, Syd. I really do. But apparently they were so out-of-it that they got drug-tested like nobody's ever been tested before. Coach was mad as hell at the time –- but understandably, though, you know? He'd invested two scholarships in them, which is a lot when you only have seventeen available and a load of talent around the country to choose from. And so," he exhaled, "Word has it that he brought in FBI-level muscle to test them."

She smirked. "The big guns?"

"The biggest. But it turns out they were clean. Surprised the hell out of everyone because they were so messed up; I heard it was like *Night of the Living Dead* or something." Remembering her encounter with them, she shuddered with recognition. Now that she thought about it, they *had been* like zombies. "So word is that they sent them out west somewhere, Dallas I think, to some special private hospital testing place or something. Very hush-hush. They didn't want the press to catch wind of it, for obvious reasons."

"And?"

"And I guess they ran some crazy-sophisticated tests, got pictures taken of their brains..."

"And?"

"And the diagnosis was brain damage."

"Jesus, Cody." She thought of the pair of them, pushing brooms and scrubbing toilets at *So What Johnny's* in their matching janitor uniforms, flushing their futures down the drain -- literally -- and she felt the tears streaking her cheeks before she even had time to wipe them away.

"Look Syd." His voice was gentle. "Like I said, this is just what I heard."

"I know, I know. I'm sorry. This is the first I'm hearing about it, and it's...it's just a lot to take in is all." She took a moment to compose herself. "So why didn't they do anything to help them?"

"Who? The school?"

"Yeah, the school!" Blood flushed her cheeks. "Didn't they want to help them? Why didn't they —"

"Help them how? Like get them medicine? I don't think you can --"

"--Or treatment or therapy or something! Or...or...I don't know! Something! They're janitors now, Cody! At some greasy rattrap! Two promising kids, on their way to a good school, then probably the NFL and now..." As her throat went dry, any scrap of her composure falling away as fast as sand in a funnel.

"C'mon Syd." His voice was quiet now, tight. "You know how the game is. You're their golden child until, well, you're *not* anymore... Then they have no use for you."

Cool sweat began to course down her back, alarm making the tiny hairs on the back of her neck prick up. Suddenly she was thinking of Marion Jefferson, of the poor woman's anguish as she described her grandson's demise.

"*Something was wrong,*" Marion had said. "*I just assumed, once again, that it was preoccupation. Oh how I wish I'd seen it then, that is was so much more than that. I would have taken him to a neurologist.*"

And Sydney had asked: "So you think something was going on in his brain? Like a tumor?"

"*Well the autopsy has since ruled out a tumor, but I think it would have been a starting point at least. To get to the root of what was making him act so crazy...*"

She was almost frantic now. "So is there someone I can talk to? The Coach probably won't talk but maybe someone else on staff?

Another player maybe? I'm not gonna cause trouble, I'm really not. Honest to God, Cody. I just need to know what happened to them. What those tests said. I just --"

"Listen Syd. Not only do I not think anyone will talk to you about this, I think it's pointless anyway."

"Pointless?" Her sad desperation was quickly being replaced with anger. "And it's pointless, *why* exactly?" Her tone had an icy edge to it, now, but Cody's retained the same gentleness.

He released a bottomless sigh: an anchor falling into a deep, dark sea, genuinely sorry to have to break the rest of the news. His voice was throaty; a gruff whisper. "After the tests, I heard they flew back east and Coach had them re-take the SATs. They might have been brain damaged but he wasn't too worried, long as they could still play the game."

"And?"

The moment that passed felt like a week.

"And it turns out they got seven-fifty."

"Well so? Isn't the NCAA minimum like seven hundred or something?"

"No Syd," he said sadly. "Combined."

"Combined like, math and verbal combined, right?"

Please let it be math and verbal combined...

"No." His voice was grave. "Combined like...the two scores together combined."

"I don't understand..."

But she did. She just couldn't admit it.

"Sydney, the Ashe brothers only scored about three hundred and change *each*."

36

1:53pm

Located on the west side of Camden, The Zion Baptist CME took up most of Bledsoe Boulevard, affording it lovely views of the rippling Delaware and the city of Philadelphia beyond: its buildings of steel and chrome sparkling in the bright of the day.

But Jarvis's mind wasn't on the view. After recovering from his afternoon migraine, he'd had a deep and dreamless sleep, only to wake up gasping in the dark, alert as if it were morning, his body restless to leave the bed, scared where his mind might lead him next.

He'd spent the next several hours on the terrace, a cup of Earl Gray in his shaky hand, cataloging his countless problems and imagining different scenarios of how they might play out, each one more disturbing than the last.

The whole business with Bruni's brother had turned everything to shit and, adding to his distress, nobody except Jarvis seemed to realize it -- not Bruni, not Sault -- no one. Iggy was the wildcard in all of this mess. Now a convicted felon, denied bail, rotting in that godforsaken jail...who knew how desperate he would become? *If* he hadn't talked already, that was. And *that* was a big 'if'. Always a profoundly stupid man, he was now a trapped criminal desperate to leave a place that turned men into animals, and animals into beasts, the souls sucked right out of them leaving empty husks behind, loose and unmoored, any spec of humanity gone like dandelion seeds in flight...What lengths he would go to save himself? The dumb fuck would be the death of him, Jarvis just knew it.

And of course there was also Heim to think of. Just how many little landmines had that goddamn fruitcake buried before he'd gone and offed his whole entire family? *Many*, logic told Jarvis. *Many*.

No thanks to Heim every little noise made Jarvis's heart bounce, sure that he was being surrounded, that the cops had finally fit all the puzzle pieces together. And why shouldn't he be scared? Once the dust settled he imagined quite easily how the police would uncover all kinds of Heim's nasty little treasures, not to mention a paper trail ten miles long, no doubt –- one that would remove any need for guesswork on their part. They'd have enough to convict them all, and anything beyond that would just be gravy. He'd never trusted him. Bringing him in on things? That was all Bruni and Sault. *Harmless*, they'd called him. *A dickless policy wonk*. Well he sure showed them, now didn't he? Dickless maybe. But there was no questioning that his balls were of absolute steel.

The Reverend's office was tidy and non-descript; the professional equivalent of a turnpike motel room. Momma would say it was the office of a "soft hands man", meaning a person who never knew a day of hard work. The décor was appropriate: crosses, bibles, religious paintings and the like, but Jarvis had a dull-pit feeling that they were merely props. Then, reflecting on how the bulk of the basis of their entire relationship had been on supplying each other money and votes –- stealing and lying and sneaking, both in abundance and in secret -- he *knew* they were.

Still, questionable ethics be damned, he knew he had to confess to the man. And, as he sat, Jarvis weighed his options. Much to his dismay, there weren't a whole lot of them anymore...

The clock on the wall now read 1:58pm, and he willed it to move, worried he might lose his nerve before the Reverend arrived. It wasn't as though he came here willingly, after all. And he was well aware the slightest spook could send him packing. But confessing was the right thing to do, and dammit, it had been too goddamn long since he'd done right.

Trying to appear relaxed in the couch, Jarvis steadied his knee that was a jackhammer against the coffee table before him, and reminded himself that confession was good for the soul.

He knew he had to let it out; the question was: just how much? All night he'd wrestled with it. Did he just start at the beginning and let the awful truth spill? Or did he start at the end and work his way back pragmatically, letting Morehouse view it from a less ethical and more technical vantage point, and thus affording Jarvis a bit more leeway, karma-wise?

Confession was good for the soul, this much Jarvis knew. But the idea of actually going through with it was another story altogether.

He was still ill at ease. Ill in the gut. The heart. Doctors and lawyers had oaths to protect –- everybody knew that much. But what about clergy? If the cops were to come snooping (maybe not even "if", but "when"...) what was to stop Morehouse from sending him up the river? For all Jarvis knew, the Rev had already handpicked his successor, the next mayor, and was just waiting for such a catastrophe to occur, and would waste no time replacing him with someone of greater affluence. Biding his time. Lying in wait. Lord knew it wouldn't be the first time the man had acted out-of-step with his profession. He could be sneaky as hell, and Jarvis knew it.

But the Reverend wasn't a stranger, not by a long shot. Jarvis and Henrietta had been parishioners of his since the 70's, and when he thought about it with a clear head, Jarvis couldn't imagine a man of God being so shifty as to sabotage another man's livelihood. Morehouse was a snake but he wasn't a serpent. He wasn't Bruni. Or worse -– Sault.

But wait a minute. Jarvis was in dire straits and knew all too well how quickly this conversation –- this confession -- had the capacity to veer off-course and toward the personal, and the thought of that made him weak at heart. Enduring the embarrassment that went hand-in hand with the disclosure of the sad state of his financial affairs, the ones that had led to his entanglement with Bruni in the first place -- to his worry over Henrietta and how she might leave him if she'd known -- was a thought that was simply unbearable. He was a pillar of this community, and was appalled at the notion losing it all, of having to emasculate himself in front of the Reverend, and have his fellow community pillar think differently of him. Of pitying him. It was enough to make him walk out the door this minute, never to return. Like so many people of Camden, he imagined the Reverend looked up to him -- he was almost sure of it. He couldn't risk losing that respect...

"Mr. Mayor?" a voice came, and Jarvis nearly leapt from his seat.

"Oh my!" He hadn't even heard the door open.

"I'm so sorry!" the young secretary in the doorway exclaimed with a blush. "I didn't mean to scare you."

"That's quite alright, my dear." *I scare mighty easily these days,* he thought with a wince.

"I apologize for the delay, but the Reverend's running a tad late. Can I get you anything while you wait? Coffee, tea?"

"What kind of tea?"

"Umm, Lipton I think?"

"No, I'm fine, thanks."

"You sure?"

"Positive."

"Okay then," she smiled, and he envied her ignorance. Her innocence. "He should be here in a jiff." And the door closed behind her.

He had half a mind to follow right behind...but somehow he remained glued to the chair. After all, there was his campaign war chest to think about. And any -- no, *every* -- upcoming election to consider. He and the Reverend had an arrangement, one that played a large part in Jarvis' re-election every four years, and they both knew it.

But then the doubts wormed their way back in again, making him wonder: how hard would the Reverend work for some schlub who couldn't even hold onto his own wife? Or one about three steps away from the slammer?

And wait a minute. If he were to tell the whole sordid story from beginning to end, Morehouse probably wouldn't give him *shit* anytime soon. After all, coming clean would mean telling him all about the money –- *all* the money –- starting five years ago, still coming to him like clockwork to this very day. Take last night: Sault had just swung by with fifty thou, no problem. Someone like Morehouse would hear that and clip off their arrangement for good. Would tell Jarvis to go screw himself the next time he came around, sniffing for his contribution. Or worse: he'd want some of it for himself.

That's it, Jarvis thought, slamming his meaty palms against his knees with finality and getting ready to rise. *I'm outta here.*

But just then the Reverend came into the office with a rush of breeze, lifting the papers on his desk and starling Jarvis so much he was collared up and away from his thoughts in an instant.

"Jarvis my good man!" Morehouse bellowed in his honey-dripped baritone. "I apologize for the delay," he said, taking the seat across from him, a veil of distraction plaguing his face until he took a good look at Jarvis, and it was swiftly replaced by concern. "Jarvis?"

Oh no he didn't, Jarvis thought with disgust. He hadn't even opened his mouth yet and already the Reverend was looking at him in a way that was almost too much to bear. As if Jarvis was in trouble. As if he needed him.

As if he was weak.

Jarvis looked away, repulsed.

But the Reverend was nothing if not professional. Calm. His voice a steady, even thing that could tame a tornado. "What is it, Jarvis? Is it Henrietta?"

Just the thought of her brought fat, jellybean tears to Jarvis's eyes. *Ah Henny,* he thought, and a mournful pain staggered him like nothing else could besides the woman he loved. And then, before he even knew what was happening, he was thinking of Heim and how he'd resorted to murdering the woman *he* had loved. And for what? Was any of this even remotely worth it? Was Bruni? Sault? The money? Any of it? *No,* Jarvis thought fiercely. *No, no, no.*

His elbows balanced on his knees, he cradled his head in his hands, letting it sway ever-so-slightly, letting the tears fall and splotch the industrial grade carpet of the office. Who knew how long the Reverend let him sit there, whimpering like a child, letting his carpet get wet...But for the first time in a long time, Jarvis Jasper knew what he had to do. It was time to do the right thing. It had been too long. He needed to come clean *today,* and not a second later, to tell it all, from beginning to end, come what may. And forget what the Morehouse thought of him personally. He was a man of the cloth, after all. If anyone would understand, it was him.

He looked up then, and caught the Reverend's eyes in his own. And, for the first time he noticed how gentle they were; how melted-chocolate soft. Kind. Wise yet charitable. The kind of eyes that knew of all sorts of secrets unspoken, and let the work of judgment fall upon those greater than he.

It all came forth then, in a rush, to the forefront of Jarvis's mind, to the tip of his tongue. He felt his hands tremble, shaking against his knees so hard he was sure the force of his tremulous knuckles could bring down the entire church, from pulpit to bingo hall to the steeple itself.

He raised his eyes but couldn't bring himself to meet the Reverend's and so they swung to the window instead, to the tidy churchyard that lay beyond: the well-worn playground used by the laughing droves of Sunday school children to the graveyard filled with the faithful. Thoughts of Momma came then, how her heart would be devastated; shattered even.

But then something caught his eye: the glint of the slide on the playground, and next to it the primitive drawings on the sidewalk -- cloudy pastel-hued hieroglyphics scrawled by children. Drawings in sherbet: the colors of naïveté -- and knew his choices had been reduced to all but one: telling the truth.

Jarvis clasped his hands together and seemed to suck the whole room of breath.

There was anticipation in the Reverend's face, but more than that there was patience. And, Jarvis was relieved to see, kindness.

"Jarvis," he said with the practiced voice of a man who had climbed mountains and lived to re-trace his path. "I can see your heart is burdened something awful, but it needn't be."

Nodding his head, feeling the tears stab like psychos at his weary, bloodless, migraine-strained eyes, suddenly he couldn't imagine why he hadn't come here sooner. Why he hadn't relieved himself of this cumbersome burden, a load so heavy, so poisonous, it was unfathomable how he'd ever carried it for five seconds let alone five years.

And as he finally found the courage to look the man in the eyes, suddenly he was unable to remember why there was ever any reason at all for not trusting the Reverend Alouicious Morehouse, and he couldn't imagine a rationale that could explain away something as foolish. Morehouse was a man who could offer him hope. Who could sustain him with faith. Or, at the very least, who could throw him a karmic life preserver.

Jarvis cleared his throat, finally ready to unburden his soul.

But when Jarvis went to speak, he found himself dry.

Swift as a cat the Reverend produced a glass and a pitcher of water, offering it forth with a gentile smile. Thus far this whole exchange had been something new and the Reverend was impatient to hear what his friend had to say. The build-up was almost unbearable, leaving the Reverend's imagination to run wild, to imagine scenarios where they were on the brink of cashing in a mother lode, conjuring up images of great wealth that would leave them both satiated for eons.

He watched as Jarvis took the glass with a grateful nod and went to take a sip when suddenly there was an explosion so huge, so cosmic, it snatched the Reverend's breath away like the cold hand of death itself, sending him flying across the room as if caught in a gale and, as he was pummeled to the floor, tumbling end over end, he found himself covering his head on instinct, praying like he had never prayed before.

Time passed. Seconds? Hours?

It wasn't until he heard his name being called by someone rushing down the hall frantic toward his office that the Reverend was able to grasp some semblance of what had happened: The picture window of his office had been obliterated –- literally annihilated -- and the innards of his office had been showered in glass, so much glass glinting in the sun it was as blinding as it was immeasurable.

"Jarvis?" Morehouse gasped, as if just remembering he was there, moving to his knees, glass falling off of him like a wet dog shaking away the rain.

Jarvis was on the ground, too, covered in more blood than the Reverend could easily comprehend. As timid as a kitten he reached out to touch a patch of it -- a wound that looked like it might have been survivable if it hadn't also been accompanied by about fifty or more others just like it -- when something in him made him recoil, rocking back and losing his balance... The Reverend's hand flew to his chest and his disbelieving eyes clung to the sight of an unmoving Jarvis until his ragged breath finally steadied into something manageable.

It was then that Morehouse realized he was covered in blood, too.

As if bitten, he flinched in revulsion. But a moment later he reached forth to touch his friend, to wipe some of the blood from his head. As he looked closer, though, he saw it wasn't just blood he was touching, but bone and brain, too.

The Reverend flew back in horror, his nausea surging, his arms flailing like a trapped animal as his hands clawed desperately at something –- anything -- anywhere to stabilize him. The chair tipped over but he was able to grasp a corner of the desk and, scrambling to his feet, stumbling backward, arms pin wheeling, he tried to regain his footing, and that's when he saw the gushing, dime-size bullet wound in his friend's temple. It was so round, so clean, it almost looked fake it was so perfectly precise. But the river of blood flowing forth and pooling on the floor left no room for doubt about the realness of it all.

Jarvis had been shot.

Assassinated.

And though he cried out his name again and again and again, he did so in vain, all the while knowing in the pit of his heart that his good friend the Mayor was dead.

37

3pm

The soft hush of rising and falling ventilators and the muted murmurs of concerned nurses explaining the unexplainable to distraught parents was the soundtrack of the Neonatal Intensive Care Unit. Sydney was hopelessly out of place, feeling as guilty as a voyeur as she passed the clusters of anguished families huddled together gathering strength from one another; hating the idea of intruding where she didn't belong. She was almost ready to turn tail and leave the Demetrius "T-Ray" chapter of the investigation an unturned stone when Diamonique Keyes suddenly appeared before her.

"I don't gotta lot of time," was the first thing she said before Sydney was even able to introduce herself. For a brief moment Sydney had a flashback of Shanice Hopkins and the way she'd all but eclipsed the interview before it had even began, and she felt herself deflate. *Maybe there is something to that Oedipus theory after all,* Sydney thought with a slight sigh.

This had become the most difficult and perplexing assignment of her career and she was growing increasingly weary with every passing hour. It was as if there were forces working against her, wanting her to fail, and she was powerless against them. It was staggering, the way she felt; like Sisyphus against the mountain. Still she collected her breath and smiled, all the while praying: *Please God, if you exist, please don't let this be another Shanice interview.*

She summoned every ounce of fortitude and stood, offering a gracious smile along with her hand to shake. "Diamonique? I'm Sydney Langston. It's so nice to finally meet you."

"I know why you came but I don't gotta lot to tell you, ai'ight? Demetrius is locked up, up damn near Canada he so far north. And as you can see I got my plate full right here, so talk fast."

Sydney forced herself to maintain her pleasantness. "I understand. I won't take too much of your time, I promise."

Although her larger-than-life eye-rolling made it clear she didn't believe a word Sydney was saying, Diamonique slid into one of the hard plastic chairs of the waiting room; her raw, tear-depleted eyes worn out and barely able to muster the strength to be suspicious. "Ai'ight. I'm here." She folded her arms across her chest. "So what you want?"

The first thing Sydney noticed about the girl was likely what *everyone* with eyes first noticed about her: Diamonique was absolutely stunning. Even as weariness ravaged her face, there was a picturesque, almost unspeakable beauty beneath the burden.

"I know this is a horrible time for you, and I'm so sorry to intrude. Believe me -- I wouldn't be here unless I had to."

"Yeah well. It is what it is."

"I really appreciate you talking to me, I do, and I --"

"Like I *said*, I don't got a lot of time, so can we fast forward through the niceties?"

Sydney shuddered at the shocking rudeness but didn't skip a beat. "Of course. So," she turned on a mega-watt smile, "it seems we have a friend in common."

Diamonique's eyebrows twisted into question marks, clearly doubting this was even remotely possible. "Oh yeah? Who dat?"

"Susan Campbell."

Diamonique's face brightened, her voice softened. "Nurse Susan?"

"She's wonderful isn't she?"

"Hellz yeah! She's been like some kinda lifesaver for me."

"And for me, too. She's my best friend's mom, and she's been like a second mom to me," Sydney said, knowing no truer words had ever been spoken.

And as began her questioning she watched Diamonique's walls disintegrate upon them having found common ground, and she was awash with relief.

She proceeded to cover the basics: what Sir Thomas More was like, how Diamonique enjoyed her time there, etc. Everything was going along well, or so she thought. But when she looked up from her notes, she saw Diamonique was crying. "I'm sorry, Diamonique... Are you alright?"

"No, *I'm* the one who's sorry," Diamonique said, swiping her face with the back of her hand. "It's just that all that seems like a lifetime ago. Demetrius and me, well, we knew with a baby on the way that the two of us was gonna have to grow up fast. But I ain't never imagined nothing like this." She laughed then, but it was vacant and sad, and Sydney's heart dropped. But just as quickly, a real smile came into flower, replacing the pain, and her face shifted into the girl Sydney imagined T-Ray had fallen in love with. Thinking of the little baby -- their baby, made from love -- smothered in wires and probes and machinery just a stone's throw away, made Sydney's heart ache. "Nurse Susan's been like an angel for us."

Sydney reached and took her hand. "Oh I have no doubt."

A silence passed, and quiet, private tears fell between them.

"Damn," Diamonique said finally, looking up toward the popcorn ceiling, her smile dying. "I don't know how it all changed so fast..."

Sydney handed her a tissue. "I have to tell you, since I started this assignment, it seems like a lot of your classmates' lives have changed dramatically rather quickly."

"Oh don't I know it," she said, blowing her pretty little diamond-studded nose. "You heard about Mailk, right?"

Sydney mentally pulled up his stats: Malik Jordan, track star, and Ebony Valdez's crush. 2.7 GPA. Voted "Best Looking". Editor of "Utopia", the school newspaper. Now a crack head.

"He was Demetrius' best friend and Miss Langston, trust me when I tell you the boy was *just* like us."

"How so?"

"Hated drugs; saw what they did to everyone else in this city, and didn't want no parts. But he started to change, too, and boom! Next thing you know..."

"When you say 'started to change, too' what do you mean? He changed like Demetrius did?"

Diamonique's face darkened. She spoke slowly. "Like we both did, I guess. For me, it was just like I started losin' my mind, or somethin'. I mean, *damn.* It was like I was goin' crazy. My head always hurt, I felt like the smarts was gettin' sucked right outta me like the world was a Hoover."

"And Demetrius...did he feel the same way?"

She looked away. "Naw. With him it was dif'rent."

"Different how?"

"I dunno."

"Better or worse?" Sydney asked, sensing the answer.

"Oh, worse. Much, much worse." She spoke as if each word was a fruit hand-plucked from a tree. "See, me and Demetrius...we been together since we was fourteen, ai'ight?" Her fingers drew circles along the mocha skin of her legs, round and round they went, the soft sheen of them reflecting the sparse light. "I ain't never knew my daddy...and my momma... well, she was no good." She chuckled then, but it was humorless. "She was some kinda junkie in the worst way. And T-Ray...well, he been my whole family, my whole life ever since..."

Sydney thought of Ben then. Of the Campbell's, and felt a swell of kinship.

The tears in Diamonique's eyes were fierce. "I would do anything for that man, and him for me. We straight up soul mates. I know him better than he knows hisself, so I could see changes in him before he could. Before I could see them in myself, an' 'cause that man been so good to me –- he my heart, you know? –- I was always more scared for him. 'Cause trust me –- them changes done scared me in a bad way."

"What kinds of changes?"

She shrugged; eyes elsewhere. "Guess it all started 'round junior year. He used to come down and watch me at cheerleadin' practice." She smiled then, nostalgic. "He'd sit in 'dem bleachers, writin' away in his little notebook, workin' on lyrics. I'd look over and damn if he didn't have his nose buried in that little notebook of his, he'd be over at the water fountain, drinkin' like he'd just gotten out of the desert." She laughed then, remembering. "He was at that fountain so much we started callin' him Joe Camel, 'cause he was always drinkin'.

Turns out he was diabetic, but we didn't know nothin' about it at the time. His manager wanted him to get a routine physical and he came up diabetic. But that wasn't no big thing, you know? We knew lots of people who had the diabetes; It wasn't like it was gonna affect his career or nothin'. But then there were other things..." her voice weakened, and Sydney noticed her hands were trembling. She took them in her own.

"It's okay," she said softly. "Take your time."

"Well at first he wasn't sleeping, but I didn't think much of it. So many things were happenin' so damn fast...but all good things, you know? He was like a kid on Christmas Eve most of the time." Her smile was far away. "But then it started to drive him crazy, you know? No sleep can do all kinds of crazy shit like that. And then before you knew it he was forgettin' things. Not big things, but enough to be annoying, you know? And we just thought it was from no sleep...Like his mind was playin' tricks on him or somethin'. Then..." she blushed. "Then...he didn't want to...you know."

"Didn't want to what?"

"Do it no more."

Sydney was confused for a moment. "Do what?"

"*It.* You know. Have sex. And that wasn't like him at all. That man was like an animal. So I went to the library at school and started doin' a little research. I thought he might be depressed or somethin'. I mean, who *wouldn't* be living with that witch?"

"Shanice?"

Diamonique's voice fell down a well. "Yeah."

"She's a bit...difficult, huh?"

"*Difficult?*" she said drily. "His moms is straight-up crazy. She's gotten worse since he got locked up, but if you axe me, she ain't never been right in the head."

"How so?"

"All that she-devil ever wanted was a meal ticket, whether it was some dude or her own son. All Demetrius did was give, give, give, an' all that bitch did was take, take, take." A brutality boiled to the surface then. "An' you wanna know she ain't ever even met her grandbaby? T-Ray's baby! Her own son! What kind of a person does that?" Her eyes were pools of hot angry tears. "She thinks he's retarded so she don't want nothin' to do with him. But if T-Ray had made it? If he was on the radio an' TV an' we was livin' in some big ass house, gettin' paid out the ass, she'd be all up in our shit. We wouldn't be able to get rid of that ho. An' you think she cared for one second about how my man was feelin'? That he might be sick? Hell no! All she cared about what was whether or not he was makin' it to the next show, makin' money."

Nothing good would come of discussing Shanice, and Sydney knew it. So instead she tried to steer the conversation to something that better served her purpose. "So T-Ray wasn't acting himself? And it was unrelated to the diabetes?"

Diamonique exhaled; the tsunami of rage aborted for the moment. "Yeah, they was two separate things. He wasn't himself, but it was more than that. He started gettin' sick all the time. His stomach always hurt. No matter what he ate he'd be throwing it the hell back up. And sometimes he had the shits so bad it scared him."

Sydney gulped. "Scared him?"

"Yeah." Her voice was so raw, so tormented. "'Cause it had so much blood in it."

A nurse appeared in the doorway. Her smile was kind and her voice timid. "You ready, Diamonique?"

Diamonique nodded as she rose, wiping away tears: "I'm sorry. I wish I could help you more."

"No, no. Please don't be sorry. You've been a huge help, Diamonique. Really."

"They're gonna let me feed my baby today," she said, smiling at the nurse, and Sydney saw a twinkle of happiness sparkling in her eyes that was almost heart-breaking in its hope.

"That's awesome news," Sydney smiled.

"If you wanna know more, Dee'll be able to help you."

Sydney was confused. "Dee?"

"Dee Cassius. He's the head of the record label. He knows Demetrius almost as good as me."

"Almost," Sydney said, and Diamonique smiled a grateful smile.

At the doorway the young girl turned. "I just want you to know that no matter what he's done, he's..." her voice failed her for a moment but she composed herself fast, almost seamlessly: the way survivors do. Set her spine straight. "Even though he's locked up, he's still a good man, Miss Langston. No matter what, he still tryna take care of us. He loves his son. He loves me." She wept openly now. "Demetrius might not be the same man he used to be, but he's still a good man, you hear me? Trust when I tell you, Miss Langston, he still got love in his heart."

38

4:45pm

The home of *Deez Beatz Recordings* was within in a long, low-slung North Camden commercial-front with blacked-out windows and a steel front vault door that made Sydney nervous.

The suspicious stares from people on the street in conjunction with the buzz from various minute motion-detector video cameras stationed like vigilantes around the perimeter were unwelcome reminders that she was in a neighborhood most sane people avoided.

The disconnected voice of a woman came through the speaker and, after Sydney had identified herself, the steel door unhinged to reveal a young Asian woman with long blonde hair in a shrink-wrap dress and impossibly high stilettos extending a soft hand and a megawatt smile.

"Hello Miss Langston. Welcome to Deez Beatz."

Sydney walked in and was stunned: it was like a high-end penthouse bachelor pad. Sleek chrome, shiny glass, pricey works of abstract art and buttery leather furniture adorned the lobby; hardly what she'd expected, given the building's exterior.

"It's so nice to meet you, Miss Langston," the woman said as she led Sydney through a metal detector and casually removed the bag from her shoulder before handing it over to a mountainous security guard.

"Please," she smiled, "Call me Sydney."

The guard was as wide as he was tall; a great behemoth of a human that began pawing through her bag with the laser beam intensity of a bomb-sniffing dog.

"Sydney then." The girl smiled, and Sydney couldn't help but wonder if she was one of the girls from the rap videos that Deez Beatz produced. She was certainly built like one. "My cousins go to Sir Thomas More. They just adore you. What you did for those kids... well. You're a hero."

Sydney laughed. "I wouldn't go that far."

"Well you're a hero here in Camden."

"She's clean," the guard rumbled, handing back Sydney's bag.

"Shall we? He's expecting you."

As they walked through a series of corridors, the number of gold and platinum records on the walls was astonishing. She had never been a fan of rap music, and though her research confirmed Deez Beatz was a successful entity, she had doubted it based on the address alone. But clearly she was wrong; without question this place was a launching pad for success stories; a home to ghetto prodigies.

The young woman approached a thick wooden door and knocked tentatively. When she wasn't rebuffed, she opened it and motioned for Sydney to enter.

Across the room he sat, and Sydney saw at once that Dee Cassius was three hundred pounds of suave, slick, unquestionable cool. Bald head, enormous stature, flashy bling, and trendy glasses -- dressed head-to-toe in understated Prada -- he was seated behind a sprawling desk that actually made him look proportionate to the rest of mankind, but once he stood, it was clearly only an illusion.

"Miss Langston," his silky baritone announced, oozing like caramel.

"Thank you so much for seeing me on such short notice, Mr. Cassius. I hope you don't mind answering a few questions for me."

His smile was molasses: easy, slow and saccharine on the eyes. "Of course not," he said, taking his seat and motioning to one of the two empty chairs across from him made of pure white, succulent suede. "Please join me."

"Thank you," she said, sitting gracefully. She drew her notepad from her messenger bag. "But before we begin, may I ask you a question? Off the record?"

His smile was amused; purely Cheshire. "Sure."

"You've obviously got a very successful venture here," she said, motioning around. "May I ask why you've chosen to make this neighborhood your home?"

A moment passed where his face remained unchanged but Sydney saw something pass through his eyes. Something dark that belied the bright sheen of his smile.

The seconds passed like decades.

Her eyebrows arched in polite demand for explanation.

He shifted in his seat but never let go of her gaze. "We have our reasons."

For a time neither one said anything.

Then he clasped his hands atop his considerable belly and, as if she'd never even asked the question in the first place, he began: "I was so intrigued by your interest in T-Ray. Ever since his incarceration, the public's interest has fallen off considerably, as I'm sure you can imagine."

"Well yes; I can. His life certainly has taken a different turn." She cleared her throat. "In fact, I just came from the NICU."

"Oh," he said, his face suddenly showing its age. "I'm so sorry."

"Why?"

"Because you met Diamonique I'm sure?"

Sydney was a bit confused. Still she answered. "Yes, I did. Why do you ask?"

"Well this is not who they are. Or, I guess I should say, who they *were*. They've changed a great deal, and not in any discernibly positive way, I'm afraid."

Pen poised, she asked: "Could you expand upon that please?"

His smile was indulgent. "Well you've met Diamonique. She was a bit...how do I put this delicately? Rude? Am I right?"

"Well yes, at first. But we have a friend in common..."

"So she softened up a bit, yes? Well good for you. You got off lucky. 'Cause let me tell you, she can be vicious. And this attitude of hers, if that's what you want to call it -- it's all new. Diamonique used to be the sweetest girl. As polite as a lady-in-waiting."

"Well she's been through a lot...I don't hold it against her."

"No, I imagine not." He offered nothing more but an indecipherable smile.

Uncomfortable under his stare, Sydney shifted in her seat. "And T-Ray?"

"He was as solid as they come. Thoughtful, forward thinking, generous to a fault. A real diamond in the rough." His warm chuckle was that of a proud father. "And you'd never met a man who loved his girl more. When they were together, time stopped. They only had eyes for each other. That's what makes all of this so hard."

"'All of what', exactly?"

He waved his hand vaguely. "All of it. They were just so peaceful. Diamonique and T-Ray doted on one another like you've never seen. They were selfless, compassionate. Passionate. Each one caring more about the other's happiness more than their own. It was truly a sight to behold, those two together. Yes they were young, and all young love is enviable. But they were above and beyond. Watching those two was like watching love in Technicolor." His face fell. "They were not supposed to end up like this."

"Like what?" she asked, but feared she already knew the answer.

His smile remained, but any joy had been robbed from it, and it had morphed into something heartrending and almost unbearable to witness. "Like everybody else from Camden."

"You've known them for a long time, I take it?"

His voice was tender. "Since they were kids. They've been together since we discovered T-Ray, and from Day One they had a glow about them. A holiness. I don't know whether it's from the stress of the baby, bein' sick an' all, or of T-Ray being in jail...but Diamonique has changed." And, for the first time, he seemed speechless -- or if not speechless altogether, then searching for articulation. "There's a hardness there now that was never there before."

"And T-Ray?"

His dark face fell pitch-black. "He ain't even *close* to the same person."

"So what changed?"

He cleared his throat. "I can't say because I just don't know."

"Well then how did it change?"

"Well..." he sighed, "It was gradual. At first it was attributed to the diabetes, but that was under control fairly quickly."

"And then?"

"Well...other things began to happen that just didn't make no sense."

"Like what?"

"Like he began forgetting lyrics. It didn't interfere much with our recording at first but, before long, live shows started presenting a problem."

She nodded as she scribbled in her notepad.

"Then he had a dry spell where he couldn't come up with anything new."

"Well that can't be all that unusual, can it?"

"No, not at face value. Our clients are artists -- their creativity ebbs and flows; we recognize that. He is certainly entitled to have his slumps -- they all are. We respect bouts of writer's block. But this was different. It became so he wasn't turning a single worthwhile thing out, and he didn't even seem to care. In time, though, I think he became depressed over the lack of creativity, which again, is not unusual among the artistic. But then..."

There was a long pause, forcing Sydney up from her notes. "But then?"

"But then he started to self-medicate, and did a horrible job of it. He'd always been a casual partier -- a lightweight, in fact, compared to a lot of his contemporaries. He hated drugs, but next thing you know he's smoking weed, and before you know it, it escalated from here and there to an around-the-clock situation."

Sydney studied him but didn't speak. Waited.

Dee Cassius showed a bit of discomfort for the first time. "But that wasn't what worried us. Weed ain't crack, after all. No, we were more concerned about the dramatic change and why it occurred in the first place." His face darkened. "And, of course, the fact that he was hanging out with a new crowd. A bad one. And we feared crack might be just 'round the corner."

Sydney thought of Cody then, and what he had said about football coaches –- how you were golden child until you weren't anymore and then they had no use for you. She felt herself growing testy, wondering if the case was the same with record labels.

"Well didn't you try to help him?" she asked, a newly harvested hostility in her voice.

"I tried to talk to him –- we all did. We even arranged to send him on a sabbatical, hoping it would do his body and mind good."

"--Hoping his dry spell would get whetted."

"--Yes," he said, growing a bit vexed as well, not liking her insinuation: "And also to get him away from the bad element he was hanging with."

"And?" she all-but demanded.

"And the night before he was set to leave he committed aggravated armed robbery. Attempted murder. I'm sure you've read the articles," he said. "He's lucky New Jersey doesn't utilize the death penalty these days, else he'd be dead man walking for sure."

A thick quiet fell between them.

"Did you know their families? Diamonique and T-Ray?"

He cleared his throat. "Well they both suffered from ghetto-itis."

"I'm sorry, I'm not following...Ghetto-itis?"

He chuckled, but it held no humor. "Yeah. The 'got-no-daddy-disease'. It's the plague of the ghetto. Neither had fathers around, and while her mom was chasing the next high, Diamonique bounced from one foster home to another, and all the while T-Ray was living in chaos, trying to make sense of *his* crazy-ass mother...sad stories, but obviously very common ones in these parts." He straightened himself, his considerable girth. "But let me tell you something. We've had our share of success stories here at *Deez Beatz*, but none to the level of T-Ray. He was a rising star in every sense of the word, and what was more, you could tell he had longevity. He had that special something that said his light was gonna keep on shining. It was so inspiring."

"How so?"

"Well usually an up-and-comer makes a hit record or two, starts making money, and next thing you know he's got an entourage the size of a football squad following him everywhere, wipin' his ass for him, helpin' him spend his loot like *they're* the ones who earned it, and before a dude knows it, he's burning through money like *that's* his job, instead of making music. They forget that one hit does not a superstar make. And this business is a cold one. It'll spit you out the minute you stop producin'. Alotta these kids don't realize that. They know it intellectually perhaps, 'cause they've all heard of people like MC Hammer and shit. But they just don't think it could ever happen to them, and so they don't prepare for the future.

"But not T-Ray. He got his first big paycheck and the next day –- boom! –- That cat was down in Center City, meeting with some fancy-ass, bow-tie-wearing financial advisin' muckety-muck about how to invest it." He chuckled. "And let me tell you...You'd never seen a young kid so tight with his money! And good thing too 'cause that momma of his would've spent every last dime if she'd had gotten a hold of it. On some level he seemed to realize that.

"And forget about tomcattin'. He'd always wanted kids –- since he was a kid himself! -- But unlike a whole lotta niggas, he intended to stick around to raise them. To marry Diamonique." He smiled fondly. "Shit. Them two fools woulda had a white picket fence if it had all worked out."

"But they still can, can't they? I mean, he can't stay in jail forever...?"

His gaze fixated on the bank of tinted, bulletproof windows and beyond, as he sighed deeply and began to wax poetic. "If there was one horse I had to put my money on," he said, stroking his chin. "One young person who might rise above this City, who would make it, it was T-Ray. A life of crime was not an option for him; it wasn't even a part of the equation. Since he was eight years old he had gangbangers left and right trying to recruit him, but he always walked the straight and narrow, no matter what the cost. He was too smart for that kind of life, and he knew it. But now...now he's neck-deep in that shit, the same shit he worked so hard all those years to avoid." His expression was heartbroken. "And prison changes people, Miss Langston, but not in the way the politicians would have you believe."

She thought of Bruni then, of his brother in jail. "How do you mean?"

He offered a patient smile. "Politicians like to talk a lot about rehabilitation but, for a litany of reasons, criminals often become *worse* in prison, not better. And as much as it pains me to admit it, I have a hard time believing he can make a comeback from this."

"But never say never, right? I mean, stranger things have happened...?" She was feeling crestfallen and desperate, and was probably sounding incredibly naive but she didn't care. She was just so damn tired of these sad, sad stories, she had to hold onto hope that they wouldn't *all* have tragic endings. She just had to.

Silence settled between them like a sleepy Rhino: vast, wide, and potentially dangerous. "I've read your columns, Miss Langston," he said with a long, placid smile. "I know your penchant for the positive, and I admire it. I really do. It's a rarity in this world anymore. But I have to tell you; it was like a horror movie. It just happened so fast; the way T-Ray took a bad turn. He just isn't the same person anymore. The light is gone." He snapped his fingers. "Just like that, it's all gone. It's like something sucked the soul right out of him."

Just then Sydney's phone erupted, the jarring ring making her jump. "I'm so sorry!" Annoyed and embarrassed by the interruption, she rummaged through her bag in search of the culprit, frantic to turn it off.

When she finally found it she recognized the area code, but not the number itself. Someone was calling from Phoenix. *Cody*, she thought, though it wasn't his number, pressing the mute button, and sliding it on the edge of the desk between them. "I'm so sorry. You were saying?"

Dee Cassius went to continue but then the phone went off again just a moment later, this time on vibrate, trembling against the wood.

"Looks like you're mighty popular today," Dee said in an act of graciousness.

She felt her neck burning red. "I apologize," she said, moving to turn it off, but seeing it was the same number again, her brow creased.

"Perhaps it's important. Maybe you should answer it."

"Oh no, I—"

"Please. I insist." He leaned back in his chair, hands clasped, eyes focused back on the windows.

Aggravated, she clicked the "ON" button. *This better be good*, she thought. "Hello?"

"Hello? Is this Sydney? Sydney Langston?"

"Yes?"

"This is Jim Cavalier."

Jim Cavalier? The coach of the Cardinals? Cody's new coach? What was going on here exactly?

Baffled, she straightened in her chair. "Y--Yes?"

"You were listed as Cody's emergency contact. I'm afraid there's been an accident."

39

5:15pm

"She was getting too close for comfort," Bruni grunted before whacking the ball against the wall with the sum of his might, his racquet a weapon come alive.

"That was out," Sault said smugly before bending over to catch his breath. Bruni handed him a bottle of water and he nodded his thanks. "And you think this'll do it? You think now she'll finally drop the whole thing?"

Though panting, Bruni was indignant. "Don't *you*?" His words ricocheted against the compact walls of the racquetball court.

Still trying to catch his breath, Sault shrugged, noncommittal. "Well she did break off their engagement. Maybe there's no love lost there."

"Yeah well you haven't heard the tape, Sterling. There's still love there. Trust me," Bruni implored, swiping his wristband against his glistening forehead. "This'll work."

"And if it doesn't? Then all you did was piss off a shitload of Fantasy Footballers."

Bruni thought of Wrigley then, now back from Phoenix and now holed up in some rat trap motel on Admiral Wilson Boulevard that accepted cash, required no ID to sign in, and was used to its occupants wanting their privacy. He had his untraceable muscle with him;

people whose names Bruni didn't even know, and didn't want to. All he cared about was that they were obviously professionals who had impressed the hell out of him with their flawless takedown of Jarvis.

"Look, Sterling. That wasn't the only trick up our sleeve. In case you haven't noticed, this is war; and it's one I am fully prepared to win."

40

7:09pm

"I hate that my last conversation with him was about work," Sydney lamented, fingering the stem of her wine glass as the tears rolled down. Stacks of Chinese food and Styrofoam containers from various eateries all delivered by a worried and well-meaning Nana Jean sat steaming on the countertop behind her, sure to go uneaten.

"I know you do, darlin'," Nana Jean said gently, tucking a wayward piece of hair behind Sydney's ear. "I know."

She'd come as soon as she heard; but after hours of talking, it was time to go. They hadn't heard anything new about Cody's condition in hours, and it simply didn't do any good to speculate. He was alive, breathing, and could you ask for anything more? That's what she'd wanted her granddaughter to realize, to cherish. "Your work is something that's important to you, Syd. Don't feel bad about it. It's something that he loved about you."

Loved. It hung in the air between them like a noxious mushroom cloud: the past tense.

Nana Jean corrected herself quickly. "Loves. It's something he *loves* about you."

Sydney sighed.

So far the details had been murky, but this much she knew: Cody's crumpled body had been found alone in an alley after leaving a Phoenix bar. He'd been jumped, and the police said the weapon used had been a blunt object, presumably a baseball bat, since they'd beaten him so relentlessly the Louisville Slugger insignia had been impressed upon his torso like a cattle brand. There were no witnesses, and the police were waiting for him to regain consciousness so they could question him.

Oh Cody, she thought, with a new batch of helpless tears. *Cody, Cody, Cody.*

The one thing that stood out in the investigation, however, was that the perpetrator never took his wallet, or his Rolex. Nor his Super Bowl ring. And if robbery hadn't been the motive, what had?

She'd wanted to book a ticket immediately, to jump the next red eye from Philly to Phoenix without another word, but Cody's coach said she wouldn't be able to see him anyway, and had kindly asked her to just sit tight –- he'd keep her updated on any and all developments.

Nana Jean smiled weakly, but her voice was strong: "Listen, dear. You know I'm not a fan of your workaholism, but I am going to give you a free pass tonight."

"Wow, that's a first," Sydney said, smiling for the first time in what felt like years.

"Well, just until you hear something. It'll take your mind off everything at least, and Cody would want it that way."

Car keys in hand, Nana Jean opened Sydney's front door, before motioning to the spread of food. "You better eat something, though, darlin'. Promise me?"

Sydney smirked. "I promise. How could I pass up a home-cooked meal?"

They embraced a final time, and then Nana Jean was gone, and Sydney was left alone once again. She took armfuls of the take-out into the kitchen, knowing there wasn't a chance in hell she'd be eating any of it, at least not tonight.

Instead she took her wine and decided to take up Nana Jean on her "permission slip", deciding that work, not food, was on the docket tonight. Anything to distract her; to keep the fear at bay.

She took a deep breath. On the wall of her dining room she had summarized all of the Camden graduates' stories –- both the ones she had interviewed, as well as all the rest -- using various points to differentiate them. Throughout all of her crossover research however, the stories seemed to boil down to one thing: their success on the outside world inexplicably seemed to correlate to how the students had utilized their extracurricular time.

It wasn't surprising to her that the most successful students were the most active; she'd expected nothing less. But as she stared at the wall she began to notice something striking –- a pitchfork of lightning among the calm -- and her adrenaline surged with every passing second.

When she had first begun the project, she had targeted the graduates whom she suspected would become the most successful; the ones who had stood out as athletes or scholars, had won awards, or whom had been chosen among their peers as "the most" in any given category: likely to succeed, popular, etc.

Now, with her research and interview notes, she split this group into two smaller ones and, looking at the map of the Sir Thomas More campus, she took a handful of colored pushpins and began.

First, the easiest ones: For Cedric and Cyrus Ashe, she took two green pushpins and pressed them into the football field.

Then, leafing through her notes, she plucked a few graduates she hadn't yet been able to interview.

> La'Kisha Bailey: GPA 1.8. Basketball Dance Troupe (co-captain). Art Club. Voted "Class Flirt". Student at Castle's Cosmetology School (Philadelphia), set to graduate on time; plans to be a manicurist. Works part-time at Ida Isley's Dance Studio on Route 38.

> Alejandro Baptiste: GPA 3.3. Color Guard. Voted "Class Clown". Patient at County Psych Hospital (no history of mental illness).
>
> Deshandra Carmichael: GPA 4.1 (weighted to include advanced placement classes) Valedictorian. Marching Band (Flute). Black Student Union. Voted "Most Likely to Succeed". Working in porn.
>
> Maria Guittierez: GPA 2.7. Choir. Remedial math. Nanny for "Nannies for Hire" (reputable firm). Annual income: $66,000. Plans to open her own daycare facility one day.

Then there was T-ray's best friend, whom both Ebony and Diamonique had spoken of:

> Mailk Jordan: GPA 2.7. Track star (Hurdles). School newspaper columnist. Voted "Best Looking". Crack head.

With every pushpin, she saw a pattern developing, and it gnawed at her. Sweating now, she moved faster, her breath quickening, not wanting to yet admit out loud what she was feeling in her heart until she was sure it was, indeed, what she thought it was.

> Yoshiro Kim: GPA 4.2 (weighted due to Advanced Placement classes). Asian American Club. Knowledge Bowl. Mock Trial. Student at Temple University, current GPA 3.8.
>
> Sara Knotts: GPA 2.9. Cross-country. Environmental Club. Voted "Most Reliable". Volunteer at St. Mary's. Planned to become a nurse, like her mother and aunts. Prostitute.

Nia Sanchez-Otero: GPA 3.0. Head Cheerleader. Peer Helper. Voted "Most School Spirit". Unemployed, on welfare.

Satiri Patel: GPA 3.6. French Club. Marching Band (clarinet). Habitat for Humanity volunteer on weekends. Voted "Most Likely to Make a Difference". Rejected by Peace Corps. Whereabouts Unknown.

Ashanti Prince: GPA 3.2. Cheerleader (Football, Basketball). Member F.B.L.A (Future Business Leaders of America). Voted "Friendlist". Stripper at Gurlz Gurlz Gurlz on Admiral Wilson Boulevard.

DeAndre Quan: GPA 2.1, Basketball star. Voted "Most Athletic". Point Guard for Duke.

Then there were the kids she *had* interviewed:

Diamonique Keyes and Ebony Valdez: both had been members of the Black Student Union and both had maintained impressive Grade Point Averages of 3.9. Diamonique had been a cheerleader whom Dee Cassius had said had changed in ways he couldn't believe, while Ebony Valdez had had to quit the team due to an injury and had taken up debate instead. One had given birth to a child with severe birth defects, fathered by a one-time successful rapper now serving twenty years, while the other was at Rutgers, Pre-law.

Sydney was both floored and saddened by the drastically different paths their lives had taken, but as she watched the pattern continue to develop on the wall in front of her, knew that she shouldn't be.

Sherrod Jefferson: Aspiring actor, Honor Roll Student, Color Guard. His grandmother, Marion, had said: "I used to kid him that he was like the mailman; neither rain nor sleet nor snow could keep him from practicing."

She thought of T-Ray then, and how Diamonique said he used to come and watch her at every practice, without fail; how he would sit in the stands writing lyrics to the songs that would become so popular, watching the girl he loved –- an honor roll student, a beautiful cheerleader –- who would go on to mother his child. Theirs should have been a modern day success story; and the kind of inner-city anecdote that makes good people smile. She thought of the nickname the cheerleaders had given him, Camel Joe, because of his water fountain habit, and suddenly her thoughts drifted back to the other day when she'd watched the football team managers dragging out hoses to fill the Gatorade containers, the players lined up at the fountains until they got their fill.

You're wasting time, she admonished herself and quickly moved to her computer. All of the kids she had studied should have made it for one reason or another; whether they were academic, athletic or social standouts -– they were *all* standouts, nonetheless. But, as her push pins showed, the ones who had fared the worst had all spent significant amounts of time in the same vicinity of the campus: by the football field. Football, cheerleading, Color Guard, ROTC, Track, Band, Cross Country –- you name it; they'd all logged countless hours out there, with the Delaware shimmering in the backdrop, while the ones who had just as equal of a chance to "make it" beyond graduation -- who actually *were* now "making it" -- were kids whose extra-curriculars had kept them elsewhere, oftentimes indoors.

She was determined to find something on the Internet, although she could not say what. But something told her this trail was only just beginning.

Even so, as she began type, she found she was still conflicted because for the life of her she couldn't imagine what in the world one had to do with the other.

All she knew was that they did.

41

"Concrete Jungle"
Lyrics by: T-RAY

Rundown days
runaways
homeless ghosts
jesus saves

Johns from the 'burbs in shiny suv's
tricks on the corner waitin' to please
tryna ignore the baby seat in back
'cause *this* baby girl needs her crack

but the river,
it still flows
flows
flows
welcome home, ho

Mad pollution
Nasty-ass prostitution
baby daddy

rolls a fatty
while money-hungry trash
gang-bangin' for cash
gettin' paid
gettin' aids
chasin' that dragon
fallin' off the wagon
h-i-v
junkie
hatin' on the whores
but lovin' that horse

and the river,
it still flows,
flows
flows
welcome home, ho

wanted to leave but girl never could
now you'll die in this here 'hood

I seen pictures of the jungle
it's pure
it's clean
bright life burstin'
everythin' green

I seen pictures of the jungle
They's ways to escape
No foster care
no prison rape
it's god's country there

> this ain't no jungle
> there ain't no god here
> there ain't no god here
>
> and the river,
> it still flows,
> flows
> flows
> welcome home, ho

Sydney set aside the binder containing T-Ray's lyrics and took a long, deep sip from her merlot but it offered no comfort. But what possibly could? Cody was laying in a hospital bed 3,000 miles away, his life dependent upon machinery. And just the thought of that made her want to curl into the fetal position and die.

From her perch in the fraying lawn chair on the roof of her building she watched the windows of Philadelphia's skyline lit like dancing fireflies in the muted night sky, glittering in the Delaware River below it, separating Jersey from Pennsylvania. She'd scouted on the Internet until her eyes grew itchy and dry, her body an exhausted shell, ultimately realizing her research was drawing her into endless circles. That's when she'd called it a night, filled up her glass, and made her way up here, where her worries always seemed to wane.

It was beyond late but it mattered naught; there was no hope of sleeping tonight. She'd already left a voicemail for her boss requesting a personal day, knowing the chances were good she might take off the remainder of the week. That Roger O'Dell might insist so.

She took another healthy gulp, savoring the burn in the pit of her rumbling stomach. She hadn't eaten in what felt like weeks, but the idea of doing so was incomprehensible. She felt unnatural, like her life belonged to someone else anymore; like it was something she was watching from afar. It was eerie and disconcerting, causing her to look over her shoulder, not sure what she might find.

It was times like this when her mind always found its way back to the one place she wished it wouldn't. As she watched the cars trickle like a trail of beetles over the bridge, her eyes swept over Camden below and before long, the face of her father was soon looming before her.

He had been good-looking, that much was incontrovertible. "He could've had any woman he wanted," she remembered Mama saying with pride, oftentimes in light of the latest bruise or black eye, as if those were simply admission charges into a handsome man's world. "Any woman at all."

He was charming, too. That's how he'd been able to fool so many people for so long.

And then when the charm wore off, when he no longer could deceive the masses with a simple dimpled smile, he'd still had one last defense, and no small one at that: he'd had his badge to protect him, and behind that, the force of a hundred men or more who would die before betrayal; who'd lie to protect an oath, a fraternal code, an unspoken bond of brotherhood...

How could Mama have fought against that? Already so beaten and so broken...How could she -- or any woman, for that matter -- have hoped to find justice when all of the jurors seemed so indifferent to the plight?

A latent memory surfaced then, one so painful she always fought to temper it: Her legs swinging, her scabby knees taunting her to pick at them, even though Mama made her promise not to; the hard wood of the bench beneath her as she waited for what seemed like forever, all the Camden policemen in their crisp uniforms bustling about, scary men in silvery chains shouting bad words.

"I'm sorry, Melanie. I really am," the Chief was saying, his hammy arm draped around Mama's thin shoulders, his belly bouncing as he walked her from his office toward the precinct's front door. "But there's simply no proof. And there's nothing we can do."

Who wouldn't have felt helpless? She wondered as the wine warmed her from the inside straight out to her chilled flesh.

Holding back tears Mama had simply nodded at him. "No proof, huh?" was all she said, as she pulled a young Sydney to her feet with her good arm, the other one shattered and useless in a sling: the latest result of an irrational rage. "Let's go, sweetie," she said, and left the station with her head held high, ignoring the Chief as he called after them to 'take care, now'.

A week later, Sydney's mom was dead.

And her Dad? Charged with murder in the first degree.

Working in Camden had brought to the surface so many memories she'd rather forget. And now with Cody...she needed to forget about both the past *and* the present. She needed to clear her mind, but knew the wine wouldn't do it. Hoping to at least distract herself, she picked up another binder, this one full of scrawled notes, and tried to get absorbed in the material.

The meetings with Diamonique Keyes and Dee Cassius had solidified things in a way that was difficult to articulate; all she knew now was that her feelings about this assignment had been correct from the start: something was definitely wrong, and she knew now that the source of what was wrong, that "something", was the school itself.

Even though it sounded ludicrous, and she was almost embarrassed to admit it, she knew it was true nonetheless. There were just too many coincidences, too many parallels in the plethora of sad stories, the dots too similar not to connect.

And what was more was that her feelings were just too intense, every one of which stemming from an insatiable intuition that seemed to be asking her –- no, *begging* her -- to listen to her gut, to follow her nose, to refuse to doubt.

The strongest connection among these children she had both studied and interviewed had all arose from the same keystone: Sir Thomas More Tech, and as foolish as it sounded, they all seemed to be worse off for having been there, when the school had been designed to provide the very opposite effect.

But just look at the outcome: while the graduation rate had been high, only a handful of drop-outs there compared to the 65% at Camden High, more than half had completely crashed in life afterwards. Grade Point Averages, high marks on SATs, impressive athletic and extracurricular achievements...none of it seemed to matter now, just a few years later. And these weren't just minor failings either; ones that could be attributed to simple immaturity or the kind of fumbles everyone seems to earn before they get the hang of adulthood. After all, what twenty year old *doesn't* make mistakes? But these were such huge failures -- smoking crack, jail, porn, prostitution -- that would affect their lives indefinitely. And these kids just seemed too damn smart to willingly take those dead-end roads. It just didn't make sense.

Frustrated, she tossed the binder aside and opted instead for one of the several library books she had checked out -- this one at least fifty years old if it was day. Leafing through *A Portrait of Camden*, her thoughts remained wrapped around Cody, leaving her mind unable to process any of the words on the pages as they flipped past.

She reached the mid-section: a series of glossy pages of black and white photographs, and she found herself thinking sarcastically: *Oooh pictures. I can handle that. Maybe not words at the moment, but pictures – yes. I can handle that.*

Taking another sip of merlot, her focus desultory, she almost quit and set the book aside but just then something caught her eye. Brow cinched, she looked closer, setting her glass down slowly, wanting to make sure she was *really* seeing what she was seeing.

The black and white photo was taken from a road -- MLK Boulevard, perhaps -- with the bridge and the Delaware aglitter in the distance. It was a ribbon cutting ceremony of some sort, with smiling men in suits and fedoras, celebrating the opening of McDougal Industries, a thermometer factory.

Sydney felt her pulse quickening. It was as though someone had jabbed her with an electric prod because all of a sudden she was alert -- more alert than she had been since the news of Cody.

She peered closer at the photo until her heart began to race with an understanding she could no longer deny.

Cradling the book, she scampered down the fire escape, its aged iron rattling beneath her, and through the window she'd left open into her apartment.

On her wall she scanned the tacked-up tapestry of background information regarding the project: various notes and cut-out articles, Xerox copies and blown-up photos -- including a print of Sir Thomas More Tech, circa 2010, where it sat like a proud peacock upon that tuft of land; a prim cherry on a picture-perfect cupcake.

She glanced down at the photo from the book one last time before holding it up next to the photo on the wall, her hands trembling.

Side by side there was no mistaking it: McDougal Industries, thermometer factory, had indeed once occupied the same land as Sir Thomas More Tech. Years before anyone had had the inclination to cultivate young minds there, it had been the home of billions of mercury-filled thermometers. Glancing back and forth until there was no possible doubt, Sydney stumbled back against her drafting table desk.

You needn't be a scientist to know that mercury was unhealthy; the list of maladies related to mercury exposure was as wide as it was long. A second later she was seated at her drafting table, firing up her computer and Googling everything mercury-poison-related.

The very first site she visited detailing mercury toxicity and its symptoms left her mouth agape. Almost at once the puzzle was pieced together for her.

Damage to brain dysfunction, personality changes, memory loss, disruption of the nervous and reproductive systems, birth defects...

Every single student she had focused on had displayed something from the list, and Sydney felt herself reel at the speculation. Each website she went to featured more of the same and after while she knew it was pointless to continue; site after site, page after page, word after word...the information she read was as redundant as it was irrefutable. The school and the factory had occupied the same plot of land, and the factory had clearly left a morbid, lasting impact. There were simply no two ways about it, and suddenly she was propelled into some foreign orbit where impossible things could suddenly become true and real.

Thinking of all those innocent kids who not only went through a battery of tests to be admitted to Sir Thomas More, but had placed their dreams there, offering them up like sacrifices to a god, and how something so far beyond their control, reaching from beyond the grave it seemed, had robbed them blind...it was dizzying.

Her heart was frantic, but she would not rest until she got to the bottom of it.

42

Tuesday
1:13am

While Sydney had spent the majority of the night franticly piecing together bits and pieces from her research, her notes, from the information in the books and from the internet, all guided by her own intuition, Ben had been up, as well, doing a great deal of thinking of his own.

For the longest time he hadn't known whether or not Kat was the right person for him, but by calculating a baby into the mix, any doubts had seeped away. Or if not seeped away entirely, they'd certainly retreated.

They might have had their differences, but didn't everybody? Sure they came from different backgrounds –- different worlds, really –- but Kat would make a fine mom. Wife. She'd throw herself into both roles just like she did everything else, not accepting anything less than excellence on her part; rising to each and every occasion and exceeding expectations handily. He'd be proud of her. To have her as his. (He tried hard not to think about her meteoric career, and how there was no way in the world she'd entertain being a stay-at-home mom, and all of the other ways their parenting philosophies were likely to differ...)

Thoughts ran like downspouts to his father, too, God rest his soul, and how idyllic his own childhood had been; what he could look forward to with a child of his own. He imagined the joy he'd bring to his mom, too -- Susan Campbell was born to be a grandmother -- and how this turn of events might even prompt Zoey to return to the fold. She was of babysitting age now and the Zoey he knew and loved wouldn't pass up any opportunity to take care of a baby, especially Uncle Ben's. With any luck she'd hear about her cousin-to-be and abandon all the Emo and Goth crap for a more civilized way of life without any further intervention on their part.

Well...one could hope anyway.

Then there was Beth to think of...Her drug-addled body and the way she'd abandoned her own child for life on the streets. Imagining how sick one must be to do such a thing made him fiercely paternal and protective of both Zoey and this unborn child of his, and only intensified his resolve to do the right thing.

The only wild card would be Kat's family: traditional, rigid Irish Catholics hailing from Marblehead and Hyannis Port who wouldn't like the news of an unwed pregnancy one bit, especially the Old Man, their lives set to their own set of ethics, no matter how ironic and ridiculous. Hypocritical even.

But the joy of a baby, a new life, would melt even the strongest icebergs, wouldn't it?

Ben could only hope.

Light was creeping into the night outside, staining the sky milky gray while Van Morrison crooned from his IPod. He was on his couch, staring at the ceiling, fighting sleep, thinking of Kat and the endearing way she liked to chew on the end of her pen when she thinking hard; how her lips tasted like strawberries; and whether the baby would have blonde hair like hers –- thick and straight -- or his curly, unruly brown, when he heard the frenzied knock at the door.

He'd barely unlocked it when Sydney came rushing in like a gale, her face a-flush, thrusting a Fed-Ex package into his arms ("This was by the door") and jabbering on from the moment she'd crossed the threshold.

"Wait Syd –- hang on a sec..." he said, setting the package aside and trying to wipe the sleepy cobwebs from his mind. "You're giving me a lot here. Slow down, will you?"

She took a deep breath, attempting to compose herself. "Okay, okay. I know this is going to sound crazy, it really is, but..."

The tale she unloaded was almost too much. Gesticulating as she paced, light fought through the blinds, illuminating her motions against the far wall like frenetic shadow puppets, leaving him feeling dizzy as he watched, her manic energy making him more and more claustrophobic with every word she breathed.

"...And everything points to this one thing. It was the school. There's something wrong with that place, Ben, I just *know it*. Something was making those kids sick, and I think it's the mercury."

"Okay, okay," he said, holding up his hands traffic-cop-style. "This is –- this is --"

"Crazy, right? I know. But just hear me out. Please."

He didn't want to; in fact, it was the last thing he wanted; the very last thing of the entire fucking planet to be exact.

But this was Sydney.

He sighed. "Alright, alright." Sigh. "Just...just go back, okay? Start from the beginning."

She exhaled loudly, exasperated, but continued just the same. She spoke of Cyrus and Cedric Ashe –- about how their promising football careers had morphed into janitorial work; their IQs diminished, their hopes obliterated. About T-Ray and Diamonique, and their little baby born defected. About Ebony Valdez and how she'd had to quit cheerleading and was therefore no longer in contact with the football field, and how this might have made all the difference for her. Then about Sherrod Jefferson, and all the others.

When he'd the entire story not once but twice more, he exhaled and said: "I'm sorry, Syd."

Her face morphed from exhausted to quizzical in an instant.

"Sorry? For what?"

He leaned back, running his palms against his thighs. "I'm sorry because I can't help you."

"Wait a sec –" her face screwed into incomprehension. "You don't believe me?"

He had expected this. "I'm sorry but –"

And just then an unprecedented ire blossomed within her. "Are you fucking kidding me, Campbell?! You don't *believe* me? I'm telling you that –"

"Hey listen. Relax. It's not that I don't believe you, it's just that—"

"What? What is it then?" Her anger had been replaced by vacuity that accompanied a complete lack of understanding, and the pained look on her face made him look away.

"Syd," he sighed, "it's a bunch of things. For one, the school –- no wait, -- the fucking *football field* was making these kids sick? It's ludicrous. I'm sorry, but it is. You think people can just build things wherever they want? No matter how powerful they might be, there's a hell of a lot of work involved, Syd. Shit, to put up a Popsicle stand in this state you need months of negotiations under your belt. And a school? A three hundred a twenty million dollar school?" he all-but screamed. "There's a *ridiculous* amount of red tape involved. Miles and miles of it, Syd. There's untold numbers of bureaucrats involved, applications, zoning approvals –" He seemed exhausted just by thinking about it. He exhaled. "Listen." Exhale. Re-group. "OK, just listen. Please?"

"Go."

"Ok...so if the site was contaminated there's just no way it would have happened. *No way.*"

"But –"

Ben refused to be interrupted. "Second of all, all these kids...who knows why some made it and some didn't? This is Camden we're talking about. Most of these kids never had a chance to begin with. I'm not the least bit surprised most of them didn't make it. I'll bet if you looked at the statistics and saw –-"

But then he saw her face; deflated and pained, incredulity piercing her doe-like eyes. "You don't believe me."

"It's not that I think that –"

"Wait a sec," she said, shaking her head in disbelief. "I have to interrupt you. I just need to know one thing. Is this because it's Bruni's school?"

"What do you mean?"

She rolled her eyes. "What I *mean* is, if you weren't working for this guy, would you believe me?"

"Syd..."

"Then what is it?"

But Ben could offer her nothing.

"Never mind," she said, and, before he knew it, she had turned and walked away.

The last thing he heard was her flip-flops whispering against the hard wood, the door clicking shut behind her, and the chill left in her wake had never made him feel more alone.

43

10:48am

The graveyard was virtually empty, save for a small knot clad in black and navy, huddled together like a painful bruise at the top of a knoll. But even if it had been crowded, Ben would've had no trouble finding the right funeral: the line of news vans and reporters were idling, painful reminders.

The heat of the morning was brutal. Wiping his brow, hating that he had to be in a dark suit on such a hot day, Ben tried his best to ignore the stares from the reporters who probably recognized him –- and, inexplicably, the mass of rubberneckers who'd felt the need to show up -- feeling guilty, like the intruder he was; no different than the uninvited invading such a private affair.

But, at the same time, he felt justified: Herb Heim had been stalking *him*, not the other way around. And, what was more, he had no idea *why* he'd been stalking him, and it was driving him nuts. If he didn't try to get to the bottom of it, the likelihood of him having a good night's sleep for the next string of months was negligible.

He made his way toward the group of sweltering mourners, taking care to turn off his cell, hoping his plan would succeed despite its roots in stupidity. All he'd wanted to do was offer his condolences to the family, introduce himself, and hope one of them might recognize his name or face, might remember Herb mentioning it at some point.

He planned to play dumb, if he *were* recognized, just hear the person out. And because his mom had always told him you are more apt to learn by listening rather than talking, he had no plans of mentioning Herb's calls to him –- not until it seemed appropriate, at least. Was it well thought out? Not terribly. In fact, it was a pretty crappy plan, and he knew it. But it was something.

But, as he drew close and took a discreet spot atop the knoll, bowing his head respectfully, he quickly realized no spot would be discreet enough; and the heat he felt from the suspicious eyes boring into him as if he'd just mooned the crowd vanished his hopes for any type of warm reception.

Regret was instantaneous as his feelings of being invasive began to escalate. All he could think of was the faces he was deliberately avoiding, and for the first time it occurred to him that they were not just mourners but *in mourning*. He pictured them watching the same news reports he'd seen; the shock and horror he'd felt must have been multiplied by thousands -– no, millions -– because they'd not only known the cast of characters involved in this tragedy, but cared for them. Thinking of the two little Heim girls he felt sick; the relentless sun not helping in the least. It was almost too much to bear.

Though his head was still bowed his eyes flickered upward and then, from beneath his eyelashes he noticed a pair of shiny Mary Janes and the skinny legs of a little girl fidgeting within them. The glare of the black patent leather made him feel queasy as he imagined Zoey in them, waiting for her mother to be lowered into the ground, smelling the freshly churned earth just as he was, knowing on some level life would never be the same, but having no idea how much. It was only a matter of time, really; after all, hadn't his mom just said Beth was shooting up in her neck now?

What the hell am I doing here?? His legs were unsteady; he suddenly felt seasick on dry land.

"Excuse me, sir," a deep voice boomed, and Ben looked up to find a member of the funeral parlor staff smoothing his black tie against his chest like the professional griever he was. "This is a private ceremony. Are you a member of the family?"

Ben glanced over at the sparse group of Heim's occupying the hilltop, staring at him with something very close to hate, and he shook his head, knowing it was pointless to lie.

"Then will you please...?"

But he didn't need to finish; Ben was already on his way.

Embarrassed was not the word. Ben felt like the world's biggest schmuck and was suddenly very, very glad he hadn't introduced himself to a soul. It was a stupid plan anyway. *What was I thinking?*

The throng of reporters eyed him curiously as he approached, trying to decide if he was important enough to interview. Just then his cell erupted.

"How's it going?" Digger asked even before he'd had a chance to say hello.

"It's going," he grumbled.

"You don't sound too excited for an expectant daddy."

Ben stopped in his tracks. *She told him?*

"She told you?"

They hadn't discussed this yet. He hadn't even told his own mother yet. In fact, they hadn't told her family yet, either, and he'd spent all night trying to picture it, too, how it would all go down, how the Old Man would finally come around, maybe even apologize for being so hard on Ben to begin with.

But if Digger knew, then maybe Kat had told her family. Without him...

His anger went from zero to sixty. "When?" he growled, gripping the phone till he was white-knuckled.

"Hey, take it easy," Digger chuckled. Ben's blood pressure surged. "I was just calling to say congrats."

Ben's stride grew stronger as he approached the reporters, hot-red-lava rage poured from his pores, and even though he saw the man in fatigues coming his way, he barely registered it, despite the man's swift gait and laser beam intensity squared on Ben.

"I understand that," Ben said through clenched teeth, "But—"

And then he heard the whistling. He almost didn't notice it at first but then his connection with Digger began to fade and it became omni-present, forcing him to stick a finger in his ear to block it out.

"Listen Ben —"

"No, Digger. *You* listen." His fury was an avalanche. "I asked you a simple question. I--"

And then it happened so fast, no matter how many times he re-played it in his memory, it would never really make any sense.

First his elbow was knocked, fumbling his finger from his ear.

"What the fu—" he said, spinning around as the man in the fatigues was walking by, almost in slow motion, his mouth moving and Ben grappling to understand what was going on.

"Stay away from the school."

"What?" Ben spluttered.

Fatigue Man looked him straight in the face, his eyes gray like bullets or tombstones, and just as desirable. "You heard me, you nosy little fuck," he said, his tone so shocking, so menacing, Ben felt chill bumps shooting through his hair follicles from ear to ankle. "Or ka-pow." He made a child's gesture of a finger pulling a trigger on an imaginary gun, and perhaps it was this silly gesture combined with the utter gravity of the message that made it so scary. It was a crazy man's gesture, but one you'd be a fool to discount.

Struck silent by surprise, Ben could do nothing but stand there, the phone dangling in his now-limp hand, hearing Digger call his name over and over.

When he finally re-gained his composure he had forgotten all about the phone and began running, calling out: "Hey! Wait!" till his voice was something close to hoarse.

But Fatigue Man was already long gone, somehow absorbed by the crowd of spectators, the chilling sound of his whistling twisting and disappearing into the thick humid day like smoke from a fire that had never been started.

44

10:59am

Jarvis was dead; that was a good thing.

He was now just a memory -- soon to be a distant one, with any luck -- which made things better of course, but Bruni was still left to wonder and worry about whether or not he'd spilled his guts before he'd gone. He doubted he'd said anything to the wife. After all, he'd kept her in the dark for years about the sorry state of their finances; why go singing now? But he'd been shot in the preacher's office of all places, which gave Bruni cause to be concerned. Had he told him anything before the shots were fired, and if so, how much?

Luckily stray bullets striking unintended targets were a common occurrence in Camden, leaving little reason to believe the cops would probe much further. They'd likely focus their attention on the gangs and their latest activity, on recent beefs or reasons for retaliation... They wouldn't have much reason to assume it was an assassination, and even less reason to speculate Bruni had any involvement. So at least he could rest easy on *that* point.

And whatever snooping the little reporter was doing was about to come to an end. They had let her go as far as she was going to go, which was plenty. And if for some reason she wouldn't give up this story, they had recourse. Plenty of it. Roughing up her little boyfriend was only the tip of the iceberg.

Even better was that Ben was now on the hook with him. By getting his niece admitted into St. Andrews, and pretty damn fast, too –- no easy feat by anyone's standards –- Ben was indebted to him indefinitely. Plus he had a kid on the way now –- a happy little accident that shoved him further into Bruni's pocket. Ben needed him. And judging from his little encounter with the reporter last night, he was not about to join her on her wild goose chase.

But it was always the little things. No matter how much optimism he allowed himself to feel he knew it would be the accumulation of the little things that brought him down. They always did.

And, like it or not, Bruni's confidence was shaken, and based on last night: visible.

"What's going on, Dino? I want to know," Micki had demanded, hand on hip, blocking him from leaving his study.

He hadn't wanted to get physical but she'd left him with no choice.

"Micki," he'd hissed, grabbing her wrists and pinning her against the doorjamb. "Enough."

The look in her eyes had seared in his mind, and it wasn't the fear he saw that bothered him so much but the suspicion. *Just how much did she know?* He could kick himself for being so careless over the years, for speaking so freely around her. The woman he saw now was not the same one he always felt he could trust. Through Iggy he'd learned the hard way that loyalty could not be taken for granted; what was to say she wouldn't turn on him, too?

The sting of his brother avoiding him had not dulled, but Dino was so preoccupied with other more pressing things at the moment that he had been able to bat it away from his immediate mind.

But now thinking of it, of the nerve of Iggy not taking his calls, of refusing his visit, was enough to make him want to off Iggy after all. He could do it, too –- it wouldn't be hard. Just another jailhouse slaying nobody on the right side of the law would care about. A mere footnote as far as the press went.

But did he dare? Heim, Jarvis...then his own brother? While people might not connect them to him, the fact of the matter was that they *were* connected to him.

Add to that the pressure of the election and the way this opponent of his was suddenly growing balls, picking at his fundraising and holding press conferences like he had some kind of relevance; some kind of chance. But the press was paying attention, and that's what worried him.

He also had something else to think of. In Heim's last email before his death he had mentioned he was going to be returning his most recent payment. It was some sort of symbolic gesture to show them he was no longer under their thumb apparently, but as of yet Bruni had not received the money. And what could he do? Ask Micki about it? Sure, that'd go over well. "Um excuse me honey, have you noticed anything unusual in the mail? Say twenty thousand dollars??" Not a chance.

But by far most pressing was what to do about Iggy. Just the thought of this made him a little lightheaded, his fury was so great. He'd been basically lying to Jarvis and Sault all along, pretending Iggy didn't worry him, wasn't a threat. But he did, and he was. Now with Jarvis out of the picture, he only had to keep up appearances for Sault. But how long could that last? Sault was smart. If he didn't get the answers he wanted, he'd by-pass Bruni without second thought. And he didn't take kindly to lies. What kind of retribution was he capable of if he found out Bruni hadn't talked to Iggy? If he found out Iggy had refused to see him? All it would take was the simple bribing of a guard or two and he'd know everything. Then where would they be? The last thing Bruni could afford was their alliance falling to pieces now, right when everything else was, too. No, he couldn't afford that one bit.

It was something he hadn't wanted to seriously consider before but now he had no choice. Iggy had always been weak, always unreliable.

Dino had taken care of him his entire life, but what did Iggy know about loyalty? All he cared about was saving his own hide. He'd sell Dino out in a heartbeat, and as much as it pained him, Dino knew it.

He hated to be backed into a corner, left with no choice, yet here he was. Between the reporter's suspicions, Heim turning into a loose cannon, Jarvis' unraveling, his brother's treachery and his wife's nosiness, he was beginning to feel inundated under the weight of the mounting pressure.

But there was still time to untangle this mess, there was.

Even if it meant adding to the body count.

45

12:02pm

The chair scraped against the linoleum of the cold, drab room, and as Ben eased his lanky body into the hard plastic of the seat, his eyes bounced around; for once in recent days he didn't just imagine he was being watched, he *knew* it one hundred percent.

The C.O.'s eyes were unapologetic as they bore through, suffocating him, and just when he thought he could take it no longer, the door swung open and Iggy Bruni shuffled in, hands and feet shackled, flanked by two more guards.

He took his time getting situated before finally looking in his eyes, but whether it was for drama's sake or just because the shackles made normal movements difficult, Ben didn't know.

"So, Mister Campaign Manager. What brings you here?" Iggy demanded. "I assume my brother sent you."

"No, no," Ben said quickly, confused. "Not at all. He doesn't even know I'm here."

Iggy's eyebrows shot up. "Is that so?"

"I uh, actually, um —-" his eyes flickered between the trio of C.O.'s standing watch and listening close. "I wanted to talk with you."

Iggy took a long time answering. "About?"

"Well, as I'm sure you can imagine, your trial has had an impact on your brother's re-election and I, uh, was just wondering if any reporters have tried to make contact with you."

The silence that gelled between them was a frosty as it was thick, and Ben suddenly felt sheepish, kicking himself for coming. After all, this man's life was at stake; or at least his freedom; his day-to-day a struggle in survival...and here was Ben, whose greatest worry in life at the moment were headlines. He felt petty, and couldn't blame Iggy for telling him to fuck-off, which is exactly what he expected to hear when Iggy moved forward and opened his mouth, but instead –- surprising Ben –- he laughed deeply and said: "My brother. Fucking bastard. Can't even accept my phone calls, the prick. All his talk about legacy and family loyalty...it's all bullshit."

Ben couldn't believe what he was hearing. Why would Dino avoid his brother's calls? Why spend all that money on his defense just to let him rot? It made no sense.

"Let me tell you a little something about my brother..."

It was a story he'd been waiting to divulge for years –- Ben could just tell -- and as each word dropped from Iggy's mouth, Ben's eyes grew wider and wider and wider.

46

12:12pm

Lilies, dahlias and potted pansies filled the big old house on The Banks, bundles of beauty gracing every floor. But while they were lovely, they were beginning to get on her damn nerves. Not only was the combined smell hard to take, but no sooner would Poppy find a vacant space to fill with a newly delivered vase than the doorbell would ring again and another batch would arrive, and she'd be off, huffing and puffing, in search of somewhere else to stick them. Plus it was so hard to keep track of them all, of who sent what, in addition to each of the covered dishes that had been delivered by hand or left on the stoop in the days since Jarvis had been killed. She tried to remember the best she could, to record the deliveries in a notebook just like her sister had asked, but the steady stream of mourners and their offerings was beginning to take its toll. She felt guilty for thinking so, but that was nothing new because all she felt was guilt anymore. After all, how many times had she wished the Mayor dead? And now here it was, her dream come true, and she felt so perverse and cruel for wanting such a thing that now all she wished for was to trade places with him.

Just looking at her sister was enough to bring tears of shame. Poor Henny had never been such a sight: wailing and moaning, her lip quivering from sun-up to moon-down, her appetite gone, her pretty face ashen and trounced.

So vice-like was Poppy's feeling of culpability that she tried to avert her gaze as much as possible, worried her sister would discover the reason behind the blame in her eyes and know once and for all just how horrible of a human being she had become.

The whistle of the kettle whisked her back to the moment. She took it and began to pour through the steam into the matching teacups, her hands shaking.

If only she could do something to make things right; if only there was one thing that could ease her sister's pain, she'd do it. The Lord had to know she didn't mean all those things horrible things she'd said and thought, the way she and LaShay would mock them, the malice they tossed around as casually as confetti. She shuddered at the memory of it as she pushed her way through the swinging door and into the dining room where Henny and the Reverend were huddled over a mass of official-looking documents and a calculator. The mood was anxious, and Poppy was grateful that neither one of them seemed to notice that she was there.

"I just don't understand," Henrietta was saying again and again, her voice so confused it sounded strangled.

The Reverend was just as hard to look at, with his visible cuts and bruises, the bandages covering the larger ones, his face so gaunt and ghostly it reminded her of those haunting faces she'd seen in pictures from those German war camps. He had Henny's hand in his, looking pained as he tried to explain. "I wish I had an answer for you, I really do. But when Jarvis left this earth, he took the answers with him."

Poppy navigated her way around the cardboard boxes on the floor, the ones that had been brought from locked drawers in Jarvis's office down at City Hall, and placed the two steaming cups before them. She backed away and waited against the wall to see if they needed anything else.

"It just doesn't make sense...we had our troubles but nothin' ever like *this*..."

The Reverend's voice was gentle, almost heartbreakingly so, and Poppy found herself feeling guilty over him, too, for all those times she cursed the man, blaming him for her financial woes. *He never forced me to no bingo,* she thought with a lump in her throat. *Not to no Atlantic City, neither...*

"Henrietta, please. You simply cannot torture yourself by questioning the past. Not now. It won't serve any purpose."

Poppy felt her face flush. *If only there was a way to make things better...*

"Right now you need to grieve for the man you loved, and take care of the most pressing affairs."

"But how can I? Look at all this!" she said, her voice a desperate falsetto as she shoved forth a pile of papers. "Now I don't even know if I can afford a casket!"

And then at once Poppy knew; there was a way to make it all better. To rectify her wrongs; maybe even reconcile with the Lord...

"But Henny," she blurted. "What about all that money he been gettin' from the engineer? Why can't you use that?"

Two sets of eyes swung to her, both taken aback by the fact that she was there, in the room with them at all.

A long, dense silence filled the room slowly, like smoke from a smoldering fire.

Finally Henrietta's eyelids lowered to half-mast and her eyes narrowed to beads. Her lip uncurled to release a voice that was so low it was almost guttural -- but sharp, too, like a poisoned arrow. "What damn money?"

47

1:37pm

To say she was disappointed was like saying the sky is big. There could have been a hundred and ten reasons for Ben to deny her, but she couldn't think of even one that she might find acceptable at the moment. The battle between being confused and being angry raged within her, but she knew she had to push it all away and instead focus on the task at hand.

She'd made countless phone calls, but always got the same response: Cody was still under duress and unable to speak to the doctors, the authorities, much less anyone else. Questions clawed at her mind but she refused to let herself wonder at just how bad his mental and physical state had become. Imagining such a strong and capable man beaten down and helpless was just so painful it was almost too much to bear.

She needed to clear her mind, and as she laced up her Nikes she felt the cool breeze coming from the Delaware and knew this run was just what the doctor ordered. Running always helped her organize her thoughts, her temper, her emotions, and bring her back to center. And if there was ever a time she needed those things to happen, it was now.

After so many endless hours of studying the video of her in her apartment, of listening to her talk on the phone, of watching her every move, Bo Wrigley was nearly giddy at the idea of finally being able to see her in person, in all her glorious perfection.

He almost hated having to report back his findings to Bruni; he wanted to keep her all to himself. And now Jesse Timms had muscled into the act, nudging him from where they crouched in the bushes along the river's edge and smirking as he watched her.

"You weren't kiddin', Wrigley," he said with a wry smile, his eyes glued to the binoculars. "She's damn near perfect."

And she was. Her long bronze legs settling into a rhythmic show horse gait, her mane of sandy blonde hair a banner behind her. It was almost a shame to kill something so beautiful, and this thought combined with squatting among the brush and breathing in the briny air brought back memories from his childhood, of him and his father, hunting.

He remembered the chilliness of the morning air as they watched the doe taking a morning drink from a cool lake; of the crunch of leaves beneath unsuspecting hooves; of the raw anticipation of it all. He remembered bringing the scope to his eye with shaky hands that grew steadier as he pointed, as his father hissed in his ear: "Atta boy, Bo. Get her."

And as he watched Sydney, the way she bobbed along so innocently, so oblivious -- half-expecting her to pause and take a cool drink from the river behind her -- he felt the same electric thrill course through his limbs. *Bob, bob, bob...*he thought to himself.

Sitting duck.

48

4:55pm

His cell phone rumbled against the passenger seat and though he didn't recognize the number, he left one hand on the wheel and answered it anyway.

"Yo Campbell," came Chip Wesley's voice.

Given how irritated Chip had been the other day at The Statehouse, Ben was surprised to hear from him. "Hey, dude. What's going on?"

"Look, I feel bad about the other day. I have a lot going on and I...I was just annoyed by the whole thing. I thought it was a waste of time, you know? That you were being paranoid..."

Ben unleashed a laugh but it was sarcastic and humorless. "Thanks for the vote of confidence, man."

"Yeah, well. I'm apologizing now, alright?"

Ben feigned mock surprise. "Chip Wesley apologizing? This is a first."

"Alright, alright," Chip said, vexxed. "Quit busting my balls, okay? I'm being serious."

Listening closely for the first time, he heard the quickness of his tone, the desperate quality it had, and knew he *was* in fact serious. Ben's heart caught in his throat. He didn't like where this was headed. Still, he acted as casual as possible. "So what's up?"

"I saw how bad the whole Heim thing had you shook, and I gotta be honest -- not finding his personnel file was weird as hell. It's been eating at me ever since. It's...it's just fucking impossible that it could be missing. *Impossible. Especially* given the length of his tenure. And I...I...Well, there's just no way anyone could have taken it...and who would want it anyway...all it had it in it was..." his voice drifted. "Anyway, I have to admit it, bro," he said with an empty attempt at a laugh. "It got me a little shook, too."

There was a pause. Ben heard a horn in the background -- a strange horn -- not a car, but more like a ship. Shouting children. A woman with a foreign accent calling out something indecipherable. "Where are you?"

Chip must not have heard him, for he continued talking. "So I did a little more digging..."

"And?" Ben felt himself holding his breath, wanting to let it go but unable to.

"And, well...I found something. I don't know if it's anything but..."

"What is it?" Ben asked, edging forward in his seat, clutching the steering wheel like a life preserver. "What did you find?"

"Like I said, it could be nothing. But. Well. I asked my buddy in IT if there was anything, you know, on Heim's computer."

"Like what?"

Chip grew agitated. "Like fuckin' *anything*, dude. About Bruni. About *anybody*."

Ben snorted. "You mean you were worried about your boss."

"Hey look Campbell, I'm trying to help you out, alright? And yes, I was looking out for my boss. She *is* the Governor, you know. The most powerful one of all fifty fucking states, remember? And in case you haven't noticed, that *is* my fucking job. Last thing I need is for her to get tangled up in some bullshit, okay? Your boss isn't the only one in this goddamn state running. She needs to get re-elected, too, you know."

"Relax, relax. I was just messing around."

"Fine." He was pissed. "Mess around all you want but—"

"Look I'm sorry, man. Please. Go on."

Chip exhaled hard, like breathing wasn't coming naturally for him all of a sudden. "Well it turns out there was some sort of glitch."

"Glitch? What do you mean?"

Chip exhaled again, this time even deeper. "They're still working on it but it seems that Heim's hard drive is missing."

"Missing?"

"Yeah and—"

"From his computer at the Statehouse?"

"Yes."

"That's a pretty big fuckin' glitch, dude."

"I know, but —-"

"But what?"

"But...well, it might be nothing." But his voice betrayed that sentiment, and they both knew it. Ben had known Chip since their freshman year at Rutgers when they were both still gangly kids, looking to find their way. They didn't have secrets; they couldn't have kept them from one another if they'd tried.

"Well I hate to break it to you, dude, but it doesn't sound like you mean that, not for one second, Chip."

"Well...that's because there's more."

Oh fuck me. Ben sighed, feeling his head begin to spin, not sure he wanted to hear what was coming next.

"So I started asking around, you know, on the down low. And I talked to some of the State Troopers on the Governor's Detail, asking if they'd heard anything from their brethren about the investigation."

"All the papers are saying it was just a domestic dispute." And Ben should know; he'd read every single article and watched every news segment on the Heim case so many times he could likely recite them from memory.

"Yeah, well." Chip cleared his throat. "It might be. But I have my doubts."

Just then Ben heard a siren wailing in the background. He thought of the number Chip had called from, the one he didn't recognize. "Wait a sec – Dude, where are you calling from?"

Chip hesitated, then stammered: "Uh...Don't worry about it. Just listen. So here's the deal: the hard drive is missing from his home computer, too. Now look, it might just be –"

"*What?!*"

"Wait a sec, just listen –"

"Just *listen?* Are you kidding me? So you can tell me that it might just be a coincidence or some bullshit? Is that what you're going to tell me next?" Ben demanded.

"Just hang on a sec, alright? I don't know if it is or it isn't, and neither do you, okay?"

"Alright," Ben grumbled.

"Alright," Chip exhaled. "But that's not all."

Ben swallowed hard. "Go on."

"Okay. This is where it gets weird. So you know how Heim was just some bureaucrat who worked for the DEP?"

"Yeah?"

"Well it turns out he's the one who signed off on Bruni's school."

"So? What the hell does that mean?"

"Well it's a bit complicated but...well, in layman's terms, it couldn't have gotten built without him."

"Some government drone?"

"Yeah, well. It is what is. Just stay with me, dude."

"Okay..." Ben said slowly, simultaneously trying to let it sink in, and trying desperately to be of the mind that it was useless information. But, thinking of Sydney, of what she had told him, was unable to do so.

"All I know is that at best this situation might just be messy; it might just fuck up your campaign. That's at best. At worst...well, all I'm saying is that there might be some bad people involved, and if I were you, I'd stay the fuck away. In fact, I'm *not* you, and I'm staying the fuck away."

"So some hard drives are missing and what? You're scared?" He almost laughed at the improbability of it. "Scared of who? Bruni? Why?"

"That project cost the state three hundred and twenty million dollars, Ben. And that money didn't just fall from the sky, you know. Those were taxpayer dollars. And for the vendors there was a ton of money to be made, not to mention a ton of national media coverage. There was a lot at stake. If there was any impropriety involved -- any at all -- people might go to great lengths to cover it up."

The blood drained from his face. "What are you saying?"

"I'm saying take a goddamn look around you! Heim's dead. Jarvis Jasper. Both were connected to the school. Two hard drives missing might be a coincidence, but two deaths? All of it in the same week? I don't know, man. This is just getting too weird, and my days of helping you out with this are over. I don't want anything more to do with it. I have a wife, a kid on the way...I don't need this shit. I don't know what this Heim dude did or didn't do, I don't know who he knew or didn't know...all *I* know is that this situation is looking weirder and weirder and I don't want any parts of it."

"You're scared?" But it was a statement not a question.

There was a long pause. "Well, yeah, I am. This could end your career, mine...it could..."

Ben felt the hand of fear rake its nails down his back, moving in time with the soundtrack of Sydney's words: *There's something wrong with that school, Ben. Something was making those kids sick...*

"This is crazy," he heard a weak voice say, surprised to realize it was his.

"Look." Chip's voice had a new tone to it, one much softer; it was the weary sound of someone having been whitewashed. "If you won't take my advice and stay out of it, just promise me you'll be careful, okay? Last thing I need is to see your dead ass on the news next."

"Yeah," Ben said, his voice faint, thinking of Sydney's face as he'd watched her walk away. His best friend had come to him for help and he'd turned his back on her. She'd been scared, too – scared like Chip. But he'd all-but laughed in her face; and worse, let her leave.

Another blasting horn snapped him back to the here-and-now. "Where are you calling from?" Ben demanded, but then he knew: Chip was calling from a pay phone. Who knew where they had them anymore, but fear had motivated Chip enough to find one.

"There's one last thing," Chip said, ignoring his question. "As you can imagine, State Troopers, FBI, everyone, went through everything in that house."

"And?"

He hesitated just long enough for Ben to know that this would be bad news. "And...Apparently they didn't find anything unusual anywhere, except in Heim's study."

"Yeah?" He croaked.

"They found a safe...completely empty except for a torn piece of paper and an address jotted down."

"An address?"

"Yeah. It was yours."

49

Wednesday
12:12am

Ben hadn't expected anyone to be at Bruni's campaign headquarters this late. If anyone were to be there besides him, it would have been Marlena Torres, fundraising extraordinaire, but he knew she was in Philly at tonight's fundraising event, counting checks and rubbing elbows with the swanky guest list meandering about Sterling Sault's extraordinary penthouse.

Still, he saw a single light burning as he pulled up, and it gave him such a start that he'd sat in his car for several minutes, debating whether he should go in, just go home, or cut to the chase and call the police.

Why the fuck is a light on?

He sat there, just staring, thinking of bricks in his bag, of Herb Heim, and Chip and Sydney and their theories...before he finally came to the conclusion that someone had just forgotten to turn it off.

It wasn't a long shot, after all, and with that thought came scant relief and enough encouragement for him to turn off the car and head inside. But no sooner had his shoes hit the gravel of the parking lot than he got a bad feeling. At once he wanted to turn back, to head home, but chastised himself instead. *Christ Campbell, you're turning into a real nut, you know that?*

He forced himself forward and, not sure why, he took care not to let his keys jangle as he unlocked the back door and stepped gingerly through. Just inside the door he paused, his ears perked like a Doberman's, waiting to flesh out any foreign sounds.

Hearing none, he cringed at once as the floorboards creaked beneath his weight. He spent so much time here he felt he knew every inch of the headquarters as well as his childhood home, yet suddenly he felt out-of-place, like an amateur cat burglar fumbling to learn the nuances of his latest target.

But why?

He didn't know. All he knew was that he hadn't felt this strange since Herb Heim. Wait. That wasn't true. He hadn't felt this strange since the other day when that whistling freak-in-fatigues approached him at the graveyard and, at the mere recollection of that exchange, the hairs on his body sprouted like insect antennae and he found himself gulping –- hard –- his Adam's apple a boulder, swollen with fear.

He wanted Sydney to be wrong. Chip. He wanted to discount what they said, rule out their warnings, prove them foolish. But more than that he wanted to continue on with the campaign, win, and marry Kat with pride, knowing he'd earned whatever job the Senator would hook him up with, and look forward to becoming a dad. He wanted Zoe and his Mom to be safe. He wanted to be able to repay Bruni some day for helping them. Which was why he now found himself at Headquarters. He had no idea what he'd find, or what he was even looking for; all he knew was that he needed to prove that Bruni was a good guy; to them, and to himself. That Sydney's findings were a fluke; that Heim was simply a nut case...

But after his meeting with Iggy, there was no more denial; there simply couldn't be.

And then he heard it. It was faint, and if he hadn't been creeping, had just walked right in without hesitation, he might have missed it. But no, there it was. Soft, but somehow substantial.

A squeak.

Coming from the Senator's office.

Ben gasped despite himself. There was no way Bruni was here. He never was at Headquarters at this hour but, more importantly, he had a fundraiser tonight at Sault's, and the biggest one of the campaign at that. It was, quite simply, impossible.

But if it wasn't him, then who? Aside from Ben nobody on the staff would ever have the guts to enter Bruni's office without explicit permission, let alone have the key to do so while the place was empty.

And that's when the blood in Ben's veins officially turned to ice. Only two people had a key to the Senator's office; Bruni himself was one, Ben the other. Ben felt in his pockets and counted the keys through his denim, ticking them off silently. *Apartment. Car. Mom's house. Bruni's office...*

And there it was again. Ben nearly jumped at the sound, his heart banging with the same gusto as a snare drum.

Ben grabbed his head with both hands, feeling that same sick feeling he'd been having ever since he'd left Kat in Boston –- that same out-of-control free-fall feeling, like falling in a dream and jumping awake just before making contact with the earth.

And as he threw open the door, he steadied himself against the jamb, swaying from the shock of what he saw.

50

12:17am

At first glance, to the average person, Dino Bruni may have appeared normal, content even, as the ice clinked in his crystal glass while he gazed through the tall, broad quartet of windows up towards the night sky, the stars both piercing through and muted by the Philadelphia pollution.

But Ben knew the man's nuances well enough to know better than that, and he knew that if he'd been *truly* relaxed in his captain's chair, the heels of his Ferragamo's would have been on the desk with ankles crossed, his silver mane of hair coiffed to perfection, all accompanied by a serene smile on his face as a result of the cunning thoughts in his mind.

But tonight was different, and Ben sensed it immediately -- innately -- almost on a molecular level. And it wasn't just because Bruni was never at Headquarters at this hour, or on a weekend; nor was it because his hair, usually smooth and slicked silver was bunchy and wretched into spikes, as if he'd been yanking it, almost willing it away. And it wasn't just because he was supposed to be at a fundraiser tonight, or that he *loved* to be at fundraisers in general...it was all of these things, but the thing that got to him the most was definitely the last.

Bruni loved everything about fundraisers: the money he made, being man of the hour -- all of it. The way people swarmed about, gravitating toward him. Admirers, one and all.

Ben's presence was rarely required, but during the odd times he was forced to go he would spend a good chunk of the time watching his boss work the room, shaking hands, accepting business cards and praise, bathing vendors and constituents alike in the warm glow of his charisma, and Ben would marvel at how naturally it suited him, this courting process. How easily he made each person he spoke to feel like the only one in the room.

Then, in between handshakes, during those rare and split-second flashes of idleness, Ben would watch on as Bruni surveyed the scene, silently counting all of those who came to pay homage and sustain his campaign war chest.

Ben knew Bruni loved every minute of those events; even loved his trashy wife next to him, for the night at least, giggling and working that nugget of pink gum between her molars like nobody's business while she slugged down cheap Pinot Grigio as vigorously as from a famed vineyard as a box propped up on the tailgate of a van.

So what he was doing here tonight, on the evening of not only the biggest fundraiser of the entire campaign -- the one given by one of his closest friends no less -- was anyone's guess. All Ben knew was that he didn't like it one bit. And despite the all-encompassing weirdness of the night, or perhaps because of it, he pushed away his fears and pushed forward, letting the door snap back against the wall.

Bruni's shoulders shuddered a bit, but he didn't turn.

"Evening, Ben," he drawled, and took a long swallow from his drink. His voice was thickened by the scotch, and for some reason this made Ben relax a bit. Bruni liked his booze, and especially on a night when he was to be "belle of the ball" at Sault's, where the top-shelf booze was always plentiful, it would have been odd to find him *not* a little liquored up.

So maybe everything was fine.

Maybe he'd just had a fight with Micki, or had gotten tired. Or maybe was just sad over the passing of Jasper. *Yes, maybe that was it.* They had been friends for years after all. Just because he had said he was OK didn't mean the grief had ended. *I'm an idiot.* Ben thought to himself as the adrenaline begin to seep away, almost wanting to laugh at himself for his paranoid conclusion jumping. *Of course that's it.*

That was, until Bruni turned, and Ben saw his face. Dark circles dominated the jaded eyes and sagging jowls, making him look ages older and more than a little beleaguered. It was a dreadful sight, made worse by the sparse light. For a man who normally took such exceptional, excessive pride in his appearance, he looked frightening.

"Howdy," Ben said in a voice that he hoped conveyed a measure of ease. "How was the event?"

Bruni attempted something like a smile but it was plastic, and taut, and it didn't last long. Instead of answering he held up a bottle. "Drink?"

But before Ben could say a word, one was being poured. One without the luxury of ice, he saw, but the scene was precarious enough without Ben ruffling any feathers.

"Here you are," Bruni said and Ben moved toward it. "Cheers." But the toast was hollow, and the look in Bruni's eyes gave Ben the creeps. Bruni held his gaze in a way that was almost hostile. "Have a seat." It was not an invitation, but a command.

Ben slid against the soft chair and took a sip of the scotch. It was good stuff, very smooth. *Shit, it's been a long week,* he thought with another sip. *Heim. Digger. Kat. Fatigue Man. Iggy.* And another –- this one more like a gulp. And then before he knew it his glass was empty and Bruni was pouring more.

"So," Bruni drawled. "What brings you here tonight?"

Booze was definitely helping Ben feel better, but his guard was still up. He knew he had to play the part until he figured out what was going on, and he best not let Bruni grow suspicious in the meantime.

He offered one of his charming, lazy smiles, and said a silent prayer it would work. "Just trying to get your ass re-elected."

Bruni laughed at this -- harder than Ben would have normally thought necessary. "Well," he said, wiping his Sinatra-blues, still chuckling. "Thanks for that."

There was an almost painful pause that felt elongated, as though a pendulum was swinging between them.

Ben looked up and saw Bruni's face grow stone cold serious, his intention embedding itself into himself like thorns. "So what *really* brings you here, Ben?"

Ben snapped back to the situation at hand, wiping away any other thoughts. He grinned a scotch-drinking grin and tipped his glass before emptying it. "I'm serious, Dino -- I came here to do work tonight."

Bruni turned then, looking back at the skyline, and gave no indication as to whether or not he believed him. Ben waited for a comment, and when none came, he took another long swallow and inspected Bruni's profile, at his furrowed brow; the way his hand came to his face, his index finger resting above his upper lip and his thumb curled beneath his chin, the dull sheen of his manicure. He could have been contemplating anything important: his re-election, war and peace, life and death. Ben watched him and felt a surge of pride that this was the man he was working for, who did good things, despite what the press liked to say these days...

But then there was Chip and Sydney. *Sydney*. Just the thought of her made him squirm, hating the way they'd ended things, wondering if she might be right. But looking at the Senator now, it seemed impossible he could do such a thing. That anyone could.

As he felt the liquor flush his face along with something else -- shame? Fear? -- he wondered if he was thinking in a linear way anymore. The scotch had gotten to him, true. But so had about a hundred other things too: Heim. The missing personnel file. The bricks. Kat. Their baby. Chip's words: *"If you won't take my advice and stay out of it, just promise me you'll be careful, okay? Last thing I need is to see your dead ass on the news next."* It was a wonder he didn't...

"So," Bruni said suddenly, interrupting his thoughts with a jolt. "How's your niece doing?"

Surprise tasered him. "Zoey?"

The Senator smirked. But *of course* he meant Zoey.

"Aw she's just great. So far so good, anyway. And I can't thank you enough. Really. If it weren't for you…"

He waved him off but a smile was evident beneath Bruni's hand. "Good. That's good. Consider it a gift." He turned then, facing Ben, his gaze intent. "That's one thing I've always liked about you, Ben."

An inquisitive grin arose then. "Oh yeah? What's that?"

Bruni's eyes were ardent, almost suffocating, and Ben felt his grin dissipate beneath them. "Loyalty. You know your duty." But then turned back to the windows, the high beams re-directed. "You're a family man, just like me. You don't take your job lightly."

"Well, thanks…"

"I'm not blowing smoke up your ass, for God's sakes," Bruni said with a fierceness that was startling. "I'm telling you that you're a real man, Campbell. You know your place in things. Take some pride in that for fuck's sake, because nobody will hand it over to you."

Ben felt a smile melt across his mouth along with a certain measure of sheepishness. It was the kind of talk a father would give and he felt a pang, thinking of his Dad then: long gone and so sorely missed. His only goal in life had been the same as the day he was born; the same as most sons: to make their fathers proud. And if it couldn't be his own father, he reasoned, Bruni was the next best thing…

"Well that means a lot to me, it really does. Thank you."

Bruni's eyes were still far away, but he offered a slight nod of acknowledgment. "Standing by family, your girl. Having a child, leaving a legacy…I can't think of anything more important."

As he continued to drink Ben's mind wandered until it landed upon Iggy, and from his scotch-laden perspective, figured Dino must be doing the same. He could hardly handle the thought of his only sister shooting up, and imagined it must be just as hard thinking of your only sibling in jail, so helpless, among the most putrid people society had to offer. It was enough to give him the chills.

But then he thought of Kat, and of the baby they'd created, and it was impossible to keep from smiling as he drained his glass.

Bruni refilled them both, emptying nearly half of his before speaking, his eyes still fixed on Philly and beyond. "Tell me something, Ben," Bruni said slowly.

"Okay..."

"Have you ever heard of Ling Chi?"

Thinking he hadn't heard right, Ben sat up in his chair. "Excuse me?"

"Ling Chi."

Ben cleared his throat. "No. No I haven't. Who is he?"

"It's not a person. It's Chinese...it's..."

And just like that Bruni seemed to morph right before him. His face became savage in a way that wasn't retrievable, almost as if all the other times Ben had seen it he'd just been looking at a series of masks -- fooled with each fold, like a different face lay within each -- and only now was the real thing finally being revealed. Bruni's eyes were lumps of coal growing colder by the moment and, as Ben watched as the Senator changed, he began thinking that this person sitting before him was not the man he knew -- the Bruni charm and poise seeming to have dissolved into thin air -- and his discomfort amplified to panic, the hairs on his arms growing rigid.

The slow burn of the scotch made it hard for him to speak, but he was at a loss for words anyway. "I, uh..."

"Ling Chi," Bruni said again, fondly, as if it *were* a person: an old friend. His voice was far away and as Ben watched him gazing out the bank of windows into the night sky, he felt as though he was immaterial in this conversation; that Bruni was in his own little world. Perhaps on his own planet.

"It's a form of execution."

Unsure of what to say but certain participation was required, Ben cleared his throat and asked: "Um...Like a water torture or something?"

Bruni's smile came fast, but it was purely deviant, and Ben felt the air slipping away from him and out of the room.

"Slow-slicing." He turned fast then, his eyes snaring Ben's and refusing to let go. "They removed portions of the body--"

Ben cleared his throat, attempting to regain his composure, but to his dismay his voice was weak and frightened. "Portions?" he gulped. "Of the body?"

Bruni's peculiar smile remained, and it unnerved Ben like nothing else. "Yes. Over a period of time."

The color drained from his face. "How long?"

"Oh," he said casually, almost sing song. "Sometimes hours, sometimes days."

"Jesus." Ben felt sick.

"They used a knife. Just one. Slow and methodical. Let them bleed till they died."

Shock strained Ben's voice to a thread of a whisper: "I don't understand..."

"Death by a thousand cuts."

"Why are you telling me this?" he croaked.

Bruni looked at Ben then as if he was noticing him for the first time. "Incrementalism, Campbell," he purred. "Gradual destruction."

"I'm still not following..."

The flicker of Bruni's chin spoke of exasperation but the melody of his tone conveyed nothing but amusement in this menacing education. "It wasn't any one big thing. Don't you see? It's the little things that ruin you. Tick, tick, tick. Slice, slice, slice." The ruthlessness of his mirth shattered any remaining doubt in Ben's mind that Bruni had finally gone and fallen off his rocker. "Always, always the little things."

This time didn't wait for Bruni to fill it; Ben reached for the bottle himself.

"Top me off while you're at it," Bruni said in a tone that made it seem like they were discussing a Bull Market, not slaughter.

They took hearty gulps and while Bruni seemed to savor his, Ben all-but chugged his, praying the scotch would wash away these horrible feelings. This was way beyond normal; it was way beyond creepy even. It was like a nightmare come alive, and that clarity sparked a fire under his ass, and as he was about to say he had to go suddenly Bruni commanded:

"Come with me!" And before Ben knew it, the Senator was on his feet swiping both sets of car keys from the corner of the desk.

Nervous now, Ben chuckled; surely he was joking.

"I'm serious. I want to show you something."

"But we..."

With a sudden air of impatience, Bruni waved him off, making it clear there would be no further discussion as he flicked off the lights, leaving Ben in the dark behind him.

51

12:33am

Considering how much he'd had to drink, Ben had to admit that he was impressed with the Senator's driving skills as he careened through the shadow-flanked streets of Camden; he observed the speed limit, kept pace with the flow of traffic, and moved seamlessly from the comforting landscape of suburbia to the pulse of the highway to the lawlessness of urban traffic.

And then Ben felt and heard it before he saw it: the unmistakable crunch of gravel beneath them as they turned off West Camden Boulevard and through the barb wired fencing of the construction site, until suddenly the work-in-progress, half-finished building stood looming before them.

They'd kept the windows down the whole ride over, and Ben was relieved to realize that the fresh air had done some good. Bruni was acting better now, more like himself, allowing Ben to relax a bit, although not totally; this little field trip was a curveball to say the least.

The building was to be sixteen stories, but only half of them had been built thus far. Shrouded in dull moonlight, it was an ominous skeleton of steel beams on the banks of the Delaware, closer than was comfortable to the bridge heading into Philly. The sight of it was unnerving as it was; but the site itself looked like a graveyard. And, with its smell of new earth upturned and raw wood like new coffins, to Ben it felt like it was a place to make peace with one's sins, for death was surely imminent.

"You coming?" Bruni asked, but it was a statement, not a question, and just like that Dino Bruni was out of the car and moving among the murky shapes cast off from the giant stationary machinery before Ben had even unbuckled his seatbelt.

He sighed but didn't move until he saw his boss's silhouette advance toward the structure and, noticing the bottle in his hand he realized that he'd brought the scotch. Flinging the door open and jogging to catch up, Ben called: "Do you really think we should be doing this?" as he eyed the multitude of "DO NOT ENTER" and "NO TRESPASSING" signs fixed to nearly every available surface.

Bruni smirked. "This is my goddamn building, in case you've forgotten, Campbell."

That was both true and not true at the same time.

"Well..."

They reached the freight elevator. "As you might remember, I secured much of the funds for its construction. Fuck, I lobbied for its entire existence in the first place, Ben. You should know that."

They were silent for the rest of the way, and Ben felt his heart thumping as the shaft propelled them to the top floor, the one least constructed.

On a mission apparently, Bruni's gait was strong, straight, and making Ben nervous as he watched. There were gaps in the floor as well as power tools and potential pitfalls everywhere but Bruni didn't seem to notice, let alone care, leaving Ben no choice but to follow.

Bruni stood at the helm, it seemed, of the top floor, the majority of which was wide open, gaping like a graphic wound, the sinuous Delaware ebbing below. He slugged straight from the bottle, making Ben wince and wonder for the millionth time what in the world they were doing there. Though he'd felt nothing but oppressive heat on the ground, the wind whistled up here, making an eerie sound as it bounced against the naked steel, a hideous song construed to keep prisoners of war awake long enough to spill their secrets.

But, after enough quiet had passed between them, Ben felt himself relaxing, succumbing to the booze and the rhythmic sounds of the rushing cars on the bridge: a soothing hum; the lights from Philadelphia a genial comfort...until Bruni spoke.

"Look at this fuckin' place," he hissed, his voice so venomous it launched Ben right out the tranquility he'd been lulled into.

With one hand Bruni was strangling the neck of the scotch bottle, the other was a fist, ready to strike, his middle finger pointed at the city of Camden below like judge, jury and executioner.

"Look at it!" he demanded, ready to lunge if Ben didn't comply. "Look at this pathetic fucking dump."

Ben took it all in and had to agree; even from this vantage point, being so far removed, it lingered below like an oozing sore. Needy. Diseased. This was Mother Teresa Territory.

"These people, these ungrateful *fucks*," Bruni spat. His face was marred by shadows but Ben could see enough of it to be frightened, to begin thinking that everything Syd and Chip believed might be true after all. It was a horrid sight, that festering anger. That shrill bitterness. The way his mouth curled into a hateful snarl as he spoke of Camden; somewhere he never spoke ill of -- at least not to Ben's knowledge -- because it was his base, his political bread and butter, and, most importantly, a place he had come from, had called home. "You wanna know something Campbell? I've busted my hump for the better part of two decades to help these ingrates, and do you think they give a shit?"

Ben was too stunned to speak.

"Trust me, they don't." He swigged from the bottle. "Millions upon millions I've secured for this shit hole and what's the thanks I get? Nothing but problems."

Ben cleared his throat, unsure of what to say but ready to take a stab at it nonetheless. "You've done so many good things. Really, you have. But --"

"Look at the stadium. Just look at it." The lights shone bright off his eyes and Ben thought of how Bruni Park had been such a staple of

Camden's boys growing up. "Mine. All fucking mine. Brought that here singlehandedly, and don't think for one second it wasn't a pissing match. Christ, the Governor wouldn't speak to me for months, the rotten cunt. And that theatre?" He said swinging himself around to point at the amphitheatre, his voice rising and his unsteady feet wobbling, making Ben nervous as he watched. "We've had every big act from shit to shinola play there, and all because of *me*. I created that forum —- it was my fucking baby from day one, just like the school." He took a hearty gulp again, but interrupted himself halfway through, as if he just remembered something. "And that's another thing," he said, his voice now lowered to nether octaves, conveying just how pissed off he really was. "That goddamn school. Those fucking kids," he said, turning to Ben, whose fear of the situation was suddenly replaced by all-consuming curiosity. "They wouldn't have had a prayer without me. Not one. *Nada*. They would've all ended up as self-fulfilling-prophetic pieces of trash. And you know it, and I know it, and *everyone* knows it, but everyone's too fucking PC these days to say it out loud. Everyone's too scared to just come out and admit these fucking kids were lucky as hell to be given a chance. Yeah, it may have been a compromised one, but at least they had a chance. Fuck, it was better than anything they'd been given before. And if something happens, *I'm* the bad guy?" His voice practically screeched. He took a swig. "For real? For REAL? Go *fuck* yourself. You gotta be kidding me. Those kids..." his voice drifted off, and Ben wondered if fatigue had gotten the better of this tirade.

He went to rise, suddenly worried it was drunkenness and not fatigue that had made Bruni drift, that any second the man could teeter right over the edge and land himself six feet under. Ben moved fast toward him but just when he got close, close enough to grab his arm, Bruni shocked him by grabbing his.

Up close Bruni's eyes were watery, but the coals were still black, still burning. His grip was firm to the point of painful but Ben was more startled than anything.

"I *bled* for that school, Campbell. Do you hear me? *Bled*. I wouldn't have gone through it all if..." he lost his train of thought but picked up a new one. "You only have so much control, you know? There's only so many people you can control. And you think I had any help?"

Ben had no idea what he was talking about and was pretty sure Bruni didn't know himself...

But then he gripped Ben's wrist tighter, stared him into his eyes and said, clear as glass: "I fight hard for the little guy. Always have, always will. But there comes a time when reality has to set in. When you gotta count your chips and see what's what. I worked my ass off for a lotta years, doing the right thing. I paid my dues. But at the end of the day you still have to make a choice. And right, wrong, or indifferent I made mine." He jabbed a thumb at his chest. "I'm the one who had to make the decision, and I'm the one who has to live with it." His voice grew hoarse, but it was not weak. If anything, it was more powerful than ever. "Because one thing's for sure in this life, Campbell, and one thing only: you can't be a cop *and* a robber."

52

1:33am

Ever since he'd left the Senator he'd had a sick-tasting uneasiness he just couldn't get past. It wasn't until he was safely inside his apartment that the reason behind the apprehensiveness revealed itself; it was the words from the Senator himself: "*Standing by family, your girl. Having a child, leaving a legacy...I can't think of anything more important.*"

Having a child...

How had Bruni known Kat was pregnant?

Ben paced his apartment, his pulse thumping. He thought of calling Kat but knew it was out of the question. Her days of frolicking on the Cape and sunning on her Dad's yacht and whatever else she did up there had ended with the holiday weekend, and she was back in DC now, in business-mode, ready to attack The Hill.

He thought of Sydney then and moved toward his cell, but then thought better of it. He'd seen the hurt in her eyes when she'd last left him; the shock and pain and indisputable anger he'd caused when he'd turned her away. It was enough to shame him now. Make him hang his head.

There was always Digger; he could always be counted on to be up at any ridiculous hour of the night, ticking away on his keyboard in his insatiable search for other people's secrets. But why would Ben call *him*? He was still so pissed that Kat had told him about the baby that at the moment he didn't if he ever spoke to that sneaky prick again.

Then there was Chip. A call this late to his home would negate the last phone call they had and return Chip's ire like nothing else. He was a newlywed; his wife was pregnant...no, calling him was far out of the question. Then he thought of Chip calling from a pay phone, too scared to reveal where he was. *Did he know something Ben didn't? Was there reason to be worried his phone was tapped? How else could Bruni have known about Kat?* All of a sudden both Chip and Sydney's theories were starting to seem less far-fetched. The school -- no, the football field -- making people sick? A government drone that murdered his entire family somehow connected to it all? To Bruni?

Heim. And then he remembered: *"They found a safe,"* Chip had said. *"Completely empty except for a torn piece of notebook paper and an address jotted down."*

"An address?"

"Yeah. It was yours."

And just then the Fed Ex package caught his eye. He'd been walking by it, ignoring it for days now, but suddenly he knew with one hundred percent certainty who had sent it, and at that moment nothing in his life was more important than finding out what was inside.

53

Dear Mr. Campbell,
 By the time you read this, I'll be dead, and hopefully in a better place.

Oh Jesus. Ben felt his knees go weak.

 You never knew me but I hope you can understand why I chose you.

Ben stumbled and was relieved when the back of his knees hit the couch, whereupon he collapsed.

 I'm not a man of many friends, and after reading your quotes day after day in the newspaper, I figured you to be the kind of person I'd like to have for a friend.

Any lingering effects of the scotch were now gone completely, having been sucked out of him and away like vapors into the night.

 And as a friend I feel a duty to explain. Let me tell you a little bit about the man you work for...

Ben couldn't believe it. The more he read, the sicker he felt, until finally he couldn't take it anymore. He threw it aside and cradled his head in his open palms, sure he was about to wretch.

Could this really be true? Could it be that --

But then his phone rang, making him jump. His eyes narrowed on his watch: 2:32am. *Who the hell would be calling now?* Ben prayed it wasn't Bruni.

He grabbed his phone, and was shocked to see his mom's number on the screen.

"Mom?" he asked, the hairs on the back of his neck standing straight. "Is everything okay?"

"Oh Ben, thank goodness I got you. No honey. Everything's *not* okay. You need to get down here right away."

"Mom, what is it? Where are you?"

"I'm on shift, and I just heard they brought in Nana Jean."

"Nana Jean?! Why? What happened?"

"Someone set her house on fire. She's barely alive."

His stomach plummeted.

"Sydney's here but you need to hurry. They say it's bad, Ben." Her voice was cracking and Ben felt his heart going right along with it.

"I'll be right there."

And a moment later, he was out the door.

54

2:01am

The automatic doors swept open with a rush of air, lifting Ben's curls as he strode through, the bright fluorescent lights of the hospital a harsh and blazing contrast compared to the mild dove-gray night behind him. A storm was building, but the night was unflustered at the moment, almost a salve, and Ben hoped his interaction with Sydney would be just as peaceful, knowing it probably wouldn't.

He found her at the nurses' station of the ICU, her head tilted with concern as she listened to a nurse speak softly, her hair hiding her face.

He couldn't have timed it better; the nurse stepped away to take a phone call just as he approached, leaving Sydney to himself.

"Syd." He said, and she turned, startled, her red-rimmed eyes wide.

You could tell that her first instinct was joy, but then a cloud came over her fast: a visible reminder of their last exchange, and her eyes instantly fell to half mast -- skeptical and closed-off -- her face suddenly as readable and friendly as a stone, and she offered no warm welcome.

"Listen Syd, I'm sorry. I—"

Pressing her eyes closed she raised her right hand to stop him. "Ben don't, okay? Just *don't*. In case you haven't noticed I have enough on my mind at the moment and I don't need your bullshit, alright? Jesus Christ. What are you even *doing* here?"

Helpless, he watched her turn to leave and did the only thing he could think of: he reached out and grabbed her shoulders, swinging her around to face him. His eyes were kind but his tone was firm. "Sydney, I know you hate me right now and that's fine, but I came here to get you. We have to go."

She looked at him as if he'd just told her they needed to commit murder. "*Go?*"

"Yes, right now...we don't have time to —-"

"Um Campbell? In case you haven't noticed my grandmother is within an inch of her life. There is nothing —- *nothing* —- that would —-"

"Sydney I'm serious." His grip tightened. "We need to get the hell out of here right now."

"*Are you insane?*" she screeched, and the heads bobbing above the wall of the nurses' station shot up, weighing their options, wondering if they should intervene.

"Listen to me, please." He softened his grip but didn't let go. "You were right. I was wrong, okay?"

"You think that matters now? Huh? Do you? You think this is about being *right*, for God's sakes? Ben, Nana Jean is —"

"I know. I know she is. But I think I know why she's here, too. And if I'm right, which I think I am, we're gonna be next."

She moved to get out of his grip. "What are you even talking about? You're not making any sense whatsoever—"

"Sydney, listen to me. I know who did this. I know who did this to Nana Jean. Please. Just hear me out."

Her face was a jumble. "I don't understand —-"

His pulse was quick, and he watched her watching the sweat trace it way down his face. "Listen Syd. I don't have time to explain. Please just trust me on this, okay?"

"Trust you like you trust me? Believe in you like you believe in me?" she shook his hands off, trying to wriggle away. "Forget it, Ben. You've lost your mind."

But he caught her wrist and turned her back again toward him before she knew what was happening. "Syd, you were right. That school was making them sick."

Her eyes shone in the glare of the fluorescent light bouncing against the white linoleum and the pea green walls that were meant to soothe, but at the moment were doing anything but. "I don't understand..."

He shook her, just a tad, just enough to drive home his point. "The school. It was making the kids sick. And Bruni — all of them -- knew it."

The nurses were still staring, and when she turned to him, the weight of it all had registered, and so when he nodded toward the door, she let him lead her outside without another word, away from all the prying eyes and ears.

Huddled in the breezeway outside of the ICU, blue forks of lightning lighting up the sky all around, they tried to light their smokes against a furiously whipping wind.

Sydney leaned in close toward his lighter, a hand clamped against her hair to keep it from catching fire.

"Jesus Campbell," she said as she tried to catch a light from his shaking hand. "You're shaking like a leaf..."

The sky was a tapestry of marbleized charcoal and cream-colored clouds, with throbs of lightening pulsating through, and Ben knew the storm would not wait.

"Ok, so what the hell is going on, Ben? How do you know all this?"

But then he saw them: The men in fatigues at the other end of the breezeway, advancing like an avalanche, almost smirking as they spotted their prey. He grabbed her arm. "Oh fuck! Let's go!"

She looked at him in something like surprise and disgust as her cigarette dropped to the sidewalk. "What the hell? Ben! Let go of me! Now!"

"Sydney please!" he shouted over the raging wind.

"Ben this is crazy! I'm not going anywhere with you!" She was mad as hell and wasn't going to go easily. She pushed her hair whipping like ropes away from her face and wriggled out of his grip. "In case you haven't noticed, the woman who means most in the world to me is inside that hospital and --"

He chased after. "Sydney, please! You don't understand. These people are crazy. We're in a lot of danger. We're..."

She continued to ignore him and had nearly reached the entrance of the hospital when he said: "I got a letter from Heim."

She stopped at this. Turned to face him.

"Cody, Nana Jean...well, I don't have any proof -- not yet -- but I'd bet my life these guys orchestrated all of it."

"What? Why?"

"Because you were getting too close."

"Too close? Too close to what? Ben, I don't understand."

"I know you don't but I don't have time to explain. Please, Syd, we have to go *now*."

She opened her mouth to speak but just then a crack of thunder split open the sky and the rain came like a waterfall, pounding down all around, bouncing against the sidewalk, creating the illusion they were being pummeled by it from all sides.

"Syd, listen to me –" he shouted over the noise of the wind and rain. "I—"

And that was when she saw them, too: the men in fatigues coming down the sidewalk, steely eyes and jaws set hard, advancing upon them, ready to stop at nothing, and that was when he grabbed Sydney's arm once again, and they began to run.

55

2:33am

The plan had been simple: each of them were to spend no more than five minutes in their respective apartments gathering research materials, evidence, clothes, and anything else they might need for a moderately extended period away from home. They had no idea what they were up against -- at least not in any true sense -- but they knew enough to be scared.

Ben told her about Chip Wesley and the missing personnel file. How he'd been paranoid enough to take the time to hunt down a pay phone -- something all but extinct anymore -- and called from it, too scared to be involved.

"Two missing hard drives? Five people dead in one week?" Was all Sydney kept asking, but it wasn't a question, at least not one she expected him to answer.

Ben's heart went out to her -- how could it not? For these were the same questions he had asked himself at least a hundred times. But he had no answers for her, and they both knew it.

He pulled in front of her building and was ready to let her out without a word. But something made him stop, grab her hand.

"Syd, I—"

She looked at him with surprise. But then it melted into something else: a mixture of sadness, confusion, worry, grief. After a moment she said, "It's okay, Ben. I know. Let's just go get our stuff. We'll figure things out after."

He'd watched her go in, waited till the lights came on, then reluctantly pulled away, allowing himself to breathe for the first time in what felt like centuries.

But no sooner had Ben walked into his apartment than his pulse froze, and he turned tail faster than he'd ever done in his life.

The place was trashed -- utterly and completely -- couch overturned, drawers ripped out, doors dangling from jambs, dozens of books and various crap from his IKEA shelves now piled on the ground and kicked through. Picture frames smashed and spiderwebbed, even his Bible shredded and stomped on. He didn't even have to guess who'd done it. In fact, it took all of about seven seconds to review the scene before one thought came, and one thought only:

Sydney.

Normally he'd circle the block and arrive properly, without breaking any laws; but on this night he simply jerked the Wrangler into reverse and sped backwards down the block, screeching to a halt at her front door, which she came running through just then.

Her face was as white as bone: "Someone's been in my place," she panted, her eyes as wide as tires, petrified.

"I know," he said, "Get in." And she did, and soon the tranquility of downtown Piedmont was drifting away in the rearview mirror, drowning in sheets of rain.

56

3:11am

As they barreled down the highway, the wind wild and night untamable, he told her everything; as much as he knew and could anyway. Though the soft top of the Wrangler made conversation difficult it wasn't impossible, and so he started with Heim and his incident with the bricks in his bag; he then rounded it out with his dealings with Chip and ended with the man in fatigues at the funeral; only to finally come back again to Heim, with his FedEx package and the letter it contained; the unspeakable crimes it detailed.

He tried his best to keep his eyes on the road -- though it was tough with the summer storm brewing all around -- and was able to sneak occasional glances in her direction.

He watched her and his heart nearly broke at her visible pain. Choking back tears she asked: "So you think Nana Jean was a retaliation of some sort?"

He nodded, knowing the truth would hurt her, but knowing she needed to hear it just the same. "And Cody, too."

She turned her face toward the open window, trying to hide her weeping eyes. She folded her arms around her, hugging herself tight.

"I'm so sorry, Syd. I--"

She surprised him then by turning toward him, her hair flying, normally kind eyes now sharper than razors. "You *what*?" she snapped. "Let me guess." Her voice was hungry-python-friendly. "You feel guilty for ditching me when I needed you most? You feel ashamed that you didn't believe me? Or wait, how about this –- none of the above, you just feel like a piece of shit knowing you totally abandoned me and if you'd only listened to me, then maybe right now… now…Nana Jean wouldn't be –-" But she couldn't go on.

"I'm *so* sorry, Syd. You have to know that."

But no words would come. Just the thought of her Nana Jean sucked all of the bravado out of her and she crumpled, sinking into the seat beneath her.

Ben wiped the sweat and rain from his brow, wanting to ask a million questions. They didn't have much time, so he needed to ask the most important question first: "How is she?"

Sydney snorted. "Just peachy."

"Syd, c'mon…" He reached a hand out to her and, surprising them both, she took it.

Her face broke beneath the weight of her pain. "Smoke inhalation. *Really* bad smoke inhalation –- her lungs are functioning at something pathetic, like ten percent. Burns over eighty percent of her body. Oh, Ben…" Her eyes swung up and caught his, staggering him with their grief. "She's so little…how is she ever going to recover from this?"

He didn't know, and so he thought it better to say nothing. Instead he just squeezed her hand. "I'm so sorry, Syd," he said, and meant it… but his eyes were still on the clock.

She was sad, scared and pissed: much of it directed at him, and all of which for good reason. But he knew that ultimately it was a small price to pay for saving their lives.

Finally she broke the silence and in a quiet voice asked: "Who were those guys?"

But he could do nothing but simply shake his head.

"They were watching me, you know." Her voice was a trembling heartbreak. "I used my master key and went into the apartment I rented out, just to make sure it wasn't a random robbery." Her eyes lowered in shame. "There was surveillance equipment, Ben. Pictures of me on the wall..." she shuddered. "Pictures of me everywhere... pictures of...Oh God Ben," her face fell into her hands.

"It's okay, Syd." His voice was gentle, belying the white-hot rage he felt blistering within. "I'll make it okay."

Her eyes never left him until she finally gave up and swung them back toward the road, throwing her hands in the air as she asked: "Well for goodness sake, Campbell, do you at least know where we're going?"

57

3:20am

The motel room looked exactly like you'd expect a $39.99 per night motel room to look: skeevy, drab, and a place you wouldn't mind saying goodbye to in the morning. They looked at each other and shrugged.

Her bones chilled through, Sydney moved toward the bed on the far side of the room and, with great reluctance, pulled the blanket off to drape across her rain-soaked body, trying not to imagine whether or not it had been laundered, nor who had touched it last. She was shivering, but whether it was from the relentless downpour or just plain fear she wasn't sure. She watched Ben as he locked the deadbolt and jiggled the weak handle, peering through the cheap polyester curtains then pulling them tight. She searched for his eyes and even though he wouldn't show them, he knew he was a nervous as she was; possibly even more so because of all the things he knew and had yet to share with her.

They'd landed here randomly. After they'd torn out of Piedmont, he had made a series of erratic turns to throw off anyone following them, and they'd landed on Route 130, which he then took north until the torrential rain grew too much for the little Jeep to bear.

"See anywhere to stop?" His shouts had ricocheted against the thrashing canvas roof.

She had; they both had. But they all had been truck stops or by-the-hour joints, and none had looked too appealing. They'd finally settled on this rattrap; the only one they'd seen for miles that didn't have a "gentleman's club" attached to it. Still, Sydney loathed the thought of actually sleeping here.

Although, if she were being realistic, sleep was doubtful tonight anyway.

The Carefree Inn was a breezy moniker that felt anything but at the moment. But it boasted Wi-Fi and fax services, both of which seemed crucial until Ben got their room key and ushered them in, and they both remembered their laptops had been stolen in the dual raids, and neither of them had anything in hand beyond a FedEx package.

The best part of the motel at the moment was its ability to tuck Ben's Jeep snugly in between two mammoth eighteen-wheelers in the parking lot so it was completely concealed from the highway.

Actually that was second best to the fact that the place took cash. Ben figured that in addition to the double ransackings, the Senator's inexplicable knowledge of Kat's pregnancy pointed to a tapping of their phones and apartments. They –- whomever *they* were –- likely would be tracking any credit card purchases, as well, and so he had been relieved by the innkeeper's willingness to take cash, and his complete disinterest in anything beyond the re-runs playing on the miniscule TV on the shelf behind the desk.

Both at a loss for words, they looked at each other for moments longer than was comfortable, waiting for some sort of reassurance from the other. But when none came, their eyes fell away.

The only thing clear was left unspoken: Life as they knew it would never be the same.

"So."

This came finally as Ben stripped off his t-shirt, so soaked it clung like a second skin. The Jeep had been like a wind tunnel, the rain beating against it unremittingly, leaving them both shivering.

"Let me take a shower first, okay? I just need to clear my head. Then we'll talk. In the meantime, you should read this." He tossed the FedEx package from Heim onto her bed.

"O-kay," she said slowly, not liking being left alone, even if he was only gone for a few minutes and only steps away in the bathroom.

Her heart hadn't slowed since it first started racing in the hospital parking lot. She sat down on the bed and rested against the headboard, forgetting the package for a moment, and closing her eyes. Her first thoughts leapt to Nana Jean, and tears came at once. She'd looked so small in that hospital bed, the hush of the ventilator next to her, the wires and tubes running every which way. Thankfully Sydney had been unable to see the actual burns; the doctors had seen to that. But just the thought of Nana Jean struggling to escape through the smoke, fighting to breathe -- the terror she must have felt, of being all alone, while the fire ate her beloved home -- and she was powerless against her tears. Thinking of Cody only compounded things, and soon her emotions had the better of her.

She thought of her home -- her sanctuary -- trashed beyond repair, and felt like the world's biggest fool for allowing the man in fatigues to rent the apartment in her building. Why, she'd practically rolled out the red carpet for this lunatic, invited him straight into her life without so much as a background check. She tried hard not to think of all the surveillance equipment next door and what it had seen, what it had recorded...

But that suddenly seemed secondary when her thoughts returned to what mattered most: People. And with a new tide of emotion her heart ached for Marion Jefferson and Sherrod ("Forgive myself? Could you?") and T-Ray Hopkins, and even his crazy mother ("He was supposed to get us out of here..."), about the Ashe brothers ("it was like *Night of the Living Dead* or something"), and Ashanti Prince ("Being naked ain't nothin' to me no more") and all the others who had been hurt by Bruni's school....

The shower faucet squeaked alive and her eyes snapped open. She reached for the package and curled her legs beneath her, ready to read until her eyes and heart could take no more.

She would get to the bottom of all of this if it killed her.

Methyl mercury (CH3Hg+) was a neurotoxin, Heim explained in his letter, and the form of mercury that was most easily bioaccumulated in organisms, usually through food chains, but in this case through a water source: the water fountains by the football field, the ones used by all of the football and track teams, the ROTC, the Color Guard, the cheerleaders.

Just as she'd thought, the thermometer factory and their mercury-filled products had left their mark on a section of The Banks, smack dab where the new school stood, and even though the land had sat vacant for so many years, its effects were still prominent at the time Bruni and his cohorts chose it for their site for the school.

And how did Heim fit into all this? By his unfortunate luck, he had worked his way up the DEP chain-of-command by then to the rank where the task of determining what tainted ground was reusable and what was not was solely at his discretion. He had lists of hundreds of contaminated sites around the state that fell into three main categories: they were either able to be salvaged, possibly recyclable, or so putrid they were never to be touched again. And though it seemed implausible, there was little by way of oversight.

As his letter went on he explained that he'd never had any intention to do anything but the job he was hired to do. His record was impeccable, he insisted; had been for fifteen years. But when he'd visited The Banks for the last time, ready to issue his final report and render the land too infected to be used again, he'd been confronted by the Scottolino brothers and swiftly brought before Sterling Sault and Dino Bruni. He was no match for them and they all knew it. He caved at first mention of harm to his family, and had been at their mercy ever since. The money came in large chunks and regularly. Over the past five years he estimated nearly $750,000 had been delivered, like clockwork. Bruni refused to acknowledge it as a bribe; instead he called it a "thank you" in exchange for Heim's loyalty.

> The man is big on loyalty, Heim wrote. He said he wished he had a hundred men or more like me. But what he didn't understand was that I wasn't loyal; I was scared.

Sydney's heart sank.

Heim went on to say that he'd never been much of a social climber or even very ambitious, but his wife was carrying on an affair and had been on the verge of leaving him, and he'd become convinced the money would make her stay. Turns out, he was right. He'd never breathed a word of its nefarious origins, but he knew the truth, and after five years of carrying such a soul-sucking burden, he'd finally had enough. He'd wanted to end his own life but was worried that the truth would come out and couldn't bear the thought of the shame it would bring on his wife and kids, and so he planned to take them out, too –- a plan that he'd obviously followed through with.

"Jesus," she said and set the package aside, her mind a torrent.

She sat for a moment, unsure what to do, if anything. But then she snapped into action mode and did the only thing that came naturally anymore: she began to write.

58

Her hand aching from writing so fast and so furiously, Sydney took the pages of notebook paper she had scrawled on, as well as Heim's letters, and went straight to the motel office.

The man in the turban behind the desk barely acknowledged her as he took the papers from her -- his eyes still on the TV -- and flushed them through the fax.

She waited pensively. "You sure that went through?"

He looked at her as though she were an idiot.

"To *The Jerzine*? It's a magazine? Roger O'Dell was the recipient..." but then her voice trailed off under his glare. "It's just that... well, it's really important."

He looked at her for longer than was naturally comfortable before replying: "It went through, miss."

Still, Sydney was reluctant. "Okay," she said, backing toward the door, eyes still on the 1999 obsolete fax machine whining behind his desk. "If you're sure..."

She was worried but knew she had no other choice but to return to the motel room. She'd written everything she possibly could and now all her hopes depended on Roger. Now that his wife had left him he was always staying late at the office, regardless of whether there was work to do or not. She could only pray that tonight was one of those nights.

She fought through the rain pummeling the breezeway and burst into the room riding a gust of wind. She struggled to close the door behind her, the wind relentless, and no sooner had she finally gotten it shut and locked than Ben stepped out of the tiny bathroom in a plume of steam, rubbing a towel against his head. He looked to her.

"I don't understand..." she began to say, but then stopped, because she *did* understand: the school was built on poisoned land by men who knew it was poisoned and chose to build it anyway. "But why?"

The rain pounded against the room's only window, the big bay one facing the parking lot, as shadows crept through the cheap curtains, illuminating Ben's face to ghostly. "I wish I knew, Syd. I imagine money had to do with it, since it always does. Sinking poll numbers..."

Her head snapped up. "Politics?" she practically spit. "You can't be serious. Ben, please tell me you aren't serious...Peoples' *lives* are in jeopardy, Ben, people who --"

"Well think about it. Think about what was going on at the time. When they decided to build the school Camden had just been named the most dangerous city in the country for the second straight year, for the third time in five years. Everyone was embarrassed, scared, desperate, pointing fingers. You remember, don't you? I heard about it non-stop, and *I* was in DC. The Governor was furious. Day after day, week after week the press was brutal. National media swarming. Bruni and Jasper were up for re-election and needed to do something to save their asses." He shrugged. "It's the oldest trick in the playbook."

"O-kay," she began slowly, the wheels turning. "Maybe I could understand someone else doing it. Sault, for example. But Bruni? Jasper? Doing that to their own people? It's just..."

"Unconscionable, I know."

She shook her head slowly, both believing and not. "So the school..." she said steadily, "The whole thing...it was a publicity stunt?"

He took her in; the breaking naiveté in her eyes, and softened his voice: "Essentially."

A time passed, spent with both of them looking anywhere but at each other.

Sydney spoke first, her face suddenly reddened with rage. "And according to Heim, your boss was behind it all," she said, her tone just shy of an all-out accusation.

Ben grimaced at the thought. "I can't believe it either. I mean, I've always known he'd do just about anything to get re-elected, but not this." He shook his head. "*Christ* Syd, not this."

A long, heavy silence passed between them. Then suddenly Ben remembered. "You know, I was with him last night. I found him at Headquarters, drunk as hell. He took me to Camden, middle of the night."

"What?"

"I know, I know. Crazy, right? But just hear me out. It gets weirder. *Trust me.*"

"What happened?"

"He took me to a construction site, one of his latest projects."

"That Sault's spearheading, I'm sure?"

"Of course, but that's not the point. He was talking all crazy and I thought it was just the booze, but now it's starting to make sense."

She sat up. "What did he say?"

"He was looking out over the city, talking to me but really kind of just talking out loud, as if I wasn't even there. He was mad as hell, going on about all the sacrifices he's made, all that he's done for the people of Camden and how they were so ungrateful."

"So you're thinking he built the school on that ground, knowing it might hurt the kids, but justifying it because of everything else he'd done for them?"

"That, and that they were lucky to get anything at all. The way he figures it I'm sure, is that these kids were throwaways anyway. They were never going to make it; didn't have a prayer. but maybe the school would give them a boost, you know? One they wouldn't get anywhere else."

"Or it might kill them," she said drily.

"True." He sighed, "That's true."

"Jesus. Did he say anything else?"

"He asked me if I knew what Ling Chi was."

Her forehead wrinkled. "Ling Chi? What's that?"

"I didn't know either. But he started going on about it. It's some sort of ancient Chinese torture where a person gets dismembered one piece at a time. Slow slicing, he called it."

She recoiled. "Oh my goodness, that's horrible! What on earth... Why would he...?"

"I know. Weird, right? But he said it's also a metaphor for gradual destruction. About how something or someone is destroyed a little bit at a time."

"And you think he was talking about himself?"

"Well don't you? Think about it. First of all -- "

But just then the door of the motel room detonated, snapped clear off its hinges in a jarring explosion of splitting wood and the whine of metal grinding against metal, and in a flash of lightening they were all illuminated: Bruni, Sault, the Scottolino brothers, and the menacing men in fatigues.

59

"Hope we're not breaking up your little party!" Bruni cackled with a maniacal smile. "Would hate to do that, now wouldn't we, Sterling?"

The engineer's head bobbed like a channel marker in a storm, his wild eyes lit ablaze by the lightning thrashing in the sky behind them.

Sydney and Ben were planted to where they stood; two helpless stumps of deadened trees whose roots were solid and unmoving beneath the earth. They looked to each other and back at the entourage, watching them as they advanced into the room, their cache of guns catching the yellow light of the motel room and glinting like new pennies.

⚘

"So I bet you're pretty proud of yourselves," Bruni said from where he sat, watching as his minions hog-tied Ben and Sydney. His smile was thin and dangerous. "Pretty damn proud."

"Fuck you, Dino!" Ben shouted from where he wriggled face down on the ground, the cheap carpeting unforgiving, burning his face.

They laughed, and the fattest Scottolino brother dug his knee deeper into Ben's spine.

"So you think you're mister tough guy now, is that it Campbell?" Bruni laughed. "I'm so disappointed in you. I thought you and I were on the same page."

Ben looked him in the eye as best he could from where he lay. "You fucking...*fuck*. We will *never* be on the same page. You poisoned those kids, Dino. Damaged their brains. You –"

But before he could finish one of the men in fatigues had a silencer pointed at Ben's leg, threatening. The big brute nodded toward Dino.

Bruni shook his head. "Not yet. Let me just ask this little prick a few more questions before he dies."

Ben felt the blood drain from his scalp to his toes.

"So, Ben. You're quite the charmer. Here all along I thought you were a good soldier. Strong. Loyal." Bruni snorted. "Turns out you're nothing more than a snitch. Nothing more than a lowlife, disloyal –"

"Like Iggy?" Ben ventured, defiant.

Stunned, Bruni's lips sprouted a gaping hole.

"I talked to him, you know, and do you want to know what he said?"

Bruni's eyes widened at his boldness then quickly cut to Sault's before returning back to Ben and tapering into blazing black holes. "Shut up, Campbell. I'm warning you."

"He said there's a reason why he wouldn't see you! Why he –-"

"Get him," Was all Bruni said, and the man in fatigues fired.

Ben screamed in agony, the blood rushing at once from the singeing hole in his pant leg.

"Fuck you, Bruni!" he yelped.

"You wanna'nother one??" Bruni screamed back, and before anyone could move, the back of Ben's other leg was a gaping hole, the smell of gunpowder choking the air.

Sydney cried out as if *she'd* just been shot, her heart a-thunder. *Please God, no. Not Ben...*

Just then Sault interrupted, his face a screw. "What's he talking about, Dino? Iggy wouldn't see you? You never told me that." Crimson flooded his face. "How *dare* you keep something like that from me! From *ME!*"

"Don't listen to this kid, Sterling, he has no idea what he's –"

"No!" Ben shouted, fighting the pain. "Listen!" Sault turned to face him and Ben sensed at once his credibility was rising in the old engineer's mind. "Iggy wouldn't see him! I swear! And he said that he was thankful to be in jail, away from *you*, Dino! That being in that shithole prison was better than being on the outside, under your thumb, forced to do shit he didn't want to do!"

"Yeah, like poison innocent children!" Sydney chimed in.

Bruni swung around. "You shut your goddamn mouth you piece-of-shit whore, before you get a bullet in your back to match your little boyfriend's." And then he was back at Ben, his fangs bared: "You don't know what the hell you're talking about! My brother disgraced our family, nearly ruined our name, our legacy –"

But just then a large shadow was cast over the pair hogtied on the floor. "Wait. Wait just a goddamn minute." And there was Sterling Sault chest-to-chest with Dino Bruni, his face a web of rage. "You fucking lied to me, Dino. That brother of yours could *ruin* us, and you didn't give me a chance to --"

"Don't fuckin' listen to this bullshit, Sterling. I –-"

Sault pointed to Ben. "This kid isn't lying, and you know it, and *I* know it, and everyone fucking in here knows it." With each word his forefinger stabbed Bruni in the chest: "You. Fucking. Lied. To. Me."

And in the long, lingering silence that followed –- the one where the great Dino Bruni was at a loss for words for once in his entire life -- everyone knew that yes, yes he had.

"I'm going to destroy you Bruni," Sault hissed, moving toward the door, "Fucking DESTROY you." But no sooner had his hand even graced the knob than Bruni nodded to a Scottolino, and before another breath could be taken inside the cheap little 1970's motel room, a spray of blood and brain matter was plastered against the 1970's wallpaper, and Sterling Sault was facedown and dead on the 1970's carpet.

60

Thus far Sydney had been struck with fear: the engineer, the Senator's good friend no less, was just inches from her, his eyes wide and dead, and she knew she had nothing left to lose. But now anger overrode it and before she knew it she was screaming too. "The truth hurts, eh Senator? You can dish it out but can't take it, is that your story? Couldn't get re-elected on your own merits so you had to invent some? You make me sick. You're not a man; you're a fucking coward."

"Oh and the little whore speaks," he said with a wry smile. "Finally." His voice was slow and ominous. "You know, after all the footage I've watched of you in that apartment of yours I was beginning to think I knew you. But I guess *we're all* full of surprises, now aren't we?"

Her face burned at the thought of all of these strange, crazy men seeing her in her most intimate moments -- not out of embarrassment but out of pure, unadulterated rage -- and she fought even harder against the ties, knowing they would never budge but having to fight against something.

"Easy now," Bruni laughed. "Easy, girl."

From the corner of her eye she saw her best friend in the world writhing in pain, the blood gushing from his thigh in torrents so fast it made her heart sink. *How long would he last with such horrific wounds?* She didn't know, but just the thought of Bruni taking him away, just as he'd tried to take all the others she loved in her life aroused an almost inhuman craze within her.

"Don't you dare talk to me like that, you pathetic piece of shit! You think I'm scared of you? DO YOU? Well FUCK YOU!"

"Sydney, please!" Ben screamed, the begging in his fading eyes so heartbreaking she had to look away.

She felt it before she saw it: the barrel of the pistol against her temple, the hot huffing of breath coming from an unknown face just inches away. She didn't know who might assassinate her; it could be anyone of them hovering behind her, but she felt that if she was going to die, she at least needed to know why.

The fury was tempered now; not gone entirely –- not even close -- but enough so she could collect her thoughts somewhat and remember her interviewing motto: you always got more flies with honey than vinegar. "Just tell me why you did it. That's all I want to know. Then you can go ahead and kill us."

"*What*?!" Ben screeched, and in one glance she hoped she conveyed to him that she knew what she was doing.

Bruni rocked back in his chair, wildly amused. "Why?" He looked to the men in fatigues.

"Should you do the honors, or shall I?" Bo Wrigley asked.

"Oh I'll handle this one, Wrigley. It'll be my pleasure."

Bo backed away in a stagy way. "By all means."

"When I was a boy," Bruni began, waxing poetic. "The world was a different place than it is now."

"Different how?" she demanded.

He cut his eyes at her and his voice took on a demonic edge. "Different in the sense that hard work meant something, girly. That legacy and loyalty were more than just words, they were...*everything*. A handshake agreement was as good as signing your name in blood. Now look at things."

"Nothing's changed," she challenged.

"Oh but it has, girly. It certainly has. The cycle of poverty has ruined this country."

"Cycle of poverty? What about the fucking cycle of corruption, huh? What about *that*? Did you ever think that maybe if —"

But he was ignoring her. "We're only as strong as our weakest link, after all. And look at these fucking ingrates. Couldn't pull themselves up by their bootstraps to save their fucking lives. Have to be paid to take care of their own children. Don't want to work. Hands out, all the fucking time, begging for more, never fucking satisfied. Fuck them," he spat. "Fuck every last one of them. They were lucky they got the school at all."

"It practically killed them!" she shouted. "It still might!"

He was the picture of calm against her fury. "And wouldn't we all be better off with a few less worthless hood rats to worry about?"

"You crazy son-of-a-bitch!" she screamed.

A man in fatigues stepped forward, not the one who she'd rented the apartment to, the other one: the one with the thick-as-oil southern accent. "That's it, ya'll, I've had enough of this shit show. You ready to get rid of this nigger-lover *now* or what?"

The Senator's smile uncurled like the unraveling of Satan's spawn, and Sydney's blood went cold. His smoldering eyesockets stared dead-set into hers. "Oh I'm ready all right." His teeth shone in the motel's puke-yellow light. "Shut this fucking cunt up for good."

Wrigley and Timms moved forward, their faces shadowy and certain, and something else she couldn't quite identify until the ugly truth of it dawned upon her: they were excited, too, and she felt herself convulse, vomit fighting its way up her throat, threatening escape, as Ben lay squirming beside her losing more blood than was mortally possible.

There was no escape. Her options were gone, that much she knew: she was theirs for the taking. For reasons unknown to her, her thoughts were suddenly consumed by the images of her mother –- loving mom, battered wife -– and what the last moments of her life were like, as Sydney's father drained the life from her with his bare hands in some drunken rage, and then before she could stop herself, she was thinking of all of them, all victims of the same place:

of Sherrod and Marion Jefferson. Of Ebony Valdez and her fellow cheerleaders who'd morphed into whores. Of T-Ray and Diamonique and Cedric and Cyrus Ashe, and all the others she'd never even met, and she could no longer contain her rage.

"Well Senator," she said through strangled speech, "It's real easy to talk about bootstraps when you don't have a boot heel digging in the back of your neck. When you don't have police roughing you up for no reason. When you don't have to beg to feed your own family--"

"Aww," he mocked, "You're breaking my heart."

But she wasn't done, come what may. "—When you don't have to go to the government with your hat in your hand, when you don't have to rely on the promises of others to keep you existing, when you don't have the people who are supposed to work for you and protect you *poisoning* you -- people who have taken oaths before God, Senator -- people like *you* --"

"That's it!" Bruni roared. "I've heard enough from this bitch! *Get her.*"

BAM! Her eyes snapped wide and the breath was knocked out of her before she could even register that she had been shot. And when the notion of it caught up with the physical pain and shock of it all, she felt adrenaline surge through her like a mudslide, then die right there on the vine.

61

Imagining death is all we can do; nobody ever can cross that line and return to report their findings. All we can ever do is teeter on the brink. *Your life flashes before your eyes,* some say. And maybe that's true. But in Sydney's case, it wasn't. After she'd been shot her entire mind went blank, save for one thought, and it was as random as it was unyielding. She thought of Buddhism, of an article one of her colleagues had written years before. What was especially peculiar about this one final thought before her imminent death was that, A.) She was agnostic. Religion had never played a role in her life whatsoever. And, B.) That the particular article hadn't ever stood out as anything more than just something a colleague of hers had written. It didn't speak to her on any level –- at the time it was published, or any other. And, if she had had the time to analyze this bizarre thought to any degree, she might've noted that the article wasn't even very well written. But for some reason, now, with the blood of her best friend pooling all around her mixing with her own, she remembered this:

Nirvana. The word, she remembered, translated into "blowing out", referring to the blowing out of the fires of greed, hatred, delusion. The article went on to describe that while there were different types of Buddhism, the one of focus was one that believed that being alive is hell, and the only way to reach Nirvana was to ultimately have no attachments to anything. If you want to reach the highest level of human life –- of being –- you have to have all of your senses fail.

And so, she thought with an unearthly sense of calmness: *Here I am. My senses have failed.*

And they had. She couldn't see, hear, smell –- nothing. The cheap carpeting beneath her could have just as easily been an iceberg as a pit of fire or a cloud.

She was going to die, she knew it. And a sense of something came over her -– if not peace, than something quite like it, and so her head, moving as if underwater, slowed by something more powerful than she, turned to Ben and her eyes locked onto his.

"Ben," she whispered, her voice nearly beyond her control.

"Syd." Was all he said, his breath labored by the heavy blanket of pending death draped across him.

"I love you."

His eyes pressed together but whether they were grateful, tired, pushing away tears or pushing away death, she did not know. All she knew was that she was certain she heard the words: "I love you, too."

62

She felt the life leaking from her limbs, the oxygen from her lungs; the world moving around her slow and swimmy, as if she were undersea.

"She dead?" she heard a voice ask, but it was far away – too far to be real. *Wasn't it?* Her eyes felt so heavy, *so heavy...*

"Not yet," another answered, "But she will be in a second."

And just then it was if the motel was an ant hill exploded: the swat team deployed and men in black were suddenly everywhere, gigantic, lithe spiders coming through windows and seemingly out of the sky, shouting and brandishing guns and putting Bruni and his entourage onto their backs and out of commission before Sydney could even catch her next breath.

EPILOGUE

One Year Later

They were on her rooftop once again –- she and Ben -- the Ficus trees circling them like an embrace, *The Who* playing in the background:

> *Sally, take my hand*
> *We'll travel south cross-land*
> *Put out the fire*
> *And don't look past my shoulder...*
>
> *The exodus is here*
> *The happy ones are near*
> *Let's get together*
> *Before we get much older...*

"Well," Ben said, thinking of Bruni's sentencing in the morning. "Tomorrow's a big day." He tugged on his beer. "At least there was a happy ending."

She recoiled. "Yeah?" Her chin jutted toward the lights of Camden beyond and took her own sip. "Tell that to them."

"Listen Syd, I hope these guys fry, too. All I'm saying is that we're lucky in the sense that the good guys won. This ain't *Law and Order*, you know. Shit takes a lot longer in the real world. Lots of times the bad guys never get caught."

"But these bad guys have a good chance of getting off. A really good fucking chance, in case you haven't noticed. Of not even doing time at all, let alone frying," she said, her voice hoarse and defeated.

"I want them to pay, Syd, I really, really do," he said, almost to himself, but mostly as a prayer.

"But what will it matter? Fry, not fry? Pay or not pay? No matter what they're sentenced to, those kids'll never be the same. Happy *ending*, Campbell? There's no such thing here." She reached out her hand, grabbed his. "Guilty, not guilty, what does it even matter?"

"I can't believe I didn't see it sooner...I can't believe I--" His voice was creeping falsetto now, a trait he always found pitiful in a grown man, yet here he was, bleating like a lamb at slaughter, not caring who heard him weak, who judged him, who saved him.

"Ben. You can't blame yourself." She pointed her finger: "They, and they alone. *They* are the ones to blame."

"So if a judge can't punish them enough, and if the system fails once again, what's the point of all this?" he motioned around; flailed really, like a drowning man.

"A judge may sentence them, but that's not the real punishment. Having to live with their choices, with their memories of the wrong they did...They'll be haunted every day and every night, with reminders cropping up in places they'd never guess. They'll see the faces of those children around every turn. They'll---"

"But how? Even if they don't get off, and that's a big *if* -- they'll be in prison! Gray walls don't often jog the memory, Syd. Gray walls have a way of justifying things. Of making sorry men hard. Of making them think twice about repenting."

"But that's where you're wrong, Ben. That's where you don't get it." She set her beer down and turned to him, eyes pleading. "Don't you see? The walls aren't their prisons, they never will be. It's their minds. Their bodies. The skin they can't shed. Living as themselves, *that's* the prison term. The sin of their crime is its own punishment."

He looked at her, the wind pressing his tears dry against his cheeks. "They're gutless, loveless…"

"But worse than that is that they're godless. And I don't mean that in a religious way, but in a human way. Call it what you want: godless, soulless. Whatever the fuck. But can you think of a worse fate, Ben? 'Cause I know I can't."

It felt as though a million moons had passed as they sat on Sydney's roof in the early morning light, the lights of the cities of Camden and Philadelphia twinkling both anonymously and in unison softly on the horizon as Sydney wept.

> *Teenage Wasteland…*
> *It's only teenage wasteland…*
> *They're all wasted…*

Ben reached over and put his arm around her, but no words passed: there was nothing more to say.

Just breathing was an effort for him as Ben negotiated his crutches up the steps of the courthouse. It had been a year, but rehab of his shattered femurs would require years more.

And what a year it had been: They'd endured Nana Jean's death and the death of Cody's career almost simultaneously. Then Kat had given birth to a bouncing baby boy, only to have paternity tests prove that it was Tad's child after all.

But the good news was that Zoey was thriving at St. Andrews, and his mother's burden was growing lighter by the day.

They'd all be here today: Henrietta Jasper and her sister Poppy, Micki Bruni, Roger O'Dell, Iggy in shackles — all of them — all to do the same exact thing as Ben and Sydney, and testify against the Great Dino Bruni.

The men in fatigues had never been identified; they'd been caught by the swat team just like Bruni, but had escaped from custody mere hours into their capture. The police were baffled and both the FBI and CIA had been called in, but there had been no progress on their whereabouts. It was as if they were apparitions that had simply vanished as if they'd never been real at all. It was a thought that made Sydney's skin crawl, and riddled her sleep nightly. Knowing these strange, dangerous men had seen her at her most intimate moments was a thought that was too much to bear. She was in therapy of course, but just like Ben's rehab recovery, it would take time. Lots of it.

When his breath finally steadied they helped each other up the steps wordlessly as they made their way into the courtroom, just in time to hear:

"Will the defendant please rise?"

The End

ACKNOWLEDGMENTS

It often takes a village to do many things, and writing and publishing a book is one of them. And I am grateful for the opportunity to now thank mine...

This project would not have been possible without two integral people: Thank you, Craig Angelini, for your expertise in biology, and editor extraordinaire Bill Thompson.

My early readers: Many thanks to my amazing brother Wade, and dear friends Dr. Ed Arrison and Mary Ellen Angelini. And of course Rich Israel, who never lets me down.

As always, Mom and Dad, you have my eternal gratitude for all of your amazing support and generosity. We are so lucky to have you. Thank you for believing in me, even when I didn't believe in myself.

And to my family: Shea, Quinn, Genevieve, Sutton, Judd and Everly. You are my absolute most favorite people on the planet. I hope and pray you will each find your passion, chase your dreams, and never give up. You can always count on me to cheer you on. I love each of you beyond words & measure.

And Michael. From the very bottom of my heart, thank you for being the leader of this family. I am so grateful for you, and for our life. Thank you for all that you do for us; it is so deeply appreciated. I'm one ridiculously lucky girl.

And last but certainly not least: I'd like to thank the people of the Delaware Valley for all of your support and well wishes, with this project and my others. It's really true what they say: there's no place like home.

xoxo

jlc